TAX BITES & TASTY MORSELS

Who's Been Eating My Pie?

Great recipes for people who love to cook but hate confiscatory taxes.

Susie Iventosch

Eloquent Books

Eloquent Books
An imprint of Strategic Book Group
P.O. Box 333
Durham CT 06422
www.StrategicBookGroup.com

ISBN: 978-1-60911-529-6

Printed in China

Book Design: Suzanne Kelly

Dedications

To my wonderful family—Lenny, Courtney, Ari, Joel, Grams and Pops, and my devoted Tasty Morsels column readership, thank you all for your love and inspiration, and your love of good food and fun recipes.

And to my media heroes—thank you for your daily inspiration to stay informed about irresponsible, runaway, out-of-control government spending. I wish you many great meals from Tax Bites & Tasty Morsels.

Mark~

We're in dire need of both a political and a tax reformation! I'm hoping for a serious "House" cleaning in November.

Let's rock the "House" and roll the Senate!!

I hope you enjoy the book.

Cheers, Susie 8/9/10

Acknowledgments

My husband, *Lenny*—thank you for your continual support and for keeping me focused on writing my book, rather than on my political rants, and for being my barbecue expert.

My children—*Courtney, Ari, Joel and all of your food-loving friends*—thank you for putting up with dozens of coconut cakes, endless chicken dishes and many an experimental meal.

Grams and Pops—thank you for your endless support, dedication and love, and for passing on the love of family cooking.

Gigi— thanks to my grandmother for being the all-time Julia Child devotee and for the many tears of laughter shared while watching her antics in the kitchen.

Dolores Iventosch, my mother-in-law, deserves a big dose of credit for her many wonderful recipes, and her love of family and family celebrations.

John and Elaine McDonald, thank you for your friendship and advice over the years.

To all of our friends, thanks for making entertaining a fun hobby.

Thanks to all of the fine chefs and wonderful friends who so willingly offered their recipes so I could share them with you!

Special thanks to: *E. Thomas Wetzel* of the Retirement Living Information Center, *J.D. Foster, Ph.D.* of the Heritage Foundation, *Dr. Gary Underwood,* Harris County, Texas tax assessor, *Andy Heath* of Auburn, California, and to the many taxpayer associations across the country who helped me learn more about our wacky taxes than even I wanted to know. This long list includes:

Natasha Altamirano and Pete Sepp/National Taxpayers Union

Jen Rezac/Americans for Prosperity (Kansas)

Wynnton G. Cannon/League of Washington Taxpayers

Timothy Wise/Arlington County Taxpayers Association (Virginia)

Jack Wibby/Maine Taxpayers United

Emerson Read/No Home Tax (S. Carolina)

Roy H. Stewart/Granite State Taxpayers (New Hampshire)

John Marsh/Clarke County Taxpayer and Property Owners Assoc. (Georgia)

Don McIntire and Jason Williams/Taxpayers Association of Oregon

Greg Fink/PETT (People for the Ethical Treatment of Taxpayers—Florida)

Darrel Bruck/OUTRAGE (Organization United to Reduce All Government Excesses—Illinois)

Dominic M. Calabro/Florida Tax Watch

Eric Eisenhammer/Howard Jarvis Taxpayers Association (California)

Tom Jenney/Americans for Prosperity, Arizona

Marc Goldstone/Arizona Tax Revolt

Mike Bodine/GiveMeLiberty.org

Lauren Silva/Forecalifornia.com

Table of Contents

Tax Man Jerk

By Susie Iventosch

The tax man came and taxed my
road.
He taxed my house, and said," It's
code."
He taxed my savings and my debt,
before he taxed me for my pet.
He taxed me for my pop's new knee,
and taxed me for my fallen tree.
He didn't stop there, he had such
fun.
He taxed my burger and my bun.
And soon it was my grandma's turn.
He dared to tax her in her urn.
He taxed my wine, he taxed my
beer,
and then he let a great big cheer.
With tax relief nowhere in sight,
he taxed me to turn on the light.
He taxed me for each D.C. czar.
He even double-taxed my car.
He taxed me on my hunting trip,
and then to fish, he stole a tip.
The catch I mounted on the wall,
was taxed again as I recall.
He taxed my travels near and far,
by plane or boat, to him was par.
He taxed my favorite local pub,
and then he taxed my daily grub.
He taxed my corn, he taxed my
fruit.
He taxed my brand new bathing suit.
He taxed my sparklers and my pig.
He taxed my 18-wheel rig.
He taxed my bank, he taxed each
branch.
He taxed the farmer and his ranch.
He taxed the belching, farting cow.
Is nothing sacred here and now?
The ambulance ride, if in the air,
is subject to a tax quite rare.
He taxed my doctor and my nurse,
and then he taxed the dead guy's
hearse!
Illegal drugs are taxed it's true,
and even your brand new tattoo.
The movies, gambling, sex and
more,
are taxed enough to make one roar.
The playing cards are taxed at times,
and cigarettes pay extra dimes.
It seems that nothing is tax-free.
To litigate, we pay a fee.
My favorite jock from any sport
is taxed on nearly every court.
The salt we eat, the air we breathe,
the taxes make me squirm and
seethe.
He's taxed my water and my coke,
and soon he'll tax a Facebook poke.
And after Carbon Cap and Take,
we'll all be looking for a break.
He's taxed my fun and taxed my
work ...
I think the tax man is a jerk.

Message to Readers

If we were to receive a monthly bill for our taxes along with the mortgage, utility, and grocery bills, I don't think Congress would get away with such theft. At every level, our government operates backwards by first over-spending, then increasing taxpayer levies to patch the inevitable shortfall. This behavior exhibits a complete and utter lack of common sense.

Introduction

As the polls closed on November 4, 2008, I had a sudden and compassionate empathy for victims of theft. I couldn't shake the feeling my wallet had just been stolen. On Fox News, the electoral map became a sea of blue, and there I sat, future fodder for the Pickpocket Brigade. It's a hopeless feeling, being a victim.

And, Republicans had it coming. The party of fiscal conservatism fell off a cliff as politicians, beholden to special interests, chose power and greed over party principles. It's time to dispose of congressional waste.

A cleansing of Congress is in order. Personally, I would fire them all and start over. With the rare exception of those in Congress who practice fiscal restraint, both sides of the aisle have abandoned fiscal responsibility, leaving us little choice. This nation is in dire need of a political reformation to redefine the role of government and lay waste to the trough. There's an idea—a starvation diet for the congressional "Chubby Club."

Instead, we've elected a modern day Robin Hood with a large helping of spending scoundrels to assist him in his mission. President Houdini managed to "cut" taxes for 95 percent of working Americans last year. That was some kind of magic trick, because according to my Obameter and the Tax Policy Center, 47 percent don't pay income tax in the first place! This particular group essentially received a rebate check from the five percent of Americans whose taxes Obama has promised to increase. Spelled out this means redistribution of wealth. (Read Chapter VI all about

PORK and the President's $787 billion American Recovery and Reinvestment Act of 2009 to learn more about redistribution of your wealth.)

We're supposed to feel patriotic about this, according to Vice President Joe Biden. Obamahood will soak the rich to drown the poor and everyone knows by now, handouts do nothing to permanently improve one's living standards. (Just ask ACORN employees!) Consequently, the recipients of your money are likely to survive on the fiscal drip line.

Speaking of life support, Congress cooked up a $700 billion plan to bailout our failing financial industry in 2008, but before they could muster enough votes to pass it, they added $150 billion in pork. So, tax rates will rise to pay for this outrageous and unnecessary spending. This is the perfect recipe for "socialist stew."

With a promise to allow the Bush tax cuts to expire in 2011, increase capital gains, dividend, social security and corporate taxes, and a plan to continually increase entitlement programs, it's a sure bet that Obama and Congress will fatten our tax bill while trimming disposable income. There are plenty of proposed tax increases to pay for the federal government's rich spending habits: Cap and Trade energy tax, stock transaction tax, value-added tax, war tax and income tax rates as high as 49%.

Add to this a host of tax breaks the Senate has so far failed to renew for 2010, (the House voted to uphold these tax breaks), such as restructuring the Alternative Minimum Tax, which will now catch Americans with family income of $75,000 in its clutches, the loss of the deduction for state and local sales taxes, the federal college student tuition deduction, and the research tax credit for R&D. This is supposed to right the sinking U.S. economy?

Has Barack Obama *ever* taken an Econ course? How many in Congress have an understanding of basic economic principles? Too few, I suspect.

The already bloated 67,000-page tax code behemoth will become heftier with new rules and regulations. Imagine reading and understanding *sixty-seven thousand pages* of highly progressive tax code. When former Senator Tom Daschle, House Ways and Means Chairman Charlie Rangel, Treasury Secretary Timothy Giethner, U.S. Trade Representative Ron Kirk and Health and Human Services Secretary Kathleen Sebelius don't understand the tax code, can ordinary citizens be expected to?

The problem with progressive taxes is that the government is dependent upon relatively few taxpayers. And, when those who pay taxes, get angry, stop creating jobs, and move offshore as a result, voila—reduced government revenue. (Remember Atlas Shrugged?)

A better plan to reduce the deficit, raise living standards and increase national prosperity all at the same time, is to broaden the base and flatten the tax, not only simplifying, but vastly improving the process. Then, we could ship 40,000 Internal Revenue Service agents off in search of Osama Bin Laden. From experience, we know that IRS auditors can find anyone!

Many nations have successfully adopted a flat tax, and those economies are growing as a result. But, American politicians prefer to indulge the hungry tax beast by adding layers of rules and regulations. We'd better get used to it. Reading the tax code could be our sole source of entertainment once the government rapes our salaries—no more movies, books or dining out. In fact, it's a great time to brush up on your cooking skills, but don't think of opening a restaurant. The double dip recession is coming and even if you are successful, the government will take an even bigger bite of your prosperity pie.

The last time I felt like this was during the Clinton administration when the top marginal tax rate went from 31 to 39.6 percent. It all began the day I got my first check as a freelance writer. Of course I had to plan for taxes and soon my accountant became the bearer of bad news—very, very bad news.

To my shock and dismay, what I received after the heist was a pitiful 34.8 percent of my pay. (15.3% self-employment tax, 39.6% federal income tax, and 10.3% California State income tax, before a few minor deductions designed to keep me from going completely nuts.) How dare they steal my money? With a husband gainfully employed, the harsh reality that my entire income would be taxed at the highest marginal rate sent me into a panic. We were being taxed to death, and even in death, we are destined to be taxed one final time. Lowering this tax burden became an obsession.

Then the thought occurred, "At least they can't tax my food … not in California, anyway." In the Golden State, as well as 30 other states, there is no sales tax on most edible groceries. Frankly, I'm a little surprised the states give us a pass on this one, considering government's voracious appetite for tax dollars. (Never mind that food is taxed in a multitude of ways before it ever reaches us.)

As a food columnist, my kitchen has been the birthplace of many recipes and, in an effort to share my hatred of confiscatory taxes and my love of cooking, I decided to write a book about both.

Through a book full of innovative recipes, you will read about these taxes, gasp in disbelief and possibly lose your appetite, over the programs we taxpayers fund. You may learn to appreciate the meaning of Tax Freedom Day—the day in the year when we finally get to keep some of the money we earn. This special occasion was April 13 in 2009. On average, if Americans were to pay all of their taxes up front, it would take until their paycheck in late April or early May before they could keep any of it. Keep in mind, an individual's Tax Freedom Day occurs sooner or later, depending upon his income and the date varies by state, as well.

Just one year into his presidency, Obama signed into law the $787 billion American Recovery and Reinvestment Act, a $200 billion bailout of Fannie Mae and Freddie Mac, $275 billion for mortgage write-downs, and a $3.6 trillion government budget for half of 2010, (more than $1 trillion to set the stage for ObamaCare—government-run health care), a $410 billion 2009 omnibus government spending package, $15 billion for "first-time" home buyer credits, $3 billion "Cash for Clunkers", another $447 billion 2010 omnibus government spending bill and who knows what else by the time you read this passage?

White House Chief of Staff, Rahm Emanuel has suggested a 10% VAT (Value-Added Tax) to pay for ObamaCare. This type of tax, which is prevalent in Europe, is a stealth tax, since it taxes every level of production or service, from raw materials all the way to market. It's common knowledge that businesses pass tax burdens to the consumer in the final cost of goods and services, and ultimately, the VAT amounts to a national sales tax, inflicting more financial pain on consumers. This regressive tax would go against the mantra of the Obama camp, "Anyone making less than $250K per year will not see their taxes increased by a single dime, *not one dime.*"

As more and more legislatures bankrupt their states, (all but three states—Montana, N. Dakota and Texas—have a budget deficit this year) those governments have either increased taxes or plan to do so in an effort to balance the state budget. California has received billions from the stimulus package and, in addition to that, the State's legislators passed a 2009/10 budget, which included $14 billion in new taxes to be imposed upon the citizens of this state. Still, this is not nearly enough to fill the budget gap given all of the new federal mandates coming our way. California is now looking at a 2010/11 fiscal deficit of $20 billion.

As for the "new" way in Washington, or a state capitol near you, it looks exactly the same to me. Change, in the form of $3 or $4 trillion straight out of our tax-paying pockets, is definitely coming! Tax and spend. Tax and spend. Tax and spend. Where is the recipe for change we were promised?

Let's dig in, before Uncle Sam polishes off what's left of our pie!

Tax Bite

B.Y.O.B. Tax (Bring Your Own Bag!)

Beginning January 1 2010, grocery stores in Washington D.C. began implementing a 5¢ per bag tax on plastic or paper bags. The stores keep 1¢ of every bag tax, but they give customers a credit of 5¢ for every bag that they bring into the store. The balance of the tax proceeds go to the City for its little "clean-up" project. The idea is to cut down on waste and to raise money to clean up the polluted Anacostia River. The tax, approved by the City Council and signed into law in July 2009, applies to anything sold at any food retailer. But, deciphering what exactly constitutes a "food" store has posed a lot of confusion. D.C. is the only major city to tax both paper and plastic bags. In San Francisco disposable plastic bags are simply banned in large supermarkets and drug store chains, but paper bags are still okay if they are made of recycled materials and can be recycled again. The D.C. law specifically excludes bags that package bulk items like produce and bin sales of dried fruit, candy and nuts. Speaking of which, this law is completely nuts and utterly impossible to enforce. In any case, it's best to bring your own bag!

Source: "In Washington, a Lesson in Bureaucracy Comes in Every Bag" by Sara Murray WSJ 1/25/2010

CHAPTER I

Taxed from Beginning to End!

Appetizers & Employment Taxes

Just as the meal begins with an appetizer, tax liabilities must start somewhere. So let's start with the very first tax bite from our paychecks at the dawn of each year—employment tax. Otherwise known as Medicare and Social Security, this granddaddy of all Ponzi schemes makes even Bernie Madoff look like an amateur book-cooker! And, to add a little zing, when we finally reach the right age to collect social security benefits, we're taxed on that very income our tax dollars funded in the first place!

These taxes are extracted from our paychecks so quickly we hardly notice they're missing! If you work for someone else, the first $106,800 of earned income is subject to Social Security tax, (FICA), but for Medicare, there is no limit, it is assessed on every dollar you earn. Here's a little history lesson: In 2008, the first $102,000 was subject to the FICA, an increase of 4.6% over 2007. The earned income subject to FICA then bumped up to $106,800 for 2009/10, another 4.7% increase. To pay for health care reform, the Senate version includes a 0.9% employment tax hike, while Congress is considering another 2% to 8% payroll tax penalty for firms and individuals that don't purchase health insurance. In addition, Obama is gunning to apply the Medicare portion of payroll taxes to capital gains, dividends, and other forms of investment income, heretofore excluded from the tax.

Every worker pays employment tax, and, unless you are one of the lucky recipients of Obama's tax rebate, you won't get a pass any time soon. My son who earned $947 last year, owed $145 in self-employment tax.

Signed into law by Franklin Delano Roosevelt at exactly 3:30 p.m. on August 14, 1935, the Social Security Act initiated a significant change from the previous American tradition of taking care of oneself, without assurances, assistance, or intrusion by the government. This act is considered by some, though certainly not me, to be one of the truly momentous legislative accomplishments in the history of the United States.

The only momentous aspect of this legislation is that it was only 39 pages long, as compared to the 1,047 pages of the 2009 American Recovery and Reinvestment Act passed last year. Strikingly similar to last year's "stimulus" bill, the Social Security Act was never reviewed by Congress before it was signed into law.

The result of the Social Security Act was a tax burden imposed on the American people to fund old-age pensions for retired workers. But levies gradually increased over time to cover surviving spouses and minor children in 1939, disability insurance and early retirement for women in 1956, and early retirement for men in 1961. In 1965 the Medicare Act was signed into law by Lyndon B. Johnson to provide healthcare for beneficiaries over age 65.

When concerns about the sustainability of the Social Security Program began to surface in the 1980s, Ronald Reagan signed a law that introduced taxation of Social Security benefits and raised the age for eligibility from 62 to 65. Can you imagine a world where you provide the meal, and you must pay (again) to eat it?

Finally, in 2003, George W. Bush added the outpatient prescription drug benefit to the program. Don't worry. This program will only cost taxpayers $800 billion in the first 10 years of operation. Surely you're willing to share in this burden.

From 1937-1942, the Social Security tax levy for both the employer and the employee was one percent on annual income up to a maximum of $3,000 of earned income. From 1943 to 1948 the rate bumped up to two percent, and in 1948 the rate increased to three percent per year. Today, these rates are 6.2 percent for each party, capping out at the first $106,800 of income for the Social Security (FICA) portion. In addition, the supplemental Medicare (MI) tax rate is 1.45 percent for each, employer and employee, for a total of 2.9% on all income earned—no limit.

Those who are self-employed have the luxury of paying double that rate, or 15.3 percent. This is a hefty contribution to a program that is already bankrupt, and almost certainly won't benefit most of today's taxpayers, once retired. *

For the employee who changes jobs mid-year, Social Security tax starts all over again under the new EIN (Employee Identification Number), despite the fact the employee may have satisfied his entire FICA obligation at the old job. In compliance with the law, the new employer is required to deduct the employment

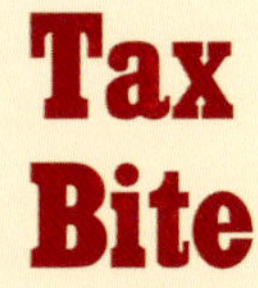

Wise Words of Tax Wisdom

"When you rob Peter to pay Paul, guess what? You can always count on Paul's support!"

Source: Dominic M. Calabro, President, Florida TaxWatch

tax as if the individual never fulfilled that year's required contribution. This is so because, despite millions, perhaps billions poured into government technology, there is allegedly no way to link one employee identification number (EIN) with another.

Funny, the IRS has little trouble locating us by social security number when they want to *collect* taxes! This means, the IRS plays the point spread on our money by having control of all interest earnings potential while we've lent it to the government for … free! Eventually this money is refunded, without interest, of course, *if* the taxpayer requests this on line 65 of his 1040 return.

**Note that self-employed persons calculate their net earnings as gross earnings reduced by 7.65%, and they deduct half of their Social Security taxes from their net earnings for federal income tax purposes.*

Tax Bite

Washington's Puffy Spending Habits

The Federal government spent more than $30,000 per household in 2009, the highest level in American history when adjusted for inflation, and $8,000 more per household than in 2008! It is a good time to be aware of exactly how your lawmakers in Washington D.C. intend to spend your money.

Source: Heritage Foundation, Budget Policy Expert, Brian Riedl.

Baked Feta Appetizer with Greek Olives and Roasted Red Peppers

(Makes four appetizer servings)

Mining through recipes is really fun to do, but it's also great when a good one just falls in your lap. That's how I discovered this dish one Saturday night. My friend Paula brought it over and I loved it, both for its simplicity and for its fabulous Mediterranean flair. She got it from her son's friend, Paige. That's how recipes work … from one good cook to another!

INGREDIENTS

1/2 pound block of feta cheese, preferably Greek, drained and rinsed

1/2 teaspoon dried oregano

1/2 teaspoon black pepper

1/4 cup coarsely chopped roasted red peppers

1/4 cup pitted and chopped Kalamata olives

2 tablespoons extra-virgin olive oil

Toasted pita bread wedges, crusty bread or crackers for serving

DIRECTIONS

Preheat broiler. Cut feta into four 1/2-inch thick slices and place in four small baking dishes for individual servings, or one large one, prepared with cooking spray. Sprinkle oregano and pepper over cheese. In a separate bowl, mix olive oil, olives and roasted red peppers. Spoon this mixture over and around cheese in baking dish. Broil about 2-4 inches from heat until edges are beginning to brown, about three to five minutes. (Keep an eye on the broiler so as not to burn the cheese!) Serve hot with pita bread wedges, crusty French or Italian bread, or crackers.

Tax Bite

A Very Long Tax Tale

As of 2006, the IRS code was 67,264 pages long and growing! When first introduced in 1913 it was just 400 pages. At last count, there were 3.7 million words in the code. Maybe this helps to explain why you can't possibly file your tax returns without the help of a tax professional. It seems neither can half of Congress nor many in the Obama Administration.

Source: FairTax.org

Dijon Dill Shrimp

(A.K.A. Ari's Shrimp, but Carol's Excellent Recipe)

When my friend brought the leftover shrimp from an Oakland Children's Hospital fundraiser to our house, my son Ari thought he had died and gone to seafood heaven. Ever since, we have called this treasured dish by its alias name: "Ari's Shrimp, but Carol's Excellent Recipe."

INGREDIENTS

50 pre-cooked medium-large shrimp
Dijon Dill Dressing (recipe below)
Fancy little toothpicks

DIRECTIONS

Marinate shrimp for several hours, or overnight. When ready to serve, remove from dressing and serve on platter with toothpicks for a cocktail party, or in martini glasses with fresh dill garnish for a sit-down affair.

Dijon-Dill Dressing

INGREDIENTS

1/2 cup olive oil
3 tablespoons white wine vinegar
3 tablespoons Dijon mustard
1 tablespoon chopped shallots
1 teaspoon minced fresh ginger root
1 clove garlic, minced
1 tablespoon chopped fresh dill
Pinch of sugar
Salt and pepper to taste

Combine all ingredients and shake in covered jar until thoroughly mixed.

Tax Bite

Taxes Take the Lion's Share

Americans work longer to pay their taxes than they work to pay for food, clothing and shelter, combined.

Source: The McPherson SentiNet

Tax Bite

$300 Billion Industry

If "tax compliance" were an industry, it would comprise 3.8 million full-time workers, spending 7.6 million hours each year in order to comply with the IRS Code. As a nation, we spend over $300 billion annually on compliance measures to file our taxes. This is equal to more than $2,000 for every one of the 130 million tax returns filed. Compliance is the total time spent filling out tax forms, record-keeping, education and other tax-related chores.

Source: FairTax.org Source: Nina E. Olson (A national taxpayer advocate at the IRS) "We Still Need a Simpler Tax Code" Wall Street Journal Editorial

Shrimp Bake Asiago (Shrimp'Cargo)

This dish is similar in style to the way escargot is normally served, but instead of snails, we use shrimp. Be sure to serve with sliced baguette, to absorb the delicious garlic butter sauce.

INGREDIENTS

18 medium-sized shrimp, peeled and deveined
1/2 cube butter, melted
1-2 cloves garlic, minced
1 tablespoon minced parsley
1/2 cup grated Asiago cheese

DIRECTIONS

In a casserole, or baking dish, lay shrimp out in a single layer. Mix melted butter with garlic and drizzle over shrimp. Sprinkle parsley and Asiago cheese over all. Bake at 425°F for about 7-10 minutes, or until shrimp is cooked and turns pink, and cheese begins to melt. Serve immediately.

Tax Bite

Big Revenue Grab

Social Security tax revenues were projected to account for 41.08 percent of total Federal Government revenue for fiscal year 2009, or $898 billion. Yet, there is still grave concern the Social Security accounts will expire by the time we baby boomers retire!

Source: USgovernmentrevenue.com

Eggplant Crostini

(Makes 15-20 crostini for hors d'oeuvres)

This appetizer is like ratatouille on a toast, with the same robust country flavor.

INGREDIENTS

1 eggplant
1 yellow bell pepper, seeds and stem removed
1 red bell pepper, seeds and stem removed
1-2 cloves garlic, minced
1 yellow onion, finely chopped
1/2 cup chopped mushrooms
2 medium tomatoes, chopped
1/2 teaspoon dried oregano (1 tablespoon fresh)
1/2 teaspoon dried thyme (1 tablespoon fresh)
Salt and Pepper to taste
1 loaf of French bread, sliced to ¼ inch.
1/4 cup extra-virgin olive oil

DIRECTIONS

Rub eggplant and peppers with 1-2 teaspoons olive oil. Roast at 450°F for 10-15 minutes. Remove from oven and cool. Chop bell peppers and scoop out eggplant pulp. Set aside. In a medium saucepan, sauté garlic, onions, mushrooms, tomatoes, herbs and salt and pepper over medium heat until onions are translucent. Add mashed eggplant and peppers to onion mixture. Mix well.

Brush thin slices of French bread (crostini) with olive oil and toast at 350°F for 5 minutes, until hot, but not too crunchy.

Spread eggplant mixture on each crostini and sprinkle with fresh-grated Pecorino Romano or Parmesan cheese. Serve warm.

Tax Bite

Stingy Serving

Will the Social Security Program Go Bankrupt? The Social Security Administrator reported in its annual report that, starting 2017, the program will pay out more in benefits than it will collect in revenue. That is not so far in the future, actually. We have good reason to be concerned about our retirement benefits. The only way to save the program is to reduce benefits, delay eligibility, or both.

Sources: http://www.ssa.gov/ and www.myretirementblog.com

Crostini of Goat Cheese, Caramelized Onions and Fig-Pear Butter

If you can't find fig-pear butter, any fig jam will work for this recipe.

INGREDIENTS

1 baguette

1/4 cup extra-virgin olive oil

4 ounces Montrachet goat cheese

4 ounces bleu cheese, crumbled

1 red onion or 6 small shallots

1/2 cup Spiced Fig Pear Butter (Earth and Vine makes a nice one)

DIRECTIONS

Slice baguette into 1/4-inch slices and place on baking sheet. Brush with olive oil and bake at 350°F for 8 minutes until slightly toasted. Remove from oven and cool. Meanwhile, mix cheeses and season with salt and pepper. Set aside. Slice onions very thin and sauté in olive oil in skillet on medium-high heat until browned and caramelized, stirring often. Set aside.

To assemble, spread one to two teaspoons cheese mixture on each baguette slice. Top with one teaspoon of Spiced Fig-Pear Butter and arrange a couple of onion slices on top. Broil until cheese is bubbly, approximately 2-3 minutes. Serve hot.

Tax Bite

Taxpayer Associations: Where toTurn When You Can't Take It Anymore!

Every state has at least one taxpayer association. Most all of these groups are taxpayer advocates that spend a good deal of time conducting research and proposing legislation to reduce the tax burden on citizens, particularly in the realm of property taxes. Check out this web site to find a group near you. http://www.ntu.org/main/groups.php

Dijon Dill Shrimp (top) and Figs with Gorgonzola (bottom).

Figs with Gorgonzola

Figs come into season twice each year, once in the spring and then again in late summer, early fall. This is a quick and tasty way to serve them that my friend Anne Stone taught me. It can be used as an appetizer or a side dish to accompany grilled meats.

INGREDIENTS

One pint basket of fresh figs
4 ounces gorgonzola cheese

DIRECTIONS

Slice figs in half lengthwise. Place a thin slice, or several crumbles of Gorgonzola atop each fig. Place on baking sheet and broil until cheese melts and browns slightly, about 3 minutes. Remove and serve immediately.

Tax Bite

Social Security Payouts

In 1937 the total of all Social Security benefits was $1,278,000. For Fiscal year 2007 Social Security benefits totaled $623,810,000,000 with a budgeted allotment of $694,804,000,000 in 2009.

Sources: http://www.whitehouse.gov/omb/budget/fy2009/ssa.html; http://www.ssa.gov/budget/2008bud.pdf; The Social Security Act of 1935; www.ssa.gov/history

Olive-Blue Cheese Toasts

Finger foods are always nice to have on hand—no pun intended! My mother-in-law taught me that olives and blue cheese team up to make a quick hors d'oeuvres or a grilled sandwich for a light meal. If you happen to have ripe black olives, diced Ortega chilies and grated cheddar on hand, make a Mexican version with a little "south of the border" flair.

INGREDIENTS

6-8 slices whole wheat or sour dough bread

1 cup green pimento-stuffed olives, finely chopped

1/2 cup blue cheese, crumbled

3-4 tablespoons mayonnaise (3-4 ounces cream cheese, softened, can be substituted for the mayo

For you mayo-haters)

1 teaspoon Louisiana hot sauce

DIRECTIONS

Using a 1 1/2-inch diameter biscuit cutter, cut bread slices into 24 rounds. Slightly toast rounds on both sides under broiler. Meanwhile, mix olives, cheese, mayonnaise and hot sauce until well blended. Place one spoonful of olive-cheese mixture atop each toast round. Broil on rack in the middle of the oven (slightly away from the heat) for approximately 5 minutes, or until heated through and slightly browned on top. Garnish with a slice of olive and serve hot.

*This makes a delicious grilled sandwich, too. Simply put the olive mixture between two full slices of bread and grill in skillet until bread is browned and inside is hot.

Tax Bite

Great Big Empty Pot

According to J.D. Foster, Ph.D. economist, Medicare trustees report that the Medicare program will present the nation with an $85.6 trillion financial hole on a perpetual time horizon (in perpetuity). This figure differs from the Medicare trustees' forecast of $36 trillion over a 75-year horizon.

Source: "A First Big Step Toward Medicare Sustainability" by J.D. Foster, The Heritage Foundation No. 2253, March 24, 2009; For more information visit: http://www.cms.hhs.gov/reportstrustfunds/downloads/tr2009.pdf

Sun-Dried Tomato-Greek Olive Tapenade on Goat Cheese

INGREDIENTS

8 ounces Montrachet goat cheese, softened to room temp

4 ounces cream cheese

1 cup sun-dried tomatoes, packed in olive oil, drained

1 cup Kalamata olives, pitted

1-2 cloves garlic, minced

Mix cheeses and pat into a round in center of serving platter, about 1/2-inch thick. Set aside. Place sun-dried tomatoes and garlic in food processor and process for 30 seconds to one minute until ingredients form a smooth spread. Scrape down sides of bowl and add olives. Continue processing until olives are finely chopped. This will take just about 15-20 seconds. To be safe, use the pulse button to reach desired consistency. Spread olive mixture over cheese and serve with crackers or sliced baguette.

Tax Bite

Cashed-Out Canisters

Federal social insurance trust funds, maintained by the Department of the Treasury, account for all income and disbursements of the Social Security programs. There are two trusts for Social Security: the Federal Old-Age and Survivors Insurance (OASI), established on Jan. 1, 1940, and the Federal Disability Insurance Trust Fund (DI), established on August 1, 1956. Though OASI pays for old-age and survivors' retirement benefits and DI covers benefits to those unable to work due to medical conditions, they are often referred to together as OASDI Trust Funds. The portion of the trust funds remaining after paying out benefits and program administration costs is theoretically invested daily in U.S. Government interest-bearing obligations (Treasury Bonds or Notes). It is important to bear in mind these trust funds are simply accounting gimmicks. There are no "trusts" in the trust funds that fall under the Social Security programs. These are simply IOUs the government writes itself and then cashes to fund these programs.

Source: www.socialsecurity.gov; J.D. Foster, Ph.D. Economics

Nutty Stuffed Mushrooms

These mushroom caps, filled with a delightful sauté of arugula, shallots, walnuts, wheat germ and white wine are sure to start your party off on the right note.

INGREDIENTS

24 medium-sized mushrooms
2 tablespoons butter
2 tablespoons extra virgin olive oil
2 large shallots, finely diced
1 clove garlic, minced
1/4 cup finely chopped walnuts
1/4 cup breadcrumbs
1/4 cup wheat germ
1 cup finely chopped arugula
1/4 cup dry white wine
1 teaspoon lemon juice
1 teaspoon soy sauce
1/2 cup finely grated Parmesan cheese
Salt and pepper to taste

DIRECTIONS

Wash and dry the mushrooms. Remove stems and chop them finely. Set aside. Set mushroom caps on a lightly greased baking sheet.

Melt butter with olive oil in frying pan. Sautee shallots, chopped mushroom stems, and garlic until soft and only slightly browned. Add wine and cook until liquid is nearly evaporated. Next add walnuts, breadcrumbs, wheat germ and arugula and continue to cook over medium-low heat for another two minutes. Add lemon juice and soy sauce. Mix well and remove from heat. Add salt and pepper to taste. When completely cool, mix in Parmesan cheese. Can be prepared a day ahead and refrigerated. When ready to serve, stuff mixture into mushroom caps and bake at 350°F for 20 to 25 minutes until tops are slightly browned and mushroom caps are cooked through.

Tax Bite

Uncle Sam's Second Helping

Beware of the FICA finks! If you change jobs during a calendar year, you start paying FICA (Social Security) taxes all over again, even if you've already satisfied the maximum annual deductions at your old job. It seems the IRS can't track your Social Security number when it isn't in their interest to do so. Uncle Sam earns the interest on your second helping of FICA tax deductions until you apply for a refund on line 65 of your 1040 tax return the following year.

Source: Our very own tax return

Warming Up to Spicy Wings

When you think of spicy wings, you probably think of Buffalo wings. That is because it was at the Anchor Bar in Buffalo, New York that this dish was invented. The wings were an instant hit and the city of Buffalo has since proclaimed July 29 as official "Chicken Wing Day." Here is our version of this famous dish.

WINGS

48 party chicken wings (include both drummettes and wings)

SAUCE INGREDIENTS

1/4 cup vinaigrette or Italian salad dressing

1/2 cup Louisiana hot sauce

1/2 cup medium-hot salsa

1 tablespoon medium 'hot' sauce (such as La Victoria's

1 teaspoon Tabasco sauce (can add this to desired heat)

1/4 cup Worcestershire sauce

1/2 cup Soy sauce

1 tablespoon brown sugar

1 teaspoon paprika

1/4 to 1/2 teaspoon cayenne pepper (depending on your heat tolerance)

1 tablespoon fresh squeezed lemon juice

3-4 grinds of freshly cracked pepper

Tax Bite

Golf Tax

If you'd like to take your mind off Social Security taxes for an afternoon, consider a game of golf. There is no better way to readjust the eye from the (tax) bill to the ball! Sadly, for those taxpayers in California, this respite from taxes could be short-lived. The 2009 state legislature proposed a "golf" excise tax on all golf-related activities, including golf play and services. Though the bill did not pass in the most recent budget, it's not dead yet. If the proposed golf tax passes, the price of a bucket of balls, or a round of golf would increase a minimum of 8.25 percent and higher in many counties.

Source: Lauren Silvan, www.ForeCalifornia.com

DIRECTIONS

Mix all of the above and pour over wings in large plastic container. Marinate in the refrigerator for several hours, or overnight, shaking/turning occasionally.

Prepare a large roasting pan with generous covering of cooking spray. Spread wings and sauce out in pan. Bake at 375°F for 1.5 hours, or until crunchy and browned. The longer they bake, the crunchier they get! Serve with homemade or store-bought bleu cheese or creamy feta dressing, celery and carrot sticks, and fresh raw string beans.

*This recipe is a bit healthier than the traditional recipe because the wings are baked rather than fried, and the butter is omitted.

Creamy Bleu or Feta Cheese Dressing

1/2 cup crumbled blue or feta cheese
2 tablespoons white wine vinegar
1/4 cup virgin olive oil
2 tablespoons mayonnaise
Dash cayenne pepper

Puree in food processor, or simply mix thoroughly by hand with a whisk. Store in refrigerator. Dressing will be chunkier if mixed by hand.

Sultry Spiced Nuts

These nuts are delicious on their own, for a bite to eat during cocktail hour, but they are also fabulous tossed into salad, or served atop curry. My friend Maureen introduced me to these tasty treasures as part of a recipe to top a cheese spread made from goat, blue and cream cheeses.

INGREDIENTS

1 cup pecans, or walnuts, or mixture, halved or coarsely chopped

2 teaspoon chili oil

4 teaspoon olive oil

1/4 teaspoon cinnamon

1/4 teaspoon cumin

1/4 teaspoon cardamom

1/2 teaspoon salt

1/4 teaspoon pepper

3 teaspoon sugar

DIRECTIONS

Mix spices with salt and pepper in small bowl. Heat oils in small frying pan. Add nuts and sauté until slightly browned. Add sugar and cook, stirring, until melted. Add nuts to bowl of spices and toss to coat well. Cool. (Be careful to hide these, or there won't be any left for the salad!)

Tax Bite

Self-Employed … Income Destroyed?

Is self-employment worth it? Possibly not, just look at this example. My son worked as a basketball referee during high school and made a whopping $957 during the 2008 tax year. After the standard deduction of $1,251 his taxable income was zero. Yet, he was still assessed $146 or 15.3 % of his earnings for self-employment (FICA and Medicare) tax. Employees pay half that amount in payroll taxes, or 7.65%–and that is bad enough already! For the self-employed in California, the combined taxes can be as high as 60.8%, increasing to 65.4% when the Bush tax cuts expire in 2011. Once the Medicare tax hikes take effect, (to help pay for ObamaCare) taxes could reach 66.3% on marginal income.

Source: Our own 2008 1040 Tax Returns

CHAPTER II

From Soup to Nutty Taxes

Soups & Sales Tax

Unless you happen to live in Alaska, Delaware, Montana, New Hampshire or Oregon, you pay sales tax on consumer purchases. Despite the fact these purchases are made with "after-tax" earnings, most goods brought home for personal benefit come with the added burden of sales tax ranging from one percent in Wyoming to 8.25 percent in California. These rates don't include the additional taxes some counties and cities levy.

If you're lucky enough to live in any state other than Alabama, Mississippi, Hawaii, Idaho, Kansas, Oklahoma and South Dakota you pay either a reduced sales tax on food items purchased for home consumption, or in the case of 31 states, no tax at all on such items.* No, this does not include alcohol, even if you plan to drink it at home!

In five of the states mentioned above (Hawaii, Idaho, Kansas, Oklahoma and South Dakota) you pay full sales tax, upfront, but some families and individuals receive offsetting credits or rebates. Beware, not everyone qualifies and rules vary. In seven states, Arkansas, Illinois, Missouri, Utah, Virginia and West Virginia you pay a reduced sales tax rate on these food items.

The same rules generally apply to pharmaceuticals in each of the states. Bottom line, if you're sick or hungry in most states, you get a pass on sales tax for those items. This is actually kind of nice, because every time we turn around we're hit with a new tax. It's a little like being in a boxing ring with Uncle Sam, only he wears gloves, and we don't. Lately, we've experienced government "spending on steroids." This is tough for taxpayers who generally operate without the assistance of steroids, which by the way are illegal (without a prescription) but if sold, can be taxed.

Now, if you plan to consume your food in the grocery store or in a restaurant, the "no tax" deal is off. If the deli counter so much as tucks a fork in with your half-pint of potato salad, you pay tax on that item in states where sales tax is imposed. This is why I recommend starting a good collection of delicious recipes so you can prepare your food, tax-free, at home! You can begin right here with 150 tantalizing and surprisingly easy recipes.

Next time you plan a trip to the grocery store, just count the number of times you've been taxed for that one trip: tax on the gasoline to power your car, for which you pay yearly registration and license fees on top of the sales tax when you originally bought it, in addition to the fact you already own the car company that sold it to you, since you're one the of benevolent taxpayers who bailed out U.S. car companies last year, and now, of course, you pay interest to yourself for the car loan you took out from the bank you've since purchased—all compliments of the U.S. government. And guess what? All of this was accomplished with after-tax dollars, so it's all at least double-taxed, if not three or four times! But most of you can seek comfort in knowing that "At least they don't tax your food!"

Tax Bite

Finland Food and Fodder Tax

You may feel better when you stop to think that Finland charges a Value Added Tax of 17% on food and fodder. This makes our sales tax look like bird food! On the other hand, tax rates on food in Italy may be as low as 4% compared with a rate of 20% for most other purchases.

Source: News Room Finland and Key Italy (keyitaly.com)

Items considered "prepared" such as rotisserie chickens, birthday cakes, or anything served to you "fork-ready" does not qualify for the tax break. See individual states for rules. Most local jurisdictions apply state rules on food taxation except some localities in Arizona, Colorado, Georgia, Louisiana and North Carolina, where food purchases are typically taxed at the local level.

La Piazza Artichoke Soup

Charles Mounzer, owner of La Piazza restaurant in Orinda, California says this is their most popular soup, and it all came about quite by accident. They had ordered two cases of artichoke bottoms for a new pizza they planned to feature on their new menu. Unfortunately, they forgot to put that pizza on the menu and, not wanting to waste the precious cases of artichokes, they concocted this delicious soup!

INGREDIENTS

2 cans artichoke bottoms
1/2 cup half & half
1 onion, chopped
2-3 tablespoons olive oil
1 large russet potato, peeled and diced
1 cup water
1 cup chicken broth (or vegetable broth)
Salt and pepper to taste

DIRECTIONS

In a large soup pot, heat olive oil over medium heat. Add onions and cook over medium-high heat until caramelized, or beginning to brown. Add the rest of the ingredients to the pot, bring to a boil, and then reduce heat to low, cooking for about 30 minutes, or until all veggies are soft. With a hand beater, beat until smooth. If you prefer to use a food processor, that's fine, but kind of messy with all the liquid. Heat to serve.

Tax Bite

Twinkie Tax

Some states have considered levying a "fat" tax on unhealthy, junk foods that, according to a predetermined formula, have higher caloric value and inferior nutritional content. Sometimes referred to as the "Twinkie" tax, this tax would be expected to result in little change in eating habits. Because dairy products constitute a good portion of "at home" fat consumption, and given the demand for most dairy products is inelastic, the fat tax is just another way to raise government revenue.

In Alabama the fat tax is a done deal for state employees. Those state employees considered obese or who have high blood pressure, high cholesterol or high glucose will have to pay $25 per month more in health insurance beginning in January 2011.

Sources: http://www.nowpublic.com/health/Alabama-impose-fat-tax, "Fat Taxes: Big Money for Small Change" www.bepress.com/fhep/10/2/2/; www.howstuffworks.com/tfat-tax.het

Sage Acorn Squash Soup

(Makes 8 cups or 4 bowls)

Acorn squash can be stuffed, sweetened for dessert, or simply baked with salt, pepper and a spot of butter. As a soup, it makes a warm, cozy entrée on a cold autumn evening.

INGREDIENTS

3 medium acorn squash cut in half, seeds and fibers removed from the center
2 tablespoons extra-virgin olive oil
1 yellow onion, peeled and finely chopped
1 medium-large shallot, peeled and finely diced
1-2 cloves garlic, crushed
2 teaspoon dried sage
1 bunch fresh sage
Salt and pepper to taste
1/2 cup dry white wine
1 1/2 cups half & half
4 cups chicken broth
1-2 teaspoons soy sauce
3-4 dashes Tabasco sauce

DIRECTIONS

Season each acorn squash cavity with salt, pepper and a sprinkling of dried sage. Place squash, upside down, in large greased baking dish and cook for 30 minutes at 350°F, or until a knife will easily pierce through outer shell. Cool. Scoop out pulp and set aside. Discard outer shells.

In a large sauté pan or soup pot, heat olive oil. Add onions, shallot and garlic and sauté just until cooked, but not overly browned. Add salt and pepper, dried sage and 2-3 sage leaves, minced.

Add squash pulp and continue to cook until heated through. Remove from stove. Puree mixture in food processor until very smooth. Add squash mixture to a large soup kettle or heavy pot. Stir white wine, broth and half & half into

Tax Bite

Maryland Flush Tax ... You'll Snicker Over This One!

The Maryland "Flush" Tax, otherwise known as the "If you pee or poop, you pay" tax, is a $30 annual fee charged to all property owners with buildings on them, whether they use public water and sewer systems or septic tanks. Non-Residential customers will be billed at a rate of $7.50 per quarter per equivalent dwelling unit (EDU) up to 3000 EDU, between 3001-5000 EDU will be charged at $3.75 per quarter per EDU, and any EDU's over 5000 for one customer will not be billed. The maximum fee for any single site is $10,000. The state expects to raise $60 million to $70 million a year to upgrade the state's 66 major sewage treatment plants to reduce the discharge of nitrogen and phosphorus that pollute the Chesapeake Bay and other waterways. The money also will be used to upgrade septic systems and fund a cover-crop program that encourages farmers to plant crops that absorb nitrogen.

Source: City of Frederick, MD.

mixture. Heat to simmering, stirring occasionally. Add soy sauce and Tabasco, stir and heat, but don't boil. Serve and garnish with a few sage leaves and a sprinkle of paprika for color.

Rustic Tomato Basil Soup

(Makes four 1-cup servings)

Segue into spring with this medley of fresh tomatoes, basil, bell pepper and Parmesan. This soup calls for fresh produce, yet creates a warm, toasty meal for those wild and woolly nights that aren't yet gentle as a lamb. Topped with a heaping spoonful of finely grated Parmesan and served with a mixed green salad and crusty bread, you don't need much else for a light spring supper. Though this soup could be pureed, we like it a bit on the chunky side for a rustic character with flavorful bites of sautéed veggies.

INGREDIENTS

1 yellow onion, finely chopped
2 tablespoons olive oil
1/2 orange or yellow bell pepper, finely chopped
1 stalk celery, finely chopped
1-2 cloves garlic, crushed
6 medium-sized tomatoes, coarsely chopped
1/4 cup basil leaves (8-10 leaves) thinly sliced
2 cups chicken broth
1 cup half & half
11/2 teaspoons Balsamic vinegar
Salt and pepper to taste
1/2 cup finely grated Parmesan cheese (for garnish)

Tax Bite

Grand Prize Winner for "Best Name" Taxpayer Association

In my research for this book, I relied on information and tips offered by various taxpayer associations across the country, in addition to government Sources. The "Best Name" award goes to PETT (People for the Ethical Treatment of Taxpayers) based in Pensacola, Florida. The group was founded by Greg Fink in response to a growing concern over continual increases of hidden taxes and user fees across the northwestern Florida region. The group soundly defeated a proposed sales tax increase to fund healthcare for indigent people in the community. This tax would've "stolen" $20 million per year from the 300,000 residents of Escambia County, while benefiting just 2,500 people. The "First Runner-Up" award goes to Darrel Bruck's OUTRAGE (Organization United to Reduce All Government Excesses) of Bradley, Illinois.

Source: NTU.org

DIRECTIONS

In a five to six-quart pot, sauté onions in olive oil over medium-high heat until soft and beginning to brown. Add garlic, bell pepper and celery to onion in pot. Continue to cook for about four to five more minutes over medium-high heat. Celery and bell pepper should still be somewhat crunchy. Add tomatoes and cook just until heated through, stirring the veggies several times to mix. Add chicken broth, half & half and balsamic vinegar and heat mixture to a simmer, stirring occasionally. Remove from heat and season to taste with salt and pepper. Garnish soup with one to two tablespoons grated Parmesan and serve hot with crusty French bread.

Tax Bite

"LOST" Tax

A Local Option Sales Tax (LOST) is a special-purpose sales tax levied at the county or city level as a means to raise funds for specific local projects such as street improvement or downtown redevelopment. Usually these taxes are voted in for a specified length of time and extensions to the original time frame must also be approved by voters. LOST taxes are levied in addition to the state and municipality's standard sales tax rate.

Source: Greg Fink, People for the Ethical Treatment of Taxpayers (PETT)

French Onion Soup au Gratin

(Serves 4)

The word "soup" stems from the idea of soaking. The Latin verb suppare, meaning to soak, was borrowed from the same German root "sup" found in the English words sup and supper. From these derived the word suppa, which became the French version soupe. This represented both the piece of bread soaked in liquid and the broth poured over the bread. The bread or toast was an important part of this dish. It allowed the diner to consume the liquid in an efficient manner, by sopping it up, eliminating the need for a spoon. French onion soup is therefore the most perfect soup!

INGREDIENTS

1/2 stick butter

5 large onions, peeled, cut in half and thinly sliced (about 3 pounds)

2 tablespoons brown sugar

1 teaspoon sea salt

1/2 teaspoon white pepper

1 tablespoon finely minced fresh thyme

*4 cups beef stock or broth**

2 cups chicken broth

1 cup dry Sherry (or dry white wine)

4 thick slices crusty French bread, slightly toasted

1 cup Gruyere (or Swiss) cheese, grated

*By using a truly homemade bouillon–beef bones and shank meat simmered for several hours with carrots, onions, celery, seasonings, and herbs, you can achieve a superb flavor, but if you lack time or ability to make your own stock, packaged beef broth is a perfectly adequate substitute, and exactly what we use.

Tax Bite

Texas Retaliatory Tax

How is this for a tax? The great state of Texas imposes a "Retaliatory" tax on foreign insurance companies that are licensed by the state of Texas to do business there. In this case, "foreign" refers to other states, not other countries. The purpose is to create an equal playing field as far as tax rates imposed by each state. So, for example, if a company is based in Oklahoma where the tax rate might be $50 per $1,000 of premium, and the same company is licensed to do business in Texas, where the tax may be only $20 per $1,000 in premium, Texas charges the Oklahoma insurer the difference between the two rates, to create a "like for like" tax environment. I always thought it was a good thing to open shop in a lower-taxed state, but in this case, it makes absolutely no difference. I'm not saying this is a good tax, but I just love the name!

Source: http://www.window.state.tx.us/taxinfo/insurance/ins_ret.html

DIRECTIONS

Melt butter in large pot. Add onions. Cover and cook over medium-low heat until wilted, about 10 minutes. Sprinkle sugar, salt and thyme over onions and toss. Cook uncovered, over medium-high heat until caramelized, stirring just occasionally. Season with white pepper.

Add sherry or wine and cook over high heat until wine is reduced, then add three cups of beef stock and simmer over medium-high heat, uncovered, for about 10-15 minutes. Add remaining stock (both chicken and remaining beef) and continue cooking over medium-low heat for about 30 minutes longer, until the broth has a rich taste.

Preheat broiler to high.

Spoon hot soup into four oven-proof soup bowls. Place a slice of French bread on each and divide cheese into four even portions and sprinkle over each bowl of soup. Place bowls on a baking sheet and broil until cheese is melted and bubbly. Serve immediately.

Tax Bite

Motion Picture Tax

In North Carolina a privilege tax of 1% is imposed on gross receipts of a person who is engaged in the business of operating a motion picture show for which an admission is charged.

Source: www.nccommerce.com

Hungarian Mushroom Soup

This soup is really easy, but tastes like you've been cooking for hours. If you really want to go easy on yourself, use the pre-sliced mushrooms.

INGREDIENTS

4 cups sliced fresh mushrooms (cremini,white, or brown mushrooms)
1 large yellow onion, chopped
2 tablespoons butter
2 tablespoons flour
1 tablespoon fresh dill weed, minced (or 1 teaspoon dried)
1 teaspoon Hungarian paprika
1 tablespoon soy sauce
1 cup milk
Juice of 1/2 lemon
2 tablespoons fresh parsley, minced
2 cups chicken broth
Dash chili pepper
1/2 cup sour cream, or plain Greek yogurt

DIRECTIONS

In a large pot, sauté onion in butter until soft and translucent. Add mushrooms and sauté until soft. Sprinkle flour, paprika and dill weed over onion-mushroom mixture, stir well and continue to cook, integrating the flour with the veggies. Slowly add milk, soy sauce and chicken broth. Mix well. Finally add lemon juice, parsley, dash chili powder, and sour cream/yogurt. Heat through, but don't boil. Serve hot.

Tax Bite

Home Rule Taxes

Speaking of outrage, some municipalities across the country have "Home Rule" authority, allowing them to impose higher rates of tax on certain goods and services than in other locales. These rules vary by state, but in the state of Illinois, the Home Rule allows for special utility taxes and extra helpings of sales tax applied in increments of 0.25% with no maximum rate. By comparison, non-Home Rule municipalities max out additional sales tax at 0.50%. Chicago may impose an additional use tax of 1.25%. The City of Kankakee, Illinois, situated just 60 miles south of Chicago, imposes a 5% utility tax on electricity, natural gas, telephone and water. And the water is taken freely from the Kankakee River at no charge! Naturally, folks expect to pay for the delivery of water to the home, but to be taxed an additional 5% on that service seems way out of line. Home Rule may be voted in by the city council in cities larger than 25,000, but in smaller towns, it must be passed by referendum.

Source: Darrell Bruck, President, OUTRAGE

Yankee Pier New England Clam Chowder

(Serves 6 one-cup servings)

Chef Michael Dunn of Yankee Pier in Lafayette, California shared this recipe and I am so glad he did. He serves it with Lark Creek's drop biscuits, which can be found in Chapter XI "Breads." Both recipes originate from the Lark Creek Restaurant Group.

INGREDIENTS

2 cups yellow or white onion, diced
2 cups celery, diced
2 cups new potatoes, diced into half-inch cubes
1 cup raw bacon, diced
1 cube butter
1/2 cup all-purpose flour
1 teaspoon fresh thyme, minced
1 teaspoon white pepper
1 1/2 teaspoons sea salt
1 cup clam juice
2 cups chicken broth
1 cup milk
1 cup half & half (can use non-fat half & half)
1/4 cup white wine or dry sherry
1 teaspoon Tabasco
1 1/2 cups chopped canned clams, or (1 1/2 pounds fresh, chopped clams)

DIRECTIONS

In a heavy pan, cook bacon over medium temperature until crispy. Remove from pan and set aside. Drain the grease, and in same pan, cook potatoes with 1/2 cube of butter until potatoes can be pierced with a knife or fork. Add remaining butter, celery and onion and continue to cook until celery and onion just begin to soften. Add flour to vegetables in pan and stir well until flour is incorporated with veggies and butter.

Tax Bite

Maine Mahogany Quahog Tax

Mahagony Quahog dealers in Maine are taxed at $1.20 per bushel. Like me, perhaps you've never heard of a quahog until this very moment, but at least it's good to know the little creatures aren't getting off scot-tax-free! Quahogs are Atlantic coast round clams with hard shells often used in chowders.

Source: Maine Revenue Services

Tax Bite

Tax Holidays

Many States offer a Tax Holiday for special occasions such as "back to school" shopping or Christmas holiday shopping and others. For a listing of these tax-exempt holidays, please visit: The Sales Tax Institute at http://www.salestaxinstitute.com/

Meanwhile, in a separate pot, mix clam juice, chicken broth, milk, half & half and wine and bring just to a boil. Add liquids to veggies in four intervals, stirring to thicken between each addition. Add thyme, white pepper, salt, Tabasco, bacon and clams. Continue to cook over low heat, stirring occasionally, for another half hour. Serve piping hot with crusty French bread.

Can freeze for reheating later.

Chicken Corn Chowder

(Serves six)

1 yellow onion, diced

1/4 cup vegetable oil

3-4 strips of bacon, cooked and crumbled

2-3 boneless, skinless chicken breasts cut into 1-inch cubes

2 medium russet potatoes, peeled or not, your choice, and diced into quarter-inch cubes

1 16-ounce bag frozen yellow corn (frozen roasted corn from Trader Joe's is excellent in this soup)

1 teaspoon fresh thyme

1 jalapeno, seeded and finely diced (I used canned jalapeno)

2 tablespoons chopped fresh cilantro

1/2 teaspoon white pepper

3-4 cups chicken broth (depending upon how thick or thin you like the soup)

1/2 cup half & half

1/4 cup dry white wine

Louisiana Hot Sauce for serving (if the jalapenos aren't hot enough for you!)

1 fresh lime, cut into wedges

Tax Bite

Only Chickens Fly Free Tax

There is no limit to the number of [chicken] hens a person may keep in New York City. In fact registration is not necessary, even though hens are considered legal pets, just like cats or dogs. But, people who are caught housing roosters, ducks, turkeys, geese or pheasants are fined between $200 and $2,000 if reported. And, they must get rid of the birds.

Sources: www.nyc.gov/html/doh/downloads/pdf/zoo/zoo-animal-healthcode.pdf and Owen Taylor, Just Food

DIRECTIONS

In a large soup pot, heat 2-3 tablespoons oil, add onion, and sauté until translucent. Add chicken to pan and cook over medium-high heat until slightly browned, about five minutes. Cover and cook for another five minutes over low heat until chicken is just cooked. Remove onion and chicken from pan and set aside. In the same pan, add another tablespoon of oil and potatoes. Cook over medium heat until potatoes are slightly browned. Add corn and continue to cook for about five minutes, stirring frequently. Return chicken and onion to pan along with bacon, fresh thyme, white pepper, jalapeno and cilantro. Add 3-4 cups chicken broth, white wine, and 1/2 cup half & half. Simmer for about five to ten minutes until hot. Soup can be prepared to this point until ready to use. When ready to serve, reheat over medium heat, but don't allow soup to boil. Serve piping hot and garnish with fresh squeezed lime and Louisiana hot sauce.

Yellow Cauliflower-White Cheddar Soup

It's not just your grandmother's white cauliflower anymore. After decades of selective crossbreeding, cauliflower is now available in four different colors: white, purple, yellow-orange and green. At a local market I discovered the purple and the yellow-orange "cheddar" cauliflower, which are excellent when steamed, and then roasted with a little extra-virgin olive oil and freshly grated Parmesan cheese. The "cheddar" cauliflower was first discovered in 1970 in the Bradford Marsh just north of Toronto, Canada, but it was very small and not so flavorful. After years of perfecting, this variety is of comparable size and flavor to the original white variety and is said to contain 25 times more beta carotene.

INGREDIENTS

1 yellow onion, chopped
2 tablespoons olive oil
1 carrot, grated
1 head cauliflower steamed until al dente and coarsely chopped. **Reserve** *broth!*
1/2 teaspoon white pepper
1/2 teaspoon sea salt
1 tablespoon butter
1-2 tablespoons flour (gravy flour is easier to incorporate, but regular flour will be fine, too!)
2-3 cups veggie broth (or chicken broth)
1/4 cup dry sherry
1/2 cup half and half (or milk)
1 cup grated white cheddar cheese

DIRECTIONS

In a large pot over medium-high heat, cook onion in olive oil until translucent. Add carrots and continue to cook for a few minutes longer. Add 1 tablespoon butter and sprinkle flour, salt and pepper over onion, carrot mixture. Cook over

Tax Bite

Sneaky Stepsister Tax

"Use" tax is the sneaky stepsister to "sales" tax. Where sales tax is usually applied to sales of taxable products within a given state, use tax is generally levied on transactions that would have been subject to sales tax if the sale had occurred in the tax-imposing state. The use tax enables states to prevent consumers from avoiding sales tax by either making "out of state" catalog or Internet purchases. Vendors who ship to other tax-imposing states are responsible for collecting the use tax, but purchasers are required to self-assess use tax if the vendor fails to collect the sales tax. This is a tricky tax, because there is a common misperception that Internet sales are not subject to tax and many business owners are unaware of use tax laws in various states. This tax is a red flag for audits. Lest you desire a meeting with a tax auditor, which is generally right after torture on most people's wish lists, you may want to check on the use tax before making your next fancy food purchase from a catalog or website.

Source: Alan Smith, Director of Sales Tax Services, Olivier & Associates, www.oatax.com/taxtipFebruary2008.htm

medium high heat, for about 3-5 minutes, stirring all the while to slightly brown flour. Slowly add veggie broth (or chicken broth) and stir with a wire whisk to incorporate flour. Add milk or half & half, sherry and cauliflower. Stir well. Add grated cheddar and stir until heated through and melted. Serve piping hot.

*Add more milk or broth to adjust consistency if soup is too thick.

Carol "The Babysitter's" Garden Fresh Gazpacho

Some call it liquid salad, but whatever you call it, this soup is refreshing and delicious in the heat of the summer. My kids' day care mom, Carol McCabe, shared this recipe years ago and we've used it ever since. Served with crusty bread, a dollop of sour cream and garnished with slices of avocado and cilantro sprigs, gazpacho makes a garden-fresh delight.

When selecting the ingredients for your gazpacho, be sure to use only ripe, fresh vegetables. It is fun to vary the vegetables that go into your gazpacho. For example, use yellow tomatoes and yellow bell peppers to create a golden yellow soup one time, followed by red or orange tomatoes and red or orange bell peppers the next. The key to making good gazpacho is to balance the mix so that no one ingredient overpowers the rest. It should be a harmonious blend of seasonal produce. It's best made several hours or a day ahead, so that the flavors have time to blend.

Tax Bite

Santa Rosa Island Surtax

Pensacola Beach on Santa Rosa Island in Florida has a unique fee structure for visitors wishing to purchase anything while visiting the island. Because the land is lease held, meaning the land under commercial and residential buildings is not sold, but rather leased on 99 year terms, the Santa Rosa Island Authority charges a lease fee to island businesses based upon revenue. Each fee is different as each lease contract is unique. Every commercial enterprise may pass the lease cost through to the customer, as long as it is not referred to as a sales tax. The bottom line, is that on top of the 6% state sales tax, there is a 1.5% Escambia County sales tax, and on top of that the SRIA fee can run anywhere from an additional 2% for professional services to 10% on concessions on the gulf pier. This can result in the customer paying between 9.5% and 17.5% in taxes and fees on their bill. The extra fees pay for services such as lifeguards, beach maintenance and bathroom upkeep.

Source: Greg Fink, President of People for the Ethical Treatment of Taxpayers; Santa Rosa Island Authority Finance Department

INGREDIENTS

1/2 bunch fresh cilantro leaves, stems removed
2 large cucumbers, peeled and seeded
1/2 orange bell pepper
1/2 yellow bell pepper
1/2 red bell pepper
1 medium red onion, chopped (can use either raw, or sautéed)
4 large tomatoes, quartered and seeded
2 cloves garlic, minced
1 tablespoon red wine vinegar
1 lime, juiced
1-2 teaspoons cumin powder
1 teaspoon California or New Mexico chili powder
1/2 teaspoon cayenne powder
1 14-ounce can of tomato sauce
1 cup chicken broth
For garnish: sour cream, fresh cilantro sprigs and avocado

DIRECTIONS

Cut cucumber, onion, bell peppers and tomatoes into medium-sized chunks. Place first 8 ingredients in large food processor fitted with a steal blade. Pulse processor six or seven times for a chunky gazpacho. Puree for a minute or two for a smoother soup. (Do this is batches if you can't fit it all into one processor bowl.) Transfer to a large glass serving bowl and add the remaining ingredients. Stir well. Chill for several hours or overnight. Garnish with avocado, sour cream and cilantro sprigs.

CHAPTER III

Tossing Up Taxes!

Salads & Property Tax

Despite all the rhetoric of boosting the economy with the federal government's $787 billion stimulus package, the most "shovel-ready" projects can be found right in your own back yard, shoveling dirt and pulling weeds to make way for this year's veggie garden. But, don't expect to see a dime from the government for your efforts, "NOT ONE DIME!"

It's unlikely you'll receive an invitation to the White House for an "Economic Super Hero" summit, but the seed purchases for your victory garden just may boost the economy out of the doldrums. Veggie seed sales are booming, and according to some reports, 2009 sales were up 40 percent over two years prior. Homegrown produce has its advantages to be sure, but cost savings to the home gardener may not be one of them.

The quaint idea of growing a family veggie garden sown on your own little slice of America can be very expensive when you take into account your annual property tax bill. The idea of saving money on produce by growing your own in the back yard is terrific, and the larger the land, the more bountiful the garden can be.

Gardening can be rewarding, but *please* don't forget the taxes you pay on the plot of land your veggies inhabit. The bigger the garden, the larger the land, the higher the taxes and this is all good for whom? Oh, yes, the government! In fact, if your garden is too prolific, the county tax assessor might get wind of it and stop by for a reassessment visit. Not good.

Property taxes vary of course by state, and by county, and in the case of some counties like King County, Washington, they vary by town and even by area within a city. For example, one portion of a larger town in King County may be assessed a tax increase one year, while other sections are not. As Wynnton Cannon, Chairman of the League of Washington Taxpayers said, "The county supervisors don't want everyone mad at them all at once!"

So, unless you live in the state of California, where the 1979 passage of Proposition 13 capped property tax at one percent of the purchase price, plus 1-2 percent annual increases on the property value, you will see a smattering of ever-rising property tax levies across the nation. These taxes are often embedded in the monthly mortgage payment, but for those that are not, the tax is usually paid in semi-annual payments. For example, in California, we pay property taxes in April and December. These make nice Easter and Christmas gifts for the government.

Many people opt out of the mortgage escrow property tax payment if they can, because they'd rather hold onto their money for most of the year, and fork it over to the government only when absolutely necessary. For anyone interested in "excising" property taxes from the escrow account, please visit: http://www.ehow.com/how_2107877_remove-property-tax-from-escrow.html

Property tax proceeds are the main source of funds for towns, cities and counties. These tax revenues specifically pay for local public schools, police/fire departments and water/sanitation services, and, even mosquito control! (Call the county if you have too many mosquitoes at your next barbecue!)

The rate of property tax varies widely by state. The property tax rate, which is a percentage of the total property value, ranged from 0.17 percent in Louisiana to 1.60 percent in New Jersey, according to a 2005 American Community Survey from the U.S. Census Bureau. Many states that do not have state income or sales tax often levy higher property taxes.

In Oregon, property taxes are based upon real market value, where in California they are based upon the purchase price of the home. In Nevada property values are reassessed every, single year and taxes are based upon the "net" assessed value, which has separate land and building components. The district tax rate is then applied to this value, and the allowable increase is capped. (In Nevada the 2009 cap was eight percent.)

In 1990, citizens of Oregon passed Measure 5, which limited Property tax to a maximum 1.5 percent of the real market value of the property. Don McIntire, President of the Taxpayers Association of Oregon introduced M-5 in the spring of 1989 in response to growing taxpayer discontent to ever-increasing property taxes. In 1989, a mobile home, or the equivalent was assessed roughly $3,000 in annual property tax, with two-thirds of that designated to fund education.

The measure, loosely modeled after California's Prop. 13 took a long, arduous year to pass. Now, one half percent is directed to Oregon's K-12 school system while the remaining one percent covers all other government expenditures. Oregon required the "double majority" rule in order to pass this measure, which meant that more than fifty percent of the voters had to turn out for the vote, and in turn, the measure had to pass by a majority of the votes.

Maine has an especially egregious property tax policy. This state socks it to resort areas in particular.

Jack Wibby is one Maine resident who was literally taxed out of his home.

"The state of Maine revalues property anytime they think they can get away with it," says Wibby, co-founder of Maine Taxpayers United, a group comprised of citizens who recognize they've been over-taxed for years at every level of government. The group's mission is to reduce state and local tax burdens and promote prudent government spending.

It is kind of odd, if you think about it. Under the 2008/09 Troubled Asset Relief Program (TARP) taxpayers were forced to pay for delinquent mortgages of those who took out home loans they couldn't afford in the first place. And, we've since learned that many had no financial stake in the home to begin with, (very small or no down payment), making it easy as pie to walk away. Meanwhile, folks who've owned their homes for years, paid off their mortgages and hoped to live out retirement in that home unencumbered of a monthly payment, must sell or rent out their homes just to pay the rapacious state and local property taxes.

Lately, citizens watch groups are taking action against the rash of property tax increases. Sooner or later, state politicians will be forced into responsible spending. It better happen before annual property taxes cost more than mortgage payments in every single municipality across the fruited plains. Otherwise, there will be a lot more vacated homes littering the landscape from Plymouth Rock to the Golden Gate Bridge, and as many abandoned veggie gardens.

Arugula Salad with Trio of Cheese, Spiced Nuts, and Orange Muscat Champagne Vinaigrette

(Serves 6)

Arugula is an aromatic, nutty and peppery salad green. It grows wild in Asia and all over the entire Mediterranean and has been cultivated and enjoyed in places as exotic as the north of Sudan. Arugula is gaining in popularity here in the United States and can now be found in most markets.

INGREDIENTS

5-6 cups arugula (loosely packed)
1 red onion very thinly sliced
2 tablespoons olive oil
1 avocado, firm but ripe, cut into small 1/3-inch chunks
1/4 cup crumbled blue cheese
1/2 cup crumbled feta cheese
Parmesan, shaved into large curls with a potato peeler (about three per serving)
1 cup Sultry Spiced nuts (see Chapter I)

Crispy Red Onions

In a frying pan, heat 2 tablespoon olive oil, add onions and cook over medium high heat until browned and crispy. Remove from heat and cool.

Orange Muscat Champagne Vinaigrette

2 tablespoon orange Muscat champagne vinegar (Trader Joe's)
3 tablespoon white wine vinegar
2 tablespoon water
1/2 cup light olive oil
1 small clove garlic, crushed
1/4 teaspoon onion powder
1/2 teaspoon salt
1/2 teaspoon freshly cracked pepper
(Add more salt and pepper as desired to taste)

Tax Bite

California Tax Grab

This may sound preposterous, but the State of California passed a measure in 2004, Prop 1A, which was designed to protect property tax revenues paid to counties and municipalities. Voters probably never knew about the stealthy clause that allows the State to "borrow" up to 8% of that revenue in times of economic stress. And, the State may borrow the money twice in any 10-year period for up to 3 years each time, as long as the loan was paid in full prior to the second helping. This can result in a 6-year period of revenue loss for counties and municipalities, because the State can pay the money back one day, and literally borrow it for the second time the following day. In addition, the State may simply take 8% from special incremental revenue districts, such as redevelopment districts, without ever paying it back! In my home town, that 8% is equivalent to 4.2% of the general fund revenue budget and 39.4% of the redevelopment general budget. This is quite a loss for small cities, with few alternative revenue sources.

Source: City of Auburn, Auburn Journal, CaliforniaCityFinance.com

Gently toss arugula, onions, avocado, nuts, crumbled blue and feta cheeses with Orange Muscat Champagne Vinaigrette. Garnish with Parmesan shavings. Serve at once.

Mouna's Celery Salad with Crumbled Blue Cheese

If you're like me, you want to have some sort of salad with every meal. But, sometimes it's such a pain in the neck to wash the lettuce and chop all the veggies. That's why I was delighted to taste Mouna's "oh so simple" salad of diced celery, blue cheese and vinaigrette.

INGREDIENTS PER PERSON

2 stalks of celery per person

1 tablespoon crumbled blue cheese

1-2 tablespoons of your favorite vinaigrette

(1/3 cup olive oil, 1/4 cup wine vinegar, fresh squeeze of lemon juice, and seasoning to taste)

DIRECTIONS

Toss all together in bowl and serve.

Tax Bite

Illegal Drug Stamp Tax

Marijuana is one crop you should not grow in your garden! Twenty states impose a stamp tax for the possession of illegal drugs, such as marijuana, cocaine and others. The tax rates are based on a scale of charges according to the sale price of the property. For example, in Kansas, stamps for 10 grams of cocaine cost $2,000 ($200 per gram) and in Kentucky, the stamps for cannabis sell for $3.50 per gram for more than 42.5 grams in possession, or $1,000 per plant if owner possesses five plants or more. The stamps may be purchased from the department of revenue and must be affixed to the drugs if and when they are seized to satisfy tax liability. The stamps have an expiration date, and if expired at the time of seizure, the individual will be charged with tax evasion in addition to charges for possession. Tax stamps will not prevent the individual from being prosecuted for possessing contraband, but only serve to prevent a charge of tax evasion. Purchases of tax stamps are said to be confidential, though some believe compliance with the law would only serve to incriminate them. Most people are unaware these laws even exist, but failure to comply can result in steep penalties. In Minnesota, failure to comply can cost up to $14,000 and seven years in jail, in addition to other criminal sentences. States imposing stamp taxes include: Alabama, Connecticut, Georgia, Idaho, Indiana, Iowa, Kansas, Kentucky, Louisiana, Massachusetts, Minnesota, Nebraska, Nevada, North Carolina, Oklahoma, Rhode Island, South Carolina, Tennessee, Texas and Utah. Don't worry, these states, usually only accept cash, so the buyer can remain anonymous!

Sources: *www.norml.org; www.ksrevenue.org/faqs-abcdrugtax.htm*

Greek Chickpea Salad

(Kathy Kaplan)
Serves 8

This salad made entirely of veggies, is dressed with a scant amount of olive oil and quite a helping of lemon juice. The seasoning derives from very thinly sliced basil and green onions. You may wish to further season with salt and pepper.

INGREDIENTS

Two 16-ounce cans chickpeas (garbanzo beans), drained and rinsed
3 plum (or Roma) tomatoes, diced
3 celery stalks, finely diced
3 scallions, finely diced
1/2 cup Kalamata olives, pitted and chopped
8 basil leaves, chiffonade (shredded fine)
1 tablespoon olive oil
Juice of 3 lemons
Salt to taste
Freshly ground black pepper

DIRECTIONS

Combine the chickpeas in a large bowl with the remaining ingredients. Toss well and taste for seasoning. Serve at room temperature or chilled (can be made in advance and stored for 3 days in an airtight container.)

Tax Bite

"Mill" Tax Rate

In many states, property taxes are expressed in "mills" which is an amount of tax per 1,000 currency units of property. This is also known as a millage rate or mill levy. To calculate the property tax due, the authorities multiply the assessed value of the property by the mill rate and then divide by 1,000. For example: a property with an assessed value of $500,000 with a mill rate of 20 would have a property tax bill of $10,000 per year.

Source: Homeowner's Guide to Property Tax in Maine

Panzanella (Bread) Salad

(Serves four as an entrée or six as a side dish)

This bread salad is delightful on a hot summer day, using the freshest of ingredients straight out of the veggie garden. Don't invite the county tax assessor for dinner!

INGREDIENTS

*6 one-inch slices of Ciabatta or crusty Italian bread cut into one-inch cubes**

1 head lettuce (romaine, or baby leaf lettuces)

1/2 bunch basil (red leafy basil is especially pretty in this salad, but traditional green works)

*3 large ripe tomatoes** (any combination of red, orange and yellow)*

1 red bell pepper

1/2 cucumber, peeled and sliced into 1/2-inch thick slices, then quartered

1/2 cup feta cheese, crumbled

1/2 cup antipasto olives, Kalamata or spiced Italian olives, drained

1 tablespoon capers, drained (optional)

**Use only the freshest, ripest tomatoes for this salad!

DRESSING INGREDIENTS

1/3 cup extra virgin olive oil

5 tablespoons red wine vinegar

1 clove garlic, minced (use more if you love garlic)

1/4 teaspoon anchovy paste

1/2 teaspoon Kosher or sea salt

1/2 teaspoon freshly ground pepper

1 tablespoon juice from tomatoes used in salad

Mix well and store in a jar until ready to use.

Tax Bite

Sad Tax (Special Assessment District)

This tax may often be confused with the actual property tax, especially since they often appear on the same bill. But, an assessment tax is a separate charge against those real estate parcels identified as having a direct and unique benefit from a particular project. These projects often include fire, school or mosquito and vector control. The real estate parcels within the Special Assessment District (SAD) are impacted.

Source: Placer County, Ca. Treasurer-Tax Collector

DIRECTIONS

Place bread squares in toaster oven at low temperature, about 200°F for about 30 minutes, or until crusty. Remove and cool to room temperature. Place bread in bottom of large salad bowl and layer the rest of the ingredients on top, beginning with lettuce, followed by cucumber, bell pepper, basil, feta, olives and capers. Pour dressing over top and let drain down to bread. Gently toss and serve.

*Can simply use stale bread, cut into cubes with or without first toasting.

Tax Bite

Minnesota Contamination Cooties Tax

This is a tax imposed annually on the contaminated value of taxable real property. This statewide tax, created in 1994 is designed to recapture tax revenues that were "lost" because property values were reduced due to contamination.

Source; Minnesota Contamination Tax Bulletin; Minnesota Dept. of Revenue

Frannie's Brussels Sprout-Heart of Palm Salad with Vinaigrette

One of my least favorite vegetables has (*had*) always been Brussels sprouts. So, when my friend Fran said she had a Brussels sprout recipe that would change my mind … I was leery. "I'll never eat Brussels sprouts … ever!" Wrong again. This salad is fabulous!

INGREDIENTS

1 head butter lettuce

18 Brussels sprouts, cut into quarters, lengthwise

1-2 tablespoon butter or olive oil

1 teaspoon Lawry's garlic salt

1/2 teaspoon pepper

One 14.5-ounce can or jar of hearts of palm spears, sliced into ¼-inch slices

1/4 cup crumbled blue cheese

1/4 cup shaved Parmesan cheese

1/4 cup cooked bacon or pancetta crumbles (optional)

4-5 tablespoons extra-virgin olive oil

2 tablespoons red wine vinegar

DIRECTIONS

Heat butter (or olive oil) in medium frying pan. Add quartered Brussels sprouts and season with Lawry's garlic salt and pepper. Sprinkle bacon or pancetta bits over all. Cook over medium-high heat for approximately 5 minutes. Stir Brussels sprouts to turn and continue to cook over medium heat for an additional 10 minutes or so, until sprouts are beginning to brown. When cooked, remove from heat and set aside.

Meanwhile, tear butter lettuce into bite-sized bits and place in salad bowl. Add blue cheese, Parmesan cheese and hearts of palm slices. When Brussels sprouts are cooked, place in salad bowl and toss with olive oil and vinegar. Serve at once.

Tax Bite

Property Tax Circuit Breaker

In many states, out of control government spending has elevated property tax rates to the point of forcing homeowners from their homes. In some cases, taxes on a home far outpace the mortgage on the same home. For folks on fixed incomes it can be impossible to pay those taxes and some are forced to rent out the home or sell in order to pay the tax. To ameliorate the situation, 31 states offer a "circuit breaker" program to prevent property taxes from overloading a taxpayer. Under the typical circuit breaker program, the state sets a maximum percentage of income that an eligible family can be expected to pay in property taxes. If the taxes exceed this limit, the state provides a rebate or credit to the taxpayer.

Source: Institute on Taxation and Economic Policy

Fresh Corn Salad with Catalina French Dressing

Despite the mad push for ethanol, which is causing higher prices and a shortage of fresh corn, corn still makes a great summer-time salad. This festive salad calls for corn, cooked then cut off the cob, cilantro, mild red chili peppers, bell peppers, basil and tomatoes, so you can have a hey day at the farmers' market picking up ingredients from nearly every vendor there.

INGREDIENTS

1 recipe French dressing (see recipe below)
6 ears fresh corn on the cob (or approximately 2 cups)
2 green onions, chopped
1/2 cup red bell pepper, diced
1/2 cup orange bell pepper, diced
1 mild red chili pepper, seeded and diced
1 large tomato, chopped
1/3 cup fresh basil, chopped
1/3 cup fresh cilantro, chopped
1/2 cup grated sharp cheddar cheese
Salt and pepper to taste
3 avocados

DIRECTIONS

Cook corn and slice kernels from cob. I like to steam the corn in a French steamer, but the corn can be cooked any way you prefer, i.e. grilled, boiled, or micro-waved. (Corn can be prepared a day or two ahead and refrigerated.)

Place all ingredients in a large salad bowl and toss with dressing. Serve over avocado halves along with warm French bread.

Tax Bite

Nebraska's Double Corn Tax

In Nebraska, corn is taxed twice, before it ever arrives to market, and then maybe again in the form of sales tax, depending upon the state it is shipped to. Thanks to the Ethanol Mandate, producers are taxed 7/8 of a cent per bushel for growing the corn. Then transportation of the corn is again taxed at the same rate. So, before corn ever reaches the retailer, it's already been taxed 1.75 cents per bushel. All that for Ethanol, which we now know is counterproductive in terms of saving money or the environment!

Source: Doug Kagan, Chairman Nebraska Taxpayers for Freedom

Catalina French Dressing

This dressing is the perfect complement to the corn salad, but if you're in a hurry or you prefer to use bottled tangy French dressing that works, too.

1/2 cup extra-virgin olive oil

3 tablespoons red wine vinegar

2 tablespoons fresh lime juice

1 teaspoon Worcestershire sauce

1 small clove garlic, minced

1/2 teaspoon sugar

1/2 teaspoon salt

1/2 teaspoon dry English mustard

1/4 teaspoon onion powder

1/2 teaspoon paprika

1 dash cayenne pepper

Mix all ingredients in a container with a tight-fitting lid. Shake well. Pour over salad and toss. This dressing is delicious with vine-ripened tomatoes, too.

Black Bean-Avocado Salad with Salsa Vinaigrette

INGREDIENTS

Two 15-ounce cans black beans, rinsed and drained

1/4 cup fresh cilantro leaves, chopped

1/2 red bell pepper, seeded and coarsely chopped

1 red onion, thinly sliced, and sautéed (in 2 T olive oil) until browned, then cooled

1 avocado, cut into bite-sized pieces

1/2 cup cherry tomatoes, halved

1/2 lime, juiced

1 head baby Romaine lettuce

1 recipe salsa vinaigrette (recipe below)

DIRECTIONS

Toss all of the above in medium sized bowl. Pour enough dressing over to coat well, but not drown!

Salsa Vinaigrette

1/3 cup light olive oil

1/4 cup red wine vinegar

1/4 cup bottled salsa

1 1/2 teaspoon onion powder

1 small clove garlic, minced

Salt and pepper to taste

Tax Bite

Tax Lien Market

Someone's loss is often another's gain, especially in the recent mortgage meltdown. There is an entire industry focusing on the secondary market of tax liens. These liens are issued against real estate properties when taxes become delinquent. Buyers scour local auctions for tax lien certificates, which produce one of two results for the investor: a payment with built-in profit by the landowner in order to release the lien, or title to the property if the delinquent taxpayer fails to pay up.

Source: http://preforeclosurefortune.com

Wild Rice Salad

Wild rice is so nutty and delicious, and when leftover and mixed with the Mediterranean flavors of sundried tomatoes, shallots, Kalamata olives, and pecans it makes a delightful and hearty salad for any time of the year.

INGREDIENTS

1 package wild rice, cooked according to directions and cooled to room temperature

2 green onions, finely chopped (or 1 large shallot thinly sliced and sautéed in olive oil)

1/4 cup sundried tomatoes, julienned and drained if packed in oil

1/4 cup quartered pecans, toasted and cooled

1/4 cup Kalamata olives, pitted and quartered

3 tablespoons extra virgin olive oil

2 tablespoons red wine vinegar

Salt and pepper, to taste

DIRECTIONS

Toss all ingredients together in a large salad bowl. Prepare one day ahead, so flavors have a chance to blend before serving.

Tax Bite

Washington's Home Seller's Tax

When homeowners in the state of Washington sell a home, they are hit with a 4% excise tax on the full sales price of a home. Sellers must not only consider the 6% Realtor commissions, but 4% excise tax to the state on top of that. According to my math, that is a 10% take from the bottom line!

Source: Wynnton G. Cannon, President, League of Washington Taxpayers

Tax Bite

Fifty-Fifty Excise Tax

In Maine, a tax of $2.20 per $500 in value is imposed when any real property is transferred. This tax is to be split evenly between grantor and grantee. Despite median home prices dropping to $150,000 in the state, this still can add several hundred dollars for both parties to the transaction.

Source: Maine Revenue Services

Roadhouse Chicken Salad

This salad has all the feeling of Buffalo wings, but without the bones or the mess!

INGREDIENTS

1 head romaine lettuce, torn into bite-sized pieces

1 to 2 avocados, peeled and sliced

4 boneless, skinless chicken breasts

4 tablespoons Louisiana Hot Sauce plus 2 tablespoons for drizzling over tossed salad

1/2 teaspoon chili powder

1 teaspoon paprika

1 teaspoon onion powder

3/4 cup walnuts, coarsely chopped, and toasted (can use spiced walnuts)

1/2 cup blue cheese dressing (use your favorite home-made or bottled dressing), or

1/2 cup Louisiana blue cheese vinaigrette (see recipe below)

DIRECTIONS

Mix hot sauce, chili powder, paprika and onion powder in a small bowl. Place chicken breasts in an airtight container, add sauce and shake well. Marinate for at least several hours or overnight in the refrigerator.

Cook chicken in 350-degree oven for about 20 minutes, or until done, or grill on the barbecue. Cool and cut into bite-sized pieces.

In a large salad bowl, place romaine lettuce, chicken, nuts and avocado and toss well with dressing. Serve immediately and, if you like it hot, drizzle a little extra Louisiana hot sauce over the top of served salads. Also, you can reserve a little of the avocado for a garnish.

Tax Bite

Homestead Exemption

In Georgia, a homeowner is entitled to a "homestead" exemption if the home is owner-occupied. The "Homestead" exemption was passed into law in 2000, and excludes the first $2,000 in home value from taxation. This provides a small, but nice tax advantage. While it is nice for homeowners, it can be seen as a disadvantage to landlords and renters, as they are not entitled to the same tax break.

Source: John Marsh, Clarke County Taxpayers and Property Owners Association

Louisiana Blue Vinaigrette

1/4 cup canola oil

1/4 cup white wine vinegar

5 tablespoons Louisiana hot sauce

1/8 teaspoon sugar

1/2 cup crumbled blue cheese

Combine first four ingredients and shake until well blended. Gently mix in blue cheese.

Suzanne's Monkey Cat Salad

This salad makes a great lunch for holiday guests, or a light dinner for those nights when you just want a salad for dinner.

INGREDIENTS

1 head romaine

1/2 cup dried cranberries

1/2 cup toasted pecans pieces

1/2 cup crumbled Gorgonzola

1-2 avocados cut into chunks

1 pound honey roasted turkey (I like to purchase a 3/4-inch thick chunk) skin removed and cut into bite-sized cubes

3 ounces Parmesan shaved with a potato peeler into wide strips,

2 large shallots, thinly sliced and caramelized in olive oil ... then cooled to room temp

1 recipe of Suzanne's M-Cat dressing

Place all of the ingredients in a large salad bowl, toss with Suzanne's dressing and serve!

Suzanne's dressing

1/4 cup apple cider vinegar

2 tablespoons soy sauce

1/2 cup canola oil

1 teaspoon onion powder

1 clove garlic, minced

Mix all of the ingredients in a shaker bottle and shake well. If you have the Good Seasons cruet, simply add the vinegar to the "V" line, the soy sauce to the "W" line and the oil to the "O" line.

Tax Bite

Telephone Pole Tax

In some states, the "right of way" that utility poles sit on is assessed property tax. In reality the pole itself is not taxed, but the tax is imposed upon the entity carrying the license to erect the pole in that location. This "right of way" is often located on private property, which is already taxed. The states claim the landowner is exempt from paying tax on that strip of land, so it is not double "property" taxed. At my house in California, we have an electric power pole located right in the middle of our acreage, but I've never seen such an exemption on our property tax bill! This "pole" tax is important, because as most folks know, businesses don't absorb tax burdens, rather customers do in the form of higher costs.

Source: Placer County Treasurer-Tax Collector

Chopped Italian Salad

(Serves 4 for entree-sized salad)

For a substantially filling "light" meal, this chopped Italian salad is a great way to go. Cubed Parmesan, salami, garbanzo beans and plenty of chopped veggies tossed in your favorite Italian dressing makes for a fun dinner at home, or a great dish to take on the road to your next potluck or picnic spot. Though there is a dressing recipe included, here, a good bottled dressing is perfectly fine, too.

INGREDIENTS

1 large head of Romaine lettuce, chopped
2 yellow, orange or red bell peppers, diced
One 15-ounce can of garbanzo beans, drained
1 1/2 cups of diced salami
4 ounces Parano or white cheddar cheese, cut into ½-inch cubes
4 ounces Parmesan cheese, cut into ½-inch cubes
1 large English cucumber, peeled and diced

DIRECTIONS

In a large glass salad bowl, layer lettuce, garbanzo beans, cucumber, salami and cheeses. Toss with dressing and serve with bread or crackers.

Dressing

1/2 cup olive oil
1/4 cup red wine vinegar
1 teaspoon Dijon mustard
2 tablespoons finely sliced fresh basil leaves
1 teaspoon dried Italian seasoning
Salt and pepper to taste

Mix all ingredients well and toss over salad.

Tax Bite

Transmission Line Tax

North Dakota strikes again taxing cooperative-owned transmission lines (of 230 kilovolts or larger) $225 per mile in lieu of property tax on lines and any substation used in delivering electrical energy. When will they ever learn? Taxes on businesses flow directly through to consumers.

Source: North Dakota Taxes

Fried Calamari and Crispy Red Onion Rings on Baby Greens with Thai Chili Vinaigrette

This salad is a take-off on a fabulous salad I enjoyed at Hotel ZaZa's Dragonfly Restaurant in Dallas.

INGREDIENTS

1 bag or roughly 6 cups of Mesclun (baby greens)

1 1/2 pounds calamari rings and tentacles

1 large red onion, thinly sliced

1/2 cup rice flour

1 teaspoon salt

1 teaspoon pepper

1 recipe Thai chili vinaigrette (recipe below)

DIRECTIONS

In a medium bowl, mix flour, salt and pepper. Dredge red onion slices, calamari rings and tentacles in rice flour mixture. Cook onions in deep fat fryer filled with 3-4 inches of oil, for approximately 8 minutes per batch. Remove from oil and place on paper towels to absorb excess oil. Then cook calamari, following the same procedure. Set aside. When ready to serve, place baby greens on individual salad plates or bowls, and divide fried calamari and onions on top of lettuce. Drizzle with Thai chili vinaigrette.

Thai chili vinaigrette

3 tablespoons Thai sweet chili sauce

5 tablespoons rice vinegar

10 tablespoons olive oil

1 teaspoon toasted sesame oil

Mix all ingredients in a dressing container with a tight-fitting lid. Shake well.

Tax Bite

Realistic Property Assessment … Every Third Year, Please!

All states that regularly reassess property values for taxation purposes do so according to their own unique schedule. While some states reassess every year, others have intervals as long as five years in between new assessments. The funniest program I found through my research was in the Lake Tahoe area of Nevada, where properties are assessed every year, but these assessments are required to produce a realistic assessment only every third year!

Source: Washoe County Assessor's Office

Rhonda's Famous Chinese Chicken Salad

My dear friend Rhonda created this delicious Chinese chicken salad, which is a big hit with adults and kids alike, and perfect for a summertime party.

INGREDIENTS

2 pounds chicken tenders

1 head Napa cabbage, thinly sliced, or chopped

3 green onions, chopped or thinly sliced

1 package Top Ramen noodles, crushed a bit

1/2 cup slivered almonds

1-2 tablespoons sesame seeds

1 recipe marinade

1 recipe dressing

Marinade

2 cups soy sauce

1 cup water

1 cup (packed) brown sugar

1 teaspoon minced fresh ginger root

1-2 garlic cloves, minced

Dressing

1/2 cup rice vinegar (or cider vinegar)

1/2 cup toasted sesame oil (can use half peanut oil)

1/3 cup sugar

1/4 cup soy sauce

Place all dressing ingredients in a container with a tight-fitting lid and shake vigorously. Taste and adjust as you see fit, by adding a little more sugar, or more vinegar to suit your tastes.

Tax Bite

Tough on Seniors Tax

According to Emerson Read, founder of Charleston taxpayer group No Home Tax, property taxes were double what they are today, before S. Carolina General Assembly Bill 388 passed into law. Still, he recounts a story of a widow who, at 94 years old, owns a home in Charleston's historic district, and pays between $15,000 and $20,000 in property tax each year. She purchased the home for roughly $65,000 in the late 1960s and today, it's obviously worth much more, particularly due to its historic location. Still, that is a lot of money to pay in property tax for a person rapidly approaching the century mark! That is why Read is pushing for further reductions in property tax, which many find more palatable than the current rates. This revenue-neutral measure boosted sales tax while reducing property tax.

Source: Emerson Read, No Home Tax

DIRECTIONS FOR CHICKEN AND MARINADE

Dissolve brown sugar in warm water. Add soy sauce, ginger and garlic. Using a fork, poke holes in chicken tenders. Pour marinade over tenders and marinate for several hours or overnight. When ready to cook chicken, barbecue over low heat. Cool and slice into bite-sized pieces. Set aside, or refrigerate until ready to assemble salad.

In a frying pan, "dry" (no oil) sauté ramen noodles and almonds until just beginning to brown. Add sesame seeds and continue to cook for just another minute or so, until seeds also are golden-brown. Remove from heat and cool. Set aside.

Place cabbage, noodles, nuts, seeds, onions and chicken in a large salad bowl. Toss with dressing and let sit for about 10-15 minutes before serving.

Tax Bite

Hungriest Tax Bites

The data below has been organized and presented by the Washington, D.C. - based Tax Foundation. The top five most expensive counties to live in based on the average annual median real estate taxes paid over each of the last three years (2005-2008) are: Westchester County NY ($7,908), Nassau County NY ($7,726), Hunterdon County NJ, ($7,708), Bergen County NJ ($7,370), and Somerset County NJ ($7,201). The five least expensive counties were all in Louisiana: Vernon Parish ($115), Allen Parish ($116), Franklin Parish ($117), Richland Parish ($118) and Assumption Parish ($123).

CHAPTER IV

Carbon-Free Carbs in Our Future?

Pasta, Pizza & Carbon Cap and Tax

Cooking is going to get more expensive if Congress musters enough votes to pass the Waxman-Markey Cap and Trade (a.k.a. Cap and Tax) legislation. The program, designed to limit U.S. carbon and greenhouse gas emissions from fossil fuels, will likely be wrought with inequities, as Congress is the grand allocator of carbon credits. Businesses can exercise the old fashioned notion of supply and demand by buying and selling carbon credits on the open exchange, but the initial determination of who gets what, remains to be seen. Don't fool yourself into thinking the program will roll out fairly. Remember, these are politicians we are talking about.

In any case, since 85 percent of our energy demand is met through fossil fuels, the estimated cost to American businesses is $646 billion, a tax that would most certainly be passed onto the consumer in the form of increased prices for nearly every product category. For the home cook, the costs would go up for everything from turning on the light switch, to firing up the grill or lighting the stove. Gone will be the days of "preheating" the oven—it will simply cost too much. I can just imagine the next big cookbook … No Oven Necessary or, Raw Food Revival, or perhaps Carb-free Cooking … and we're not talking carbohydrates!

The estimated per household costs of Cap and Trade range from $175 per year (Congressional Budget Office) to $1,400 (American Council for Capital Formation) as much as 2.8 percent of income for many in the middle class (based on $50K annual income.) Some experts have pointed to annual costs as high a $4,000 per family as a result of such policy, and according to a Heritage Foundation analysis, the Waxman-Markey energy legislation would reduce gross domestic product by $393 billion annually and by a total of $9.4 trillion by 2035.

Obama's goal of reducing greenhouse gas emissions by 14 percent below 2005 levels within 11 years, or by 2020 is going to hit Americans hard, especially, since China and India have both flatly rejected the notion of signing up for any such program. These developing nations somehow understand that capping carbon emissions would result in an economic earthquake. It begs the question, why can't our own government see it? And, remarkably, a recent study of cap and trade by the Massachusetts Institute of Technology concluded that the U.S. policies have relatively small effects on the CO_2 concentration if other regions do not follow suit. It further concluded that if developed nations are alone in limiting emissions, a scant one-half degree centigrade of global warming will be cut. Not only is China unimpressed with the legislation, they view carbon tariffs imposed on imports as a direct violation of the World Trade Organization rules.

If Congress musters enough votes to shove through Cap and Trade legislation, it could cost you a bundle the next time you fire up the barbecue, drive to the grocery store, or even turn on the light to read a recipe!

Family's Favorite Pasta

This pasta is pure and simple and simply delicious!

INGREDIENTS

1 pound angel hair pasta

1/4 cup extra-virgin olive oil

2 cloves garlic, peeled and slightly crushed, but kept intact

2 sprigs fresh thyme

2 sprigs fresh rosemary

1/2 cup Kalamata olives, pitted and coarsely chopped

1/2 cup drained and coarsely chopped sun dried tomatoes

1/3 cup pine nuts, lightly toasted

1/2 cup grated Parmesan cheese

1/2 cup crumbled feta cheese

DIRECTIONS

In a saucepot, heat olive oil, but do not bring to a boil. When hot, add garlic cloves and herbs and heat for about 10 to 15 minutes over medium heat. Turn heat off, cover pot and let sit for several hours or overnight. Before serving, discard herbs and garlic cloves.

Boil pasta and cook to al dente, drain and dump back into the cooking pot. Reheat garlic-herb infused olive oil and toss over hot, drained pasta. Add remaining ingredients and gently toss. Serve with extra Parmesan on the side.

Tax Bite

Pot Tax Approved

And, speaking of pots … in July 2009, voters in Oakland, California voted overwhelmingly (80%) to approve a 1.8% gross receipts tax on medical marijuana sold at city's four cannabis dispensaries, which took in $19.7 million in the last fiscal year. The tax is expected to bring in more than $300K to the cash-strapped city. It is the first tax of its kind in the country. San Francisco Assemblyman Tom Ammiano introduced legislation to legalize marijuana and tax it at $50 per ounce. This could generate $1.4 billion a year in taxes. The Public Safety Committee voted 4 to 3 on January 12, 2010. The measure now moves to the Health Committee.

Sources: Newsfeedresearcher.com and Politicsdaily.com

Gnocchi Alla Romana

On one trip to Europe, we stayed in a tiny little jewel of a town in the Italian Alps. Champoluc, tucked into the base of Monte Rosa, is absolutely charming with beautiful vistas and cabins perched on ledges—truly a mountain-dweller's delight. And the food was exceptional. Our lodging of choice was the creaky-floored Albergo Anna Maria, built in post-war 1948 and run by the same family today. The meal was included in the overnight stay … and it was excellent. Our very favorite dish was the Gnocchi Alla Romana and, luckily, the waitress was kind enough to write it down for us … in Italian! The gnocchi was served with just a bit of Parmesan sprinkled over it before baking, but if you prefer a sauce, then a simple marinara sauce would be a nice accompaniment.

INGREDIENTS

4 1/4 cups of milk

6 tablespoons butter

1 1/8 cups of semolina flour (available at most markets)

3 egg yolks

1/2 teaspoon salt

1/2 teaspoon pepper

1/4 teaspoon ground nutmeg

1/2 cup freshly ground Parmesan cheese

DIRECTIONS

In a medium-sized pot, heat milk and butter over medium heat until butter is melted. Slowly add flour using a wire whisk to blend in well and cook over low heat for approximately 10 minutes, stirring all the while. Remove from heat add egg yolks and mix thoroughly. Finally add salt, pepper, nutmeg, and 1/4 cup of the Parmesan. Spread the dough out onto a large smooth surface, such as countertop or cutting board, to a thickness of about 1/4 inch. Let cool completely. With a small round glass or biscuit cutter (11/2

Tax Bite

"Fuelish" Tax

Almost every state imposes and collects excise tax on gasoline, diesel fuel and gasohol in addition to the federal excise tax. Alaska is the only state that does not. It does, however collect the federal excise tax of 18.4¢ per gallon on gasoline and 24.4¢ per gallon on diesel fuel. The state with the highest combined local, state and federal tax on fuel is … wait for it … California at 64.5¢ per gallon, followed closely by New York, Hawaii, Connecticut and Illinois. When it comes to diesel fuel, California drops to third, beat out by Hawaii at 70.8¢ per gallon and Connecticut at 69.5¢ per gallon. California's total diesel fuel tax is 68.9¢ per gallon. Rounding out the top five states for diesel fuel tax are Indiana and Illinois. The most fuel-friendly states after Alaska are Georgia, Wyoming, New Jersey, Oklahoma and S. Carolina.

Source: Energy API (July 2009 figures)

to 2 inches in diameter) cut dough into rounds. The cutter will become very, very sticky and to avoid this dip the cutter into flour between each one. You may even have to wash the cutter a few times.

Butter the insides of six ramekins and place two layers of gnocchi into each one. (Place approximately 8-10 gnocchi per ramekin.) Sprinkle the remaining Parmesan cheese over each dish. Bake at 400°F for 30 minutes. The gnocchi should be slightly browned and crispy on the outside edges, but the inside will remain quite soft.

To serve, invert ramekin onto a small plate and the golden brown underside will make a very pretty presentation. (If you're not trying to impress anyone … simply serve the gnocchi in the ramekins, but be careful, as the dishes will be extremely hot.)

Tax Bite

Water Use Tax

Arizona charges a water use tax of 65¢ per 1,000 gallons to any business operating a municipal water delivery system for delivery to a customer. Water delivered to a customer for resale is exempt from the tax. This is good to know, since you need a half-gallon pot of water to cook a pound of pasta!

Source: Arizona State Legislature

Bowtie Pasta with Gorgonzola, Chicken and Sun-Dried Tomatoes

(Serves four)

White wine and basil make this dish extra-flavorful.

INGREDIENTS

One 16-ounce bag bowtie pasta
8 (boneless, skinless) chicken breast tenders
1 tablespoon olive oil
1/3 cup julienne cut oil-packed sun-dried tomatoes (drain and reserve tomatoes and one tablespoon oil separately)
1 clove garlic, crushed
1/4 cup dry white wine
11/4 cups chicken broth
1/2 cup half & half
1/2 cup crumbled Gorgonzola
2 medium shallots, finely sliced
2 tablespoons chopped fresh basil
1/3 cup pine nuts, toasted
1/2 cup freshly grated Parmesan cheese
Basil sprigs for garnish

DIRECTIONS

Heat olive oil and reserved oil from sun-dried tomatoes in large skillet. Add garlic and chicken tenders and cook over medium-high heat until browned and just cooked through, about 3-5 minutes per side, depending on thickness. Remove chicken from pan and tent with foil.

Add wine to pan drippings and cook, scraping pan, until reduced to approximately 1-2 tablespoons. Add chicken broth, half & half and shallots and cook over medium heat until bubbly and slightly thickened, for about 10 minutes, stirring occasionally. Add sun-dried tomatoes and Gorgonzola and cook until cheese is completely melted. Add chicken back into sauce along with basil. Reduce heat to low and keep sauce warm.

Meanwhile cook pasta in large pot of boiling water until al dente. Drain pasta and toss into chicken-cheese sauce. Serve pasta on plates and sprinkle with finely grated Parmesan cheese and toasted pine nuts. Garnish plate with basil sprigs and serve with French bread.

Tax Bite

8,000 Hazardous Substances Tax

Washington State's Department of Ecology determines which substances will be subject to the Hazardous Substance Tax. There are currently about 8,000 substances falling under this classification. The tax is applied to the first possession of the substance in the state. The rate is .007 of the wholesale value. The proceeds are distributed to the Department of Ecology to help clean up and manage solid and hazardous waste in the state.

Source: Washington Department of Revenue

King Crab Penne Pasta

Every time I want to eat crab, I think of all the work it will involve and usually decide against it. But, when there is a sale on Alaskan king crab legs, I jump on it, because it is so much easier to get the meat out of these big, succulent crab legs than out of Dungeness crab shells.

INGREDIENTS

1 pound of penne pasta

1 tablespoon olive oil

1 small onion, finely chopped

2 small cloves garlic, pressed

1 large or 2 small tomatoes, chopped

1 medium orange or red bell pepper, diced

6 basil leaves, chopped or snipped into small pieces

1/2 cup dry white wine

3/4 cup half & half

Salt & pepper, to taste

2 pounds king crab legs, shelled and cut into one-inch pieces

1 cup freshly grated Parmesan

DIRECTIONS

Heat oil in a large frying pan and cook onions and garlic until soft. Add bell peppers and sauté until they begin to soften, too. Toss basil and tomatoes into the pan and cook for about two minutes. Add wine and cook on medium high heat for about three or four minutes, scraping pan and stirring every so often. Add half & half, mix well and heat through. Season to taste with salt and pepper. Keep warm on very low heat.

Meanwhile, cook pasta in boiling water until al dente. Drain and place back into cooking pot. Stir all but 1/2 cup of the crab into the sauce and pour over pasta. Place extra crab on top of each serving and sprinkle generously with Parmesan.

Tax Bite

Enhanced Food Fish Tax

This is a tax imposed on the first commercial possession of certain fish within the state of Washington. The rate is charged on the value of the fish when first landed and varies depending upon the species. The tax rates range from .0009 for oysters to .0225 for shellfish, .0337 for pink and sockeye salmon and eggs, .0492 for sea urchins and cucumbers (I don't have any recipes for these two!), and .0562 for anadromous games fish, including Chinook, Coho and Churn salmon.

Source: Washington Department of Revenue

Mac'n Cheese with Crumbled Bacon

Macaroni and cheese (food for the soul) is one of the favorites in traditional American comfort cuisine. And, it can be an elegant dish, if you're willing to step outside the "box"—the Kraft box, that is. Popular folklore tells us that Thomas Jefferson served the dish in the White House in 1802. According to food history buffs, Jefferson did not actually invent the dish, but rather returned from a trip to Europe with the idea. Whatever the case, perhaps we can thank the founding father for delivering one of the most satisfying dishes to hit American soil. Create your own version by using a favorite cheese or by adding veggies or different cooked meats, such as chicken or sausage. This special macaroni and cheese is made the old-fashioned way—with real cheese, but the smoky cheddar and bacon give it a rustic flair. Rigatoni, significantly larger than macaroni, provides more surface area for the sauce to coat.

INGREDIENTS

Two 12-ounce packages Rigatoni pasta
3 tablespoons butter
2 large shallots (or one yellow onion), finely chopped
2 tablespoons flour
1/2 cup white wine
11/2 cups milk
1 cup half & half
2 cups grated sharp cheddar cheese
2 cups grated smoked cheddar cheese
6 pieces turkey or pork bacon, cooked and crumbled
Salt & pepper to taste
1-2 teaspoons paprika

Tax Bite

Exercising the Old Electricity Excise Tax Trick

In Illinois, as in many other states, there is a tax imposed on the privilege of using electricity purchased for use and consumption and not for resale. Each month, municipal systems and electric cooperatives collect this tax from each purchaser in an amount equal to the lesser of:
5% of gross receipts or
$.0032 per kilowatt-hour per customer. This tax is in addition to any sales tax imposed as well as the cost of buying the electricity in the first place.

Source: Illinois Department of Revenue

SAUCE

Melt butter in medium-large pot. Sauté shallots until soft and translucent. Add flour to butter mixture and stir with a whisk over medium heat to brown flour ever so slightly. (This creates the roux and helps remove the starchiness.) Slowly add white wine, stirring constantly, to integrate roux with liquid. Add milk and half & half and bring to boil. Continue stirring and allow mixture to gently boil until slightly thickened, 3-5 minutes. Reduce heat to medium, and add 2 1/2 cups of the combined cheeses and stir until melted. Remove from heat.

PASTA AND ASSEMBLY

Meanwhile, cook pasta in boiling water until al dente, and not mushy! Drain and rinse in warm water. Place pasta back in pot and pour warm sauce over. Add crumbled bacon and mix well. Transfer pasta into a greased 9x13 inch casserole dish and sprinkle remaining cheese evenly over top. Shake paprika over cheese for a hint of color. Bake at 350°F for about 20-30 minutes, or until heated through and cheese on top is bubbly and slightly browned. Serve immediately with French bread and a light salad.

Tax Bite

Texas Fireworks Tax

A 2% tax is added to the regular Texas sales tax for the sale of fireworks in counties approved for such sale, during the specifically approved sales periods each year. There are three sales periods, which lead up to Cinco de Mayo, July 4th Independence Day and New Years Day holidays. The sales dates are as follows: May 1-May 5 (if sold at a location that is not more than 100 miles from the Texas-Mexico border,) June 24-July 4, and December 20 through January 1. Regular sales tax in Texas is 6.25% but can be as high as 8.25% due to Local Option Sales Tax.

Source: Texas Taxes, Window on State Government

Baked Ortega Chili Orzo Casserole

My friend Shawn Klein made this dish for us before we ever had kids. Now, some 20 years later, it is still one of our favorite pasta dishes. My son used to think this dish was the absolute definition of the word "casserole."

INGREDIENTS

11/2 cups orzo (rice-shaped pasta)

11/2 cups grated Monterey Jack cheese (or Pepper Jack)

1/2 cup diced Ortega chilies

1 red bell pepper, diced

1 cup sour cream

1/2 cup grated Parmesan cheese

DIRECTIONS

Preheat oven to 400°F. In a large pot of boiling water, cook orzo to al dente. Drain and place in large bowl. Mix cooked orzo with 1 cup of the jack cheese, bell pepper, chilies and 1/2 cup sour cream. Spread into a greased 9x13 inch baking dish. Spread remaining sour cream in an even layer on top and sprinkle with remaining Jack and Parmesan cheeses. Bake for approximately 20 minutes, or until slightly puffed and cheese is browned.

Tax Bite

Fully Charged, Texas Battery Fees

For the sale, storage, use or consumption of new or used lead-acid batteries not for resale, Texas imposes a fee. For batteries of less than 12 volts, the fee is $2 and for those with a capacity of 12 volts or greater, the fee increases to $3 per battery.

Source: Texas Window on State Government

Rustic Italian Sausage Rigatoni

(Serves four)

INGREDIENTS

One 12-ounce package rigatoni pasta

2 tablespoons olive oil

1 clove garlic, crushed

1 large brown onion, coarsely chopped

1 red or yellow bell pepper, coarsely chopped

1 teaspoon dried Italian herbs, or 2 teaspoons minced fresh herbs

One package Italian or chicken sundried tomato sausage (4 large links), casing removed and crumbled

One 14.5-ounce can diced tomatoes in juice

One 15-ounce can of tomato sauce

Salt and pepper to taste

Freshly grated parmesan cheese

DIRECTIONS

Saute garlic, onion, bell pepper and herbs in olive oil until browned. Add sausage and cook over medium heat until sausage is well-browned. Add canned tomatoes, tomato sauce and salt and pepper. Cook over low heat until slightly reduced and thickened, about 10-15 minutes. Stir occasionally.

Meanwhile cook pasta and drain. Toss with sauce and top with grated Parmesan. Serve with rustic Italian bread, salad and a good Zinfandel.

Tax Bite

"Taken to the Cleaners" Tax

The state of Kansas imposes a 2.5% environmental surcharge on the gross receipts received from the dry cleaning or laundering of garments and household fabrics. The dry cleaning environmental surcharge is in addition to the state and local retailers' sales tax. A fee is also imposed on the sale of dry cleaning solvents (chlorinated and petroleum-based) by solvent distributors. The fee is determined by the number of gallons of dry cleaning solvent sold.

Source: Kansas Department of Revenue

"Please Your Palate" Pizza

Makes four small (8 inch) pizzas

Pizza was not just a dinner when my kids were young, but rather an event. We liked to make homemade pizza whenever they each had a friend over for the night. While the kids were running around playing, I made the dough and rolled it out for them, prepared the sauce and lined up all of the toppings. Then, two by two, they came in to create their own pizzas and they had a wonderful time, both making them and eating them!

CRUST

1 cup warm water (about 100-115 degrees on a thermometer, or warm to the touch)
1 package active dry yeast (or 2 1/4 teaspoons)
2 to 3 cups all purpose flour
2 tablespoons extra virgin olive oil
1 teaspoon sea salt or kosher salt

DIRECTIONS

Combine water and yeast in large bowl. Gently whisk to blend in yeast. Add 1 cup flour, salt and olive oil and mix well. Add enough remaining flour to make soft dough. (You may need more or less flour, so add it gradually.) Turn dough out onto a floured board or cloth and knead until dough is smooth and elastic, about five minutes. Transfer dough to a clean, greased bowl and cover with a slightly damp kitchen towel. Let rise in warm place (not the oven) for about one hour or until doubled in size.

When dough has risen, divide into the number of pizzas you plan to make. If you want four pizzas, then make four small balls. For two larger pizzas, make two balls. If you prefer appetizer size pizzas, make eight balls. Cover dough with a towel and let rest for 10 to 15 minutes. Then dough will be ready to roll out and top.

Preheat pizza stone or heavy baking pan for 15 minutes at 450°F. Roll out dough and place on wooden or plastic cutting board or pizza paddles. (Make sure there is a little extra flour under pizza rounds and sprinkle one table-spoon cornmeal underneath, as well. This will help to slide pizza onto baking surface.)

On top of the dough spread sauce, sprinkle grated mozzarella cheese and decorate pizza with your favorite toppings. Use large spatulas and an extra set of

Tax Bite

Wind Energy Tax

Even though we're supposed to be rewarded for "going green" Minnesota taxes the production of wind energy on a sliding scale based upon production capacity. For a large scale wind energy conversion system with capacity of more than 12 megawatts, the payment is 0.12¢ per kilowatt hour; for medium scale systems between 2 and 12 megawatts the payment is 0.036¢ per kilowatt hour, for small scale systems of greater than 250 kilowatts to 2 megawatts the cost is 0.012¢ per kilowatt hour and for those very small scale wind energy conversion systems at or below 250 kilowatts, the tax is waived.

Source: The New Rules Project/ Wind Energy Taxation-Minnesota

hands to slide pizza onto pizza stones or baking sheets that have been greased with olive oil, or cooking spray and sprinkled with cornmeal. Bake at 450°F for 10 to 15 minutes, or until desired doneness.

SAUCE

1 clove garlic, minced

1 teaspoon Italian herbs (or whatever fresh herbs you like–fresh minced basil adds a nice touch.)

2 tablespoons red wine

One 12-oz. can of tomato paste

Salt and pepper to taste

Mix all of the above. Spread over pizza dough.

Topping Ideas

For a change of pace, you may want to try goat or feta cheese, pesto, pine nuts, Greek olives, red bell pepper, roasted tomatoes, marinated artichoke hearts, and fresh mozzarella. But it's always a good idea to have the old standbys on hand for the guests: mushrooms, black olives, pepperoni, Canadian bacon, sausage and pineapples.

CHAPTER V

The Main Event

Entrees & Federal Income Tax

If any part of the meal relates to federal income tax, it is definitely the main course. Unfortunately, at 67,000 pages long, it is a very difficult recipe to follow!

Who would've thought one simple little sentence could cause so much harm? The 16th Amendment to the U.S. Constitution enacted in 1913, was just such a statement, and one that taxpaying citizens have come to rue.

"The Congress shall have power to lay and collect taxes on incomes, from whatever source derived, without apportionment among the several States, and without regard to any census or enumeration."

This one sentence allowed Congress to levy an income tax—against the wishes of the founding fathers of our nation—on income from wages and salaries, business profit, dividends from stock shares, and interest income from invested funds. And this tax has been growing ever since to meet the demands of government on steroids.

Actually, the federal income tax did have a predecessor. In 1861, Congress passed the Revenue Act of 1861, which was considered to be the origin of our current income tax. This bill established the imposition of a three percent tax on annual incomes greater than $800.

Up to this point, the government coffers had mostly been filled through excise taxes and customs duties. Within a year of implementing the Revenue Act, the law changed to collect more from high income earners and the rate bumped up to five percent for incomes greater than $10,000.

Sounds suspiciously familiar, doesn't it? The good old government gets hungrier for tax dollars every year. Except by the time the Civil War ended, the need for government revenue decreased and the tax was repealed. Can you possibly imagine today, a scenario where the government declares it needs less money, and therefore abolishes the income tax? While it's a delicious thought, it's not going to happen in our lifetime!

In fact, quite the opposite will likely happen. In 2011 the Bush Tax Cuts are scheduled to expire, which will inflict considerable taxpayer pain, but not nearly enough to pay the piper. When Uncle Sam comes to collect with his "People's Republic" hat in hand, we're destined to see income tax levies rise even further. Once again, taxpayers will be called to fill the budget abyss, caused by the epic government spending spree of 2009. Taxpayers are destined to suffer "1040 Fever" while the freeloaders (47% of tax filers), inoculated by the tax-free vaccine, will survive on the public dole.

The problem is that even if income tax rates shoot all the way to 100 percent, the resulting revenue wouldn't come close to closing the spending gap. The top one percent of taxpayers already pays 40 percent of the nation's income tax, while the top five percent generates 60 percent of all government tax revenue. Furthermore, it has been proven over and over again, that rising tax rates sap the entrepreneurial spirit, kill innovation, diminish the incentive to work, and lower tax revenues.

This is clearly illustrated by the fact that governments which have adopted a flat tax have prospered, while the economies under the influence of progressive taxes have suffered by comparison. The original 15-nation Euro Zone experienced economic growth of 2.6 percent for 2007, while the U.S. tallied a mere two percent growth. Meanwhile, the flat tax nations experienced much higher 2007 GDP growth, as high as 12.4 percent in Georgia, 10.4 percent in Slovakia and 10 percent growth in Latvia, whose flat tax rates are 12, 19 and 25 percent respectively. Perhaps more importantly, those nations that have adopted a flat tax, have never considered going back to the old discriminatory tax regimes.

Though the U.S. doesn't levy the highest personal income taxes in the world—yet, we have much to look forward to under the Obama administration. According to the Heritage Foundation we are in for a Health Care Taxapalooza, meaning tax hikes are coming for high income earners in the form of an expansion of Medicare taxes to investment income such as capital gains, dividends, rental income, royalties and annuities. In addition, workers at all income levels could be subject to new taxes on items like sugar and beer, among others.

So what to do? A serious rehabilitation program is in order for Congress to change its profligate ways. We'll never return to the halcyon days of peace and prosperity without some kind of intervention … perhaps a tax revolt? Can you say "Tea Party?" Read Chapter XIII, Time for a Tea Party, for more about that!

In the 96 years since the inception of the income tax, top income tax rates have varied from as little as seven percent in 1913 (that lasted one entire year!) to 94 percent toward the end of World War II, bouncing back and forth between 31 and 91 percent in between, and dipping to 28 percent during the Reagan years. Not surprisingly, our economic growth has continued to react inversely to these fluctuating rates. This is a wide range of rates, and as the rates changed, so did the code. What started as a few hundred pages has "blossomed" to 67,000 pages and counting. The time is ripe for a tax revolution.

CHICKEN AND POULTRY

Tax Bite

Bigger Tax Bites

The Federal government's income tax revenue increased by 42.5% in the ten years between 1998 and 2008, while the population increased by a mere 12.6%.

Source: http://www.usgovernmentrevenue.com

April's Chinese Basting Chicken

(Serves 4-5)

My husband and I first discovered this chicken dish while aboard a dive boat in the Caribbean a dozen years ago. Chef April made it one evening and we were so hungry after scuba diving all day, that we could barely contain ourselves. Even the fish were jumping out of the water to check out the enticing aroma! My kids love walking in on this dish, because it makes the whole house smell edible. Leftover April's chicken is perfect in a Chinese chicken salad, but there probably won't be any, so you might consider doubling the recipe!

INGREDIENTS

1 roasting chicken (5-6 lbs.), cleaned with neck and giblets removed from cavity
1 recipe April's basting sauce
Basting sauce
1/2 cup soy sauce
1/4 cup honey
1/4 cup cider vinegar
1 tablespoon minced fresh ginger
2 cloves garlic, crushed

DIRECTIONS

Mix above well. Place chicken in a well-greased roasting pan and bake at 425°F for the first 20 minutes without sauce. Pour basting sauce over chicken and continue to cook for another hour at the same temperature, basting every 20 minutes with sauce from roasting pan. Cooking time may vary depending upon size and desired doneness of chicken. Carve chicken and serve with Basmati rice. Pour sauce over both chicken and rice.

Aloha Chicken

(Serves 4 to 6)

Grilled pineapple gives this dish a touch of the islands.

INGREDIENTS

6 boneless, skinless chicken breasts

1 large pineapple, peeled and sliced into ½ inch slices (core removed)

4 to 6 bunches green onions, remove roots and cut greens to about 6 inches

6 to 8 extra long chives (to tie around green onions)

Pineapple Marinade (recipe below)

1 teaspoon cornstarch (dissolved in 2 tablespoons warm water)

1 cup chicken broth

Pineapple Marinade

2 cups pineapple juice

1/2 cup dry cooking sherry

1/2 cup soy sauce

1 teaspoon toasted sesame oil

2 tablespoons olive oil

2 cloves garlic, crushed

1/2 teaspoon fresh ginger root, peeled and crushed

Blend all ingredients. Pour 1 cup of marinade over chicken breasts and marinate for several hours in an airtight container. Pour 3/4 cup of marinade over pineapple slices and 1/4 cup over green onions and marinate, separately, for at least one hour in airtight containers. Reserve the remaining marinade for the glaze.

Tax Bite

Oahu's "GET" tax

Since we think of Hawaii when we consider pineapples, here is a tax—island style. Since January 2007, the county of Oahu charges an extra 0.5% surtax in addition to the state's General Excise Tax to pay for the county's mass transit fixed guide way system. The General Excise tax ranges from 0.15% to 4%. Businesses may pass this tax on to customers. The state has no sales tax per se.

Source: State of Hawaii, Dept. of Taxation.

Pineapple Glaze

Pour reserved marinade in medium saucepan and add 1 cup of chicken broth. In a small bowl, add 2 tablespoons warm water to 1 teaspoon of cornstarch and stir to dissolve. Add to other ingredients in saucepan and mix well. Bring sauce to boil, reduce to medium-high heat and continue to boil until sauce thickens and reduces in quantity to 1 cup.

Green onion bundles

Tie four to six green onions together with 2 extra long chives with a little bow. Marinate. Grill for 2-3 minutes, or until slightly crispy and browned.

DIRECTIONS FOR GRILLING CHICKEN AND PINEAPPLE

Remove chicken and pineapple from marinade. Preheat barbecue to medium-high heat. Grill chicken breasts five to seven minutes per side, or until desired doneness. Grill pineapple at same heat for approximately 2 minutes per side, until heated through and dark stripes appear.

Cranberry Cabernet Chicken

(Serves 6)

INGREDIENTS

6 boneless, skinless chicken breasts
5 tablespoons olive oil (split for chicken and sauce)
3 shallots, finely chopped
2 cloves garlic, minced
1 cup fresh, frozen or dried cranberries
1 teaspoon minced fresh rosemary
2 teaspoons Dijon mustard
Salt and pepper to taste
1/2 cup Cabernet
1/2 cup orange juice
2 cups chicken broth (split for cooking chicken and sauce)

For topping: 4 ounces cranberry-cinnamon goat cheese (available in many grocers' gourmet cheese cases), cut into six rounds.

DIRECTIONS

In a large skillet, heat oil over medium-high heat and brown chicken on both sides. Remove chicken from pan and place in a casserole dish. Pour 1/4 cup chicken broth over chicken and cover tightly with foil. Bake at 325°F for approximately 30 minutes or until chicken is just cooked through.

In same skillet, heat 2-3 tablespoons olive oil, add shallots and garlic. Cook over medium-high heat until translucent. Add cranberries and rosemary and continue to sauté until berries are heated through and beginning to brown slightly. Stir in Dijon, salt and pepper, Cabernet, orange juice and bring to a boil. Continue to boil for about 2-3 minutes. Add chicken broth and stir in well. Bring to boil again and continue to boil over medium-high heat, stirring occasionally, until sauce is reduced by roughly half. Place a round of cranberry goat cheese atop each chicken breast and pour heated reduction sauce over top immediately before serving. Cheese should begin to melt slightly.

Tax Bite

California Cell Phone Tax

If you ever take a moment to review your cell phone bill, you may be surprised to note the variety of taxes and surcharges. A Verizon bill of mine totaled $455.09, which included taxes of $7 comprised of fees for: the California Public Utility Commission, the California State High Cost Fund (A), the California State High Cost Fund (B), the California Teleconnect Fund Surcharge, the Lifeline Surcharge, the California Advanced Services Fund (CASF) and the California Relay Service Communication Device Fund. Now, I have to wonder how much each of these various entities can possibly benefit from a combined $7.

Source: My Verizon Statement 3/19/2009

April's Chinese Basting Chicken (top) and Chicken Empanadas with Lime Cilantro Sauce (bottom).

Chicken Empanadas with Lime Cilantro Sauce

Crust

2 cups all-purpose flour

1 teaspoon sea salt

1 1/2 sticks butter, cut into small cubes

3 teaspoons apple cider vinegar

1/3-1/2 cup ice water

Mix flour and salt in a medium mixing bowl. Add butter and using pastry cutter or tips of fingers, blend butter into flour mixture until all butter is incorporated into flour. Sprinkle vinegar over the top and mix into flour-butter mixture with a fork. Add water a little at a time, mixing well and adding more as needed until dough can be rolled into 8 balls approximately 2-inches in diameter.

On a floured surface such as a cutting board, or smooth countertop, roll each ball into a flat circle approximately 7-inches in diameter. Place 1/4-1/3 cup filling (recipe follows) on one half of the dough circle. Fold the other half over and seal the semi-circle all around the edges with a fork. This should seal the filling inside of pastry.

Bake on a greased baking sheet or pizza stone for approximately 20 minutes at 450°F.

Chicken Filling

INGREDIENTS

3 boneless, skinless chicken breasts

1 cup white wine

1 cup water

2 tablespoons New Mexican Chile Powder

1 can diced Ortega chilies

1/2 bunch cilantro

1 tablespoon ground coriander

1 tablespoon ground cumin

Tax Bite

HUT, Hut, (Tax) Hike

If a motor carrier operates a vehicle that is greater than 9 tons anywhere in the state of New York, the operator pays a quarterly Highway Use Tax (HUT) based upon the weight of the vehicle and the mileage driven. This tax applies to operators from any state if they use NY highways. Don't worry, if you're just passing through every once in a great while, you can always purchase the 72-hour permit for $25.

Source: NYhut.com

DIRECTIONS

In a large, deep frying pan place chicken breasts. Sprinkle with spices and diced Ortega chilies. Pour wine and water over chicken and cover pan. Bring to a boil and reduce heat immediately to low, keeping covered. Simmer over low heat for about 20-30 minutes or until chicken is cooked through. Remove from heat and cool. When cool, remove chicken from liquids and shred with two forks, or your clean fingers! Set aside until ready to complete filling. Then add the following mixture to the chicken to complete the filling.

In a separate frying pan, heat 3 tablespoons canola or olive oil and add:

1 large onion, chopped

1 clove garlic, pressed

2 poblano chili peppers, flame roasted, seeded, peeled and chopped

1 red or orange bell pepper, chopped

2 tablespoons New Mexican Chile powder

2 tablespoons ground coriander

2 tablespoons ground cumin

1 teaspoon salt

1 teaspoon pepper

1 cup grated extra sharp cheddar or Monterey jack cheese

Lime Cilantro Sauce

Blend the following together in a food processor until smooth:

1 bunch cilantro

2 limes, juiced

3 tablespoons mayonnaise

2 tablespoons sour cream

1 tablespoon white wine vinegar

1/4 cup olive or canola oil

1/4 cup feta cheese, crumbled

1 teaspoon Louisiana hot sauce

Chicken Enchiladas

(Makes 12)

This is my signature dish to deliver to friends and family when they need a little extra help getting food on the table, whether it's because they have a lot of family in town or they've been sick and unable to cook. The recipe makes a lot and can be easily doubled, and it stores well in the refrigerator or freezer!

INGREDIENTS

12 large flour tortillas (can use corn, but will need about 16 corn tortillas)

1 recipe chicken filling (recipe follows)

1 recipe Marilyn Greco's Enchilada Sauce (see Chapter X) or, substitute canned sauce

2 1/2 cups grated taco blend cheese (Monterey jack and medium sharp cheddar)

2 teaspoons paprika for garnish

1 can (3.5 ounces) sliced ripe olives

12 tablespoons sour cream for garnish (approximately 3/4 cup)

Serve with refried beans, rice and guacamole.

Chicken filling

2 1/2 pounds chicken breast tenders (skinless)

1 cup medium-hot salsa

2 cups water

1/2 yellow onion, coarsely chopped

1 teaspoon salt

1 teaspoon pepper

2 cans (4 ounces each) mild Ortega chilies diced

1 teaspoon Tabasco sauce (more or less, depending on your heat tolerance!)

Tax Bite

The "Big Enchilada" Tax

The individual income tax is the single largest source of federal revenue and has been since 1950, averaging just over 8% of Gross Domestic Product.

Source: Tax Policy Center

Tax Bite

Who Actually Pays the Taxes?

According to the Tax Foundation's figures for 2006, the top 1% of income earners paid 39.89% of the total Federal Individual Income Tax bill. The top 5% of income earners paid 60.14%, the top 10% paid 70.79% and the top 25% paid 86.27%. All told, the top 50% of income earners paid 97.01% while the bottom 50% of income earners contributed a mere 2.99%.

Source: The Tax Foundation, http://www.taxfoundation.org/news/show/250.html

DIRECTIONS

Place chicken tenders in a large, frying pan, at least three inches deep. Pour salsa and water over chicken. Add onions and salt and pepper. Cover and bring to a boil. Reduce heat to low, and simmer on stovetop for approximately 20-25 minutes, or until tenders are completely cooked through. Remove from stove and cool.

Once cooled, remove tenders and discard liquid. Shred chicken using two forks. Place chicken in large bowl. Add 1/2 cup grated cheese, 1/2 cup enchilada sauce, Ortega chilies and Tabasco sauce. Mix well. Add salt and pepper to taste.

TO ASSEMBLE:

Heat tortillas in microwave for one minute just to make pliable. Lay tortillas on flat surface and spoon about 1/3 cup of chicken filling on each tortilla. Spoon just a teaspoon or two of extra enchilada sauce over filling and sprinkle one tablespoon of extra cheese over sauce. Roll tightly into a log. Place in greased casserole dish side by side. (Can be made up to a day ahead, and refrigerated or kept frozen for several weeks, but do not cover with remaining enchilada sauce until ready to heat and serve.)

To Serve: Pour remaining sauce over enchiladas and sprinkle evenly with remaining cheese. Dust the top of each enchilada with paprika for color. Bake at 400°F for 15-20 minutes, or until cheese is bubbly and slightly browned.

Garnish each enchilada with a dollop of sour cream and sliced black olives, and serve with guacamole and refried beans on the side.

Caramelized Onion-Apple Chicken Cheddar Crêpes

(Makes eight crêpes)

The inspiration for this recipe was an "apple" themed teacher appreciation luncheon, where every dish was to include apples as an ingredient. This was easy for appetizers and desserts, but posed a bit of a challenge for entrees. In the end, we created apple-onion-cheddar crêpes, and the response was great! In this variation, we've added chicken, but it is quite delicious without, as well. This dish won first prize for the savory category at the 2007 Auburn Community Harvest Festival recipe contest and was sampled to 600 guests at the Food Bank of Contra Costa-Solano annual fundraiser in 2009 with a tremendous response.

Tax Bite

Who is NOT Paying Taxes?

According to the Tax Policy Center, an astonishing 43.4 percent of American tax filers now pay zero or negative federal income taxes. The number of taxpayers who file single or joint individual income tax returns, yet pay no taxes and may even receive government handouts, has reached 65.6 million, out of a total of 151 million. The Tax Policy Center projects the number of tax filers paying no federal income tax for 2009 will increase to 46.9% due to tax credit provisions in the 2009 American Recovery and Reinvestment Act.

Source: Tax Policy Center, a joint project of the Urban Institute and the Brookings Institution.

Crêpes (filling recipe below)

INGREDIENTS

2 cups all-purpose flour
4 large eggs
3 1/2 cup milk
1/2 teaspoon salt
1/2 cube butter (for cooking crêpes in frying pan)

DIRECTIONS

Mix flour and salt in large mixing bowl. Beat eggs and milk in a separate bowl or large glass measuring cup. With wire whisk, slowly add liquids and stir into flour until blended and smooth. Batter should be rather thin.

Heat one teaspoon of butter in a crêpe pan or flat frying pan with shallow sides. When butter is very hot, pour 1/2 cup batter into pan and holding handle, swirl pan in the air to get crêpe batter to cover entire bottom of pan. Cook on medium-high heat until browned. Flip pancake over and cook for just about 30 seconds longer. Crêpes will be quite thin—much thinner than a normal pancake. Remove from pan store in between sheets of waxed paper until ready to use. Can be made up to two days ahead and refrigerated.

Chicken-Onion-Apple-Cheddar filling

INGREDIENTS

10 chicken tenders or 4 boneless, skinless chicken breasts, sliced into 1 1/2-inch strips
2 medium yellow onions, peeled and coarsely chopped
3 medium green Fuji or Empire apples, peeled, cored and coarsely chopped
2 cups grated extra-sharp white cheddar cheese
1/3 cup extra virgin olive oil
1/3 cup dry white wine
1/4 cup sherry (I like Dry Sack for this recipe)
1/4 cup apple juice
Salt and Pepper to taste

DIRECTIONS

Heat 1-2 tablespoons olive oil in large skillet. Add chicken tenders and brown. Reduce heat to medium-low, add wine, cover pan and continue to cook until chicken is cooked through, about 5-8 minutes. Remove from heat and tent with foil. When cool and completely cooked through, shred chicken with fingers or two forks and set aside in a large bowl. Don't clean pan … yet.

Using the same pan, add 2 tablespoons sherry and heat, scraping up browned chicken bits from bottom. Add 2 tablespoons olive oil, onions and apples and cook until onions and apples are caramelized, adding extra oil, sherry and juice occasionally and as needed to keep from drying out. This process will take about 20 to 25 minutes over medium heat. Add any remaining sherry and juice and cook just until absorbed. Remove apple-onion mixture from pan and add to chicken mixture. Mix well. When cool add one cup grated cheddar, salt and pepper to taste and mix well. Store in refrigerator until ready to assemble crepes.

TO ASSEMBLE CRÊPES

Lay each crêpe out flat on a cutting board. Spoon 1/4 cup of chicken mixture into center of the crepe. Sprinkle with one tablespoon grated extra-sharp cheddar cheese. Roll up and place in greased casserole dish, seam side down. Continue with remaining crêpes until filling is used up. Sprinkle remaining cup of grated cheese over the top of the crêpes.

Heat through at 350°F until cheese on top melts and centers are hot, approximately 20 minutes.

Curried Chicken Kebabs

(Serves 6-8)

This dish may be my family's favorite dish. It requires a bit of time, but it is well-worth the effort to see the smiles and happy faces at the dinner table!

For both the marinade and the sauce you will need to make a batch of the garam masala. I have doubled the recipe so you can use half for each. Keep in mind, there are no exact quantities for this spice concoction. Garam masala is a blend of ground spices that are commonly found in Indian cuisine. The blend can be store-bought, but is better when made fresh by roasting and grinding spice pods and seeds and mixing them with garlic, ginger, cilantro and peppers. Experiment to find the blend that suits your tastes.

Tax Bite

Every American's Nightmare Debt

According to U.S. Debt Clock.org, as of March 30, 2010 the national debt hovered just above $12.67 trillion. This equated to debt share of $41,000+ for every single American—even for little kids and brand new babies, and more than $115,000 per taxpayer. When taken together all U.S. Government unfunded liabilities totaled approximately $108 trillion—nearly $350,000 per citizen. Check it out, this is an awesome site.

Source: http://www.usdebtclock.org/

Garam masala

(spice mixture–use ½ for marinade and ½ for curry sauce)

2-3 teaspoons sesame seeds

2-3 teaspoons cumin seeds

Dry toast above in pan over medium heat, stirring often. Grind into a powder in a spice grinder along with the following:

2 black or green cardamom pods

2 teaspoons mustard seeds

Add to mixture:

2 teaspoons powdered turmeric

1 teaspoon ground mace

1 teaspoon ground cinnamon

1 teaspoon ground nutmeg

1 teaspoon ground cloves

1-2 teaspoons cayenne pepper (use more or less depending upon heat desired)

3-4 cloves garlic, pressed

3 teaspoons grated fresh ginger

1 serrano chili, seeded and finely diced (use as you like according to heat)

Salt to taste

INGREDIENTS FOR CHICKEN AND MARINADE

9-10 skinless, boneless chicken breasts cut into skewer-sized chunks

For Marinade:

Mix half of the garam masala with:

1/2 cup olive oil

1 cup dry sherry

1 cup finely diced yellow or red onions

1/2 bunch chopped cilantro

Place chicken into a plastic container with tight-fitting lid. Pour marinade evenly over and seal closed. Marinate for at least several hours or overnight, turning occasionally.

When ready to cook, (be sure curry sauce is ready before cooking chicken!) discard marinade and skewer chicken. Grill over medium-high heat until cooked through and edges are just browned and chicken is cooked through, but not overcooked about 3-4 minutes per side. (Serve with basmati rice and pour curry sauce over all!

For additional sauces, serve Tzatziki (recipe below) and spicy mango chutney. I really like Sherwood's spicy hot chutney, which isn't really hot, but it is delish!

Tax Bite

Vessel Gambling Tax

In case your ship is sailing near Alaska, please note that the state imposes a 33% tax on the adjusted gross income from gaming and gambling activities aboard large passenger vessels (those ships with overnight accommodations) operating in the waters under the jurisdiction of the State of Alaska, as long as the vessel originates out of state, makes two stops in Alaskan waters and the duration of the cruise is at least 60 hours long. Gambling is illegal in Alaska, so no such ships would originate from within Alaska.

Source: www.tax.alaska.gov

For Curry Sauce:

1/2 of the garam masala spice mixture above

3-4 teaspoons curry powder

1 teaspoon turmeric

1 teaspoon cumin powder

1/4 cup olive oil

1 large yellow or red onion, finely chopped

1 green (Pippin or Granny Smith) apple, peeled, cored and finely chopped

1-2 tablespoons store bought biryani paste- (made of canola oil, cilantro, cumin, salt, chili peppers, salt, ginger and garlic–available at specialty markets or online: http://www.englishteastore.com/biryani-paste.html)

One 14-ounce can of coconut milk

1/2 cup dry sherry

1 cup chicken broth

DIRECTIONS FOR SAUCE

Heat 2-3 tablespoons oil in large skillet and add spice mixture, powdered curry, turmeric, cumin and onions. Cook over medium-high heat, stirring often and continue to cook, adding oil as needed, for 10-15 minutes, until onions are browned and spices become very aromatic. Add apples, and continue to cook until soft. Reduce heat, and continue to cook for about 5 minutes longer. Here you can add more spices, curry, garlic, ginger or chilies.Whatever your little heart desires!

Add the sherry and cook to slightly reduce. Add the chicken broth and coconut milk and again, cook over medium-high heat to slightly reduce. Once your sauce has reached your desired thickness, turn it off until ready to serve. If it should get too thick, simply add more of your preferred liquid, i.e. sherry, coconut milk, or chicken broth. Remember, though, the more liquid you add, the less intense flavors of the sauce.

Tzatziki Sauce

2 cups plain yogurt

1-2 cloves garlic

1 teaspoon fresh ginger, minced

1 cup cucumber, peeled, seeded and coarsely chopped

1/3 cup chopped fresh mint leaves

Place a large piece of cheese cloth over a bowl or a plastic container so that you have a little sieve of cheese cloth. Stabilize cloth with a firm rubber band. Place yogurt in cheese cloth and allow to sit for up to an hour, so that the liquid drains from the yogurt. Put drained yogurt in a bowl and add the rest of the ingredients. Mix well and serve cold or at room temperature. This can be made ahead of time.

Port-Balsamic Glazed Game Hens

Serves 6

INGREDIENTS

Six Cornish Game Hens
Port-Balsamic Green Peppercorn Glaze

To Prepare Game Hens

Clean hens and remove innards from cavity and season with seasoned-salt and pepper. Barbecue indirectly for approximately 45 minutes, or until done and nicely browned. Cook breast side down for the last 15 minutes, so that juices run into the breast meat. (To cook indirectly on a gas grill, use the two side burners and place hens in the center of the grill.)

Port-Balsamic Green Peppercorn Sauce

1 cup Port
¼ cup balsamic vinegar
¼ cup soy sauce
3 tablespoons Worcestershire sauce
½ cup chicken broth
1 clove garlic, crushed
1 teaspoon green peppercorns, drained from brine
1 tablespoons gravy flour
1/8 cup warm water
Salt and Pepper to taste

DIRECTIONS

Heat first six ingredients in saucepan until boiling. Add peppercorns and cook with sauce for one to two minutes. Strain peppercorns from sauce and set aside. Add warm water to flour to make a little paste. Add to sauce and continue to cook until thick and bubbly and thick enough to coat the back of a spoon. Add the green peppercorns back to the sauce just before serving.

To serve, spoon sauce over each individual game hen and pass extra sauce in a small pitcher.

Tax Bite

Tennessee's Litigation Tax

The state of Tennessee imposes a tax for litigation. The tax varies with the offense, but the least expensive tax is $1 for a parking meter violation. I wish they'd charge $1,000s for the tort lawyers to go to court. That alone might save our healthcare system!

Source: Tennessee Department of Revenue

Lime Basted BBQ Turkey

This is a great way to serve turkey in the middle of the summer. The pan drippings make fabulous gravy, too. (Follow the recipe for Lenny's Gravy in Chapter X, but use BBQ drippings instead of oven roasted pan drippings. They'll have much less fat, too.)

INGREDIENTS

Turkey

15-pound turkey (can use turkey breast, but cut marinade in half)

Marinade:

3/4 cup olive oil

1/2 cup fresh lime juice

1/3 cup soy sauce

1/4 cup Dijon mustard

2 tablespoons fresh chives, finely chopped

2 tablespoon fresh sage, minced (or 2 t dried sage)

2 tablespoons parsley (or cilantro) chopped

1 clove garlic, crushed

2-3 teaspoons Hungarian paprika

Mix all of the above ingredients and stir well. Pour half of the marinade over turkey breast and marinate overnight in a plastic container. Save the extra marinade to baste turkey while cooking.

Tax Bite

Chicago's Bottled H_2O Tax

Since January 2008, Chicago has imposed a bottled water tax of 5¢ per bottle, allegedly to combat "waste." The tax revenue has fallen far short of expectations, as citizens simply travel outside city limits to purchase their bottled water! This 5¢ tax is in addition to sales tax of 10.25% in the city of Chicago.

Source: www.taxfoundation.org

COOKING TURKEY BREAST

Remove turkey from container. Cook turkey in an indirect fashion on the barbecue. For a gas grill, turn both outside burners to high and keep the middle burner off. Place the turkey breast in a roasting pan over the inactive center burner. Cook approximately 11 minutes per pound, turning occasionally. If you plan to cook a whole turkey, cook indirectly for approximately 10 to 11 minutes per pound.

Let turkey sit for about 4-5 minutes before carving. If you want to serve gravy, use pan drippings as the base and follow Lenny's gravy recipe in Chapter X.

FISH AND SEAFOOD RECIPES

Jobe's Grilled Swordfish with Caramelized Shallot-Wasabi Sauce

(Serves 4)

My son Joel created this sauce one day when he was making dinner for us. It was amazingly delicious and simple, too.

IINGREDIENTS

4 swordfish steaks

Sauce

1/4 cup shallots, chopped and caramelized in 1 tablespoon olive oil

1 1/2 teaspoon prepared wasabi

1 1/2 teaspoons hot Chinese mustard

1/4 cup saki (or dry sherry)

1/4 cup half & half

1/4 cup soy sauce

DIRECTIONS

Preheat grill and brush swordfish steaks with a dash of olive oil. Meanwhile make sauce. In a small saucepan, sauté shallots until brown and beginning to caramelize. Add remaining ingredients and stir well. Heat to boiling and reduce temperature to low. Grill fish steaks to desired doneness. Serve with rice and drizzle heated sauce over both swordfish and rice.

Tax Bite

"Go Fish" Fees

If you wish to fish, you'll need a license. The cost varies from state to state and depends upon what you want to hook. For example, in California, if you're 16 or older, you can get an annual sport fishing license for $41.20, but if you plan to go out just for the day, you can get by on $13.40. However, if your plan is to fish on the state's bays or deltas, you'll be required to add a Bay-Delta Sport Fishing Enhancement Stamp for $6.30, and if your day includes abalone diving, the added cost is $19.70! That said, you can simply buy the lifetime fishing license for between $459.25 and $754.75, depending upon your age.

Source: California Department of Fish and Game

Tinrin's Nectarine-Avocado Salsa for Grilled Fish or Chicken

(Makes approximately 2 cups of salsa)

This is a healthy topping for fish or chicken and uses whatever seasonal fruit is available.

INGREDIENTS

6 fresh fish filets (Halibut, salmon, swordfish or ahi tuna)

4 ripe nectarines (can use mango, peaches, papaya, kiwi or pineapple) peeled and cut into bite-sized pieces

1 avocado, firm yet ripe, cut into bite-sized chunks

2 tablespoons olive oil

1 small garlic clove, pressed

Juice of 1/2 lemon or lime

1/3 cup diced cilantro leaves

Dash of sea salt

Dash of sugar

DIRECTIONS

Mix all ingredients except fish in a bowl and refrigerate until ready to serve. We served this delicious salsa over grilled swordfish, wild salmon and boneless chicken breast and it was wonderful with all three. You can substitute seasonal fruits and quantities of ingredients to suit your tastes.

To grill salmon filet, place filet skin side down on a piece of foil. Cook over medium-high flame for two minutes, then tent filet with foil and continue to cook for another six or so minutes, depending upon the thickness of the filet. For swordfish steaks, cook directly on the grill for approximately four minutes per side at medium high heat, again depending upon thickness. Remove filets from foil. Spoon fruit salsa over fish and rice.

Tax Bite

On the Hook

U.S. taxpayers propped up the commercial fishing industry by doling out more than $6.4 billion in subsidies from 1996 to 2004. Some argue this supported fisherman, but not the fish. Subsidies may be responsible for accelerating the ongoing collapse of worldwide fish stocks, and adding to the devastation of large ocean fish species, not to mention increasing the price of fish at the market!

Source: Environmental Working Group

Tax Bite

Regional Seafood Development Tax

This special tax is levied on salmon harvested in Prince William Sound and Bristol Bay by drift gill net. Hmmm … I wonder how those little salmon pay this tax? Aha … this 1% tax is collected by licensed buyers and is based on the price paid for the salmon.

Source: Alaska Department of Revenue

Nautical Nellies Pecan-Crusted Salmon

(Serves 4)

One day I received an enticing email from my editor at the Auburn Journal. In it, she described a most wonderful dish she'd had while vacationing in Victoria, British Columbia. I immediately phoned the restaurant and almost instantly the recipe was in my inbox. Thanks to Chef Lisa Hartery of Nautical Nellies Steak and Seafood House for sharing this fabulous dish that her sous-chef Adam Hunter created back in 2001.

INGREDIENTS

4 Salmon Fillets, boneless and skinless (6 oz. each)

Maple Balsamic Dressing:

1 cup real maple syrup (or honey)
3/4 cup balsamic vinegar
3/4 cup canola oil
2 tablespoons sesame oil
1/2 bunch green onions, cut in 1/4" slices
2-3 cloves garlic, minced
1 teaspoon salt
1 teaspoon crushed chilies

Pecan Crust

1 cup pecans, roasted
3 tablespoons butter, softened to room temp
3 tablespoons brown sugar

Vegetable Noodle Base

1 large bunch sui choy, (Napa cabbage) chopped
1/2 bunch green onions, cut on a bias
18 pieces snow peas, julienne
1 large tomato, small dice
1 package chow mein noodles (1 pound), cooked
Lime, fried leeks and maple syrup for garnish

Tax Bite

Taxidermied Fish Tax

In Oregon, there is an actual case of a fisherman, who after paying $25 for his fishing license, went out and caught a nice fish. Apparently, this fish was a trophy fish and he decided to take it to the taxidermist to have it mounted on the wall in his office. When the tax assessor came to determine his "personal property" tax liabilities for the business, he included the mounted fish in the list of items being taxed. So, this poor fellow was not only taxed to catch the fish, but then again for his wall art!

Source: Taxpayer Association of Oregon

DIRECTIONS

Dressing

In a large mixing bowl combine the syrup and vinegar. Gradually whisk in the canola oil until well incorporated. Add all remaining ingredients and mix well. The dressing can be made ahead of time and will hold refrigerated for two weeks.

Pecan Crust

Toast the pecans in a moderate oven, 250-300°F for 5 minutes or until they start to release their oils. Remove from the oven and cool completely. Place the nuts in a food processor and pulse to rough chop. Add the butter and brown sugar. Pulse until mixture comes together, being careful not to make a paste.

Heat oven to 425°F.

Salmon

Rub the fillets with a little olive oil. Season with salt and pepper. Sear in a large, hot sauté pan, approximately 45 seconds to a minute per side, depending on the thickness of the salmon. Place seared salmon on a baking sheet, skin side down, and crumble the pecan crust over each fillet. Place the salmon in the oven for 5-7 minutes. (Again, time in the oven depends on the thickness of the fish, be careful to not overcook the salmon.)

While the salmon is baking, return the searing pan to medium high heat. Add the first three vegetables and stir fry quickly. Add the diced tomatoes and toss to warm through. Pour the dressing into the pan, 2 ounces per serving, 1 cup total. Heat through. Add cooked and drained chow mein noodles and toss through. Divide among four bowls. Remove salmon from the oven. Place a piece of salmon on each dish.

Garnish each dish with fresh lime, fried leeks and a drizzle of maple syrup.

Halibut with Rhubarb-Shallot Cream Sauce

(Serves 4)

This is especially nice on halibut, sword fish or salmon and there's no need for lemon, as the rhubarb offers the touch of tang that tastes so good with fish. Simply grill the fish to desired doneness on the barbecue, or if you prefer to poach the fish in the sauce, place halibut in baking dish, pour sauce over and cover tightly with foil. Bake at 350°F for 15-20 minutes, depending upon thickness.

INGREDIENTS

4 wild halibut steaks

1 recipe sauce (below)

Rhubarb-shallot white wine cream sauce

(Makes 1 cup to serve over fish or chicken)

2 tablespoons olive oil

1 cup thinly sliced rhubarb (strings removed before slicing)

2 large, or 3 medium shallots, finely diced

1 cup dry white wine

1 cup chicken broth

1/4 cup cream

White pepper and salt to taste

DIRECTIONS

In saucepan, heat olive oil over medium-high heat, add shallots and rhubarb and sauté until just golden-brown. Add white wine and continue to cook over medium heat until reduced by half. Add chicken broth and repeat the process. Add cream and heat through. Remove and serve over grilled fish or chicken and rice.

Tax Bite

New York Congestion Tax

In 2008 New York City's Mayor Michael Bloomberg proposed a congestion tax of $8 per car and $21 per truck to enter the city during peak traffic hours. The congestion tax has been championed as a method to reduce traffic, improve air quality and generate revenue for city mass transit. The New York City Council voted in favor of the bill by a margin of 30-20 on March 31, 2008. Luckily for drivers' pocketbooks, the State Legislature shot down the bill the following week.

Source: thenewspaper.com, crainsnewyork.com

Seared Scallops Wrapped in Prosciutto with a Lemon-Shallot White Wine Reduction

My sister called me one day raving about this dish she'd had at a friend's house. Naturally, I had to have the recipe.

INGREDIENTS

2 pounds fresh large sea scallops

2 pounds prosciutto

Sauce:

2 shallots

Juice of one-half lemon plus the actual lemon half

1 cup dry white wine

11/2 cups cream

11/2 tablespoons soy sauce

4 tablespoons (1/2 stick) butter, cut into small pieces

1 large tomato, small dice (can substitute capers, avocado or red pepper here)

DIRECTIONS FOR COOKING THE SCALLOPS

Preheat oven to 400°F. Wrap scallops with prosciutto and secure with a toothpick if necessary. Over very high heat, and on a preheated pan or griddle, sear for one minute per side, allowing the prosciutto to brown and slightly crisp. Place scallops in hot oven for approximately one minute more. (The key to delicious, moist scallops is to not overcook them. You are basically just heating them at this point.)

DIRECTIONS FOR SAUCE

In a medium saucepan, place chopped shallot, lemon juice, lemon and wine and heat over high heat, allowing the wine to boil out, about five minutes. Add cream and reduce to half the volume. Remove half lemon, but first squeeze any leftover juice into sauce. Add soy sauce and butter and whisk until smooth.

Tax Bite

"It's a Privilege" Tax

In Mississippi, any financial company that loans money secured by tangible personal property is subject to the Finance Company Privilege Tax of 0.25% of the indebtedness acquired each quarter. Exemptions include loans secured by real property, signature loans, general merchandise dealers taking securities on sales of their own merchandise and securities held representing loans for the payment of wholesale sales price.

Source: Mississippi State Tax Commission

Hot 'N Spicy Grilled Prawns

(Serves 4-6)

There are more than 1,000 species of shrimp and prawns worldwide, living in various aqua systems from freshwater lakes to estuaries and oceans. Most of the shrimp marketed in the United States comes from the Gulf of Mexico, but due to the nature of today's global economy, your local grocer may have shrimp from anywhere in the world.

INGREDIENTS

24 large uncooked prawns, or shrimp, or 36 medium-sized prawns

6 wooden skewers

Marinade:

1/4 cup canola oil

1 teaspoon sesame oil

1/2 cup soy sauce

1/4 cup Worcestershire sauce

2 tablespoons hot La Victoria Salsa

3 dashes Tabasco sauce

1 clove garlic, crushed

1/2 teaspoon salt-free seasoning, such as Lawry's

Mix all of the above and reserve 1/4 cup for drizzling over cooked prawns. Pour remainder over skewered prawns and marinate in the refrigerator for up to several hours.

DIRECTIONS

Peel prawns and skewer four to six on each skewer depending upon the size you select. Pour marinade over prawns and store in airtight container in the refrigerator for several hours, turning occasionally. When ready to grill, drain skewers from marinade and place directly on medium-high grill. Cook until prawns are done and have turned from gray to pink. Do not overcook! Heat extra marinade in a pot on the stove and drizzle over each skewer.

Tax Bite

Tattoo Tax

Arkansas charges its citizens an extra 6% tax for getting tattoos and body piercings. Electrolysis treatments are subject to this special tax too!

Source: www.cnnmoney.com

Tax Bite

"It's Getting Personal" Tax

In an effort to find easy money in an economic downturn, the IRS is getting serious about a law created 20 years ago to tax an employee's use of a company-issued cell phone. The IRS is cracking down on this personal use as a fringe benefit and therefore subject to personal income tax. The IRS is weighing a proposal to deem one-quarter of an employee's use of a work cell phone as a personal fringe benefit. This would also limit employer deductions for the expense of the phone. This creates an accounting nightmare for employers.

Source: Martin Vaughan, Campaign for Liberty

BEEF AND LAMB RECIPES

"Nearly Missed the Veggies" Braised Short Ribs

(Serves 4-6)

I was intrigued by a recipe for braised short ribs on the cover of Bon Appetit Magazine one fall. When I finally got around to making the dish, I realized it called for no veggies, just meat and sauce. It looked a little boring, so halfway through the baking, I threw in some potatoes, carrots and onions and it made a huge difference!

INGREDIENTS

8 pounds meaty beef short ribs, as much fat removed as possible

3-4 tablespoons vegetable oil

2 medium yellow onions cut in half lengthwise, then in quarters to make 16 wedges

6 new potatoes, washed and quartered

16 ounces baby carrots

2 cloves garlic, minced

1 tablespoon minced fresh rosemary

1 tablespoon fresh thyme, minced

1/3 cup finely chopped parsley

1 tablespoon each finely grated lemon and orange peel

Salt and pepper for browning ribs and for sauce to taste

One 750 ml. bottle red wine, such as cabernet sauvignon, zinfandel or Shiraz

Tax Bite

Fart Tax (Pardon Me!)

The Environmental Protection Agency, in its infinite wisdom, has floated the idea of imposing a tax on the methane emissions (from either end) of dairy cows, beef cattle and pigs. As the largest producer of methane gas, livestock are being targeted by the EPA. The proposed annual taxes are: $175 per head of dairy cattle, $80 per head of beef cattle and $20 per pig.

Source: www.politicalhotwire.com

DIRECTIONS

Sprinkle short ribs with salt and pepper. In a large oven-proof pot with a tight-fitting lid, heat oil and brown each short rib on all sides. This may take a couple of batches, and if so, add a little more oil to the pot for each batch. Remove ribs to a plate and set aside. Discard excess fat from pot.

Using same pot, add potatoes, onions, carrots, garlic and herbs and in a little extra oil, brown veggies slightly. Remove to a bowl and set aside. Add wine and with a spatula scrape up pieces of beef and veggies from bottom of pot.

Return ribs and juices, along with parsley and zests to pot and bring to boil. Cover and transfer to 375°F oven. Cook for one hour. At this point, add veggies and potatoes to meat in pot, scattering around ribs. Cover and continue to cook for another hour, or until veggies are done and meat is very tender.

With a slotted spoon transfer ribs and veggies to a serving platter and cover tightly with foil. Bring sauce to a boil over high heat and continue to boil until reduced by half and slightly thickened. Season to taste with salt and pepper. Serve meat and veggies, spooning sauce over all.

Tax Bite

Utah Nude Tax (aka Sexually-Explicit and Escort Tax)

In Utah, owners of sexually explicit businesses, where someone appears nude or partially nude, must pay a 10% tax on gross receipts.

Source: Utah Code Title 59, Chapter 27

Mustard and Brown Sugar Crusted Corned Beef

(Serves 6)

This recipe comes from my mother-in-law, who didn't make it very often, but when she did, I turned into a little piggy, because I absolutely loved the flavors and the crunchy, mustardy crust that formed while baking. It's great for St. Patty's Day, or any day!

INGREDIENTS

1 4-pound corned beef brisket

1/2 cup mustard (can either use French's or Spicy Brown such as Sierra Nevada Porter Spicy Brown—French's gives a nice tangy flavor, spicy brown is a wee bit more subtle)

3-4 tablespoons brown sugar

1 tablespoon soy sauce

DIRECTIONS

Brisket

Remove brisket from plastic wrap and rinse well to remove brine. Place in large pot and cover with water. Bring to boil. Reduce heat to medium and simmer for three hours until tender in the center. You should be able to easily stick a fork into the center. Remove from liquid and set aside. Trim any excess fat from brisket.

Crust Mixture

Mix mustard, brown sugar and soy sauce and spread over entire brisket–all sides. Prepare roasting pan with oil or cooking spray. Place brisket in roasting pan and bake at 350°F for 30 minutes or until crusty and browned on the outside. Slice across the grain into 1/2-inch thick slices.

Tax Bite

Nevada Live Entertainment Tax

Just in case you spend St. Patty's Day in Las Vegas, remember the state imposes a special tax on live entertainment establishments. The tax is structured as a two-tier levy, based upon the maximum occupancy of the facility where the live entertainment is taking place. The tax rate is applied to admission charges, food, beverage and merchandise sold at the venue. For facilities that hold between 300 and 7,500 the rate is 10% and for larger facilities that can hold 7,500 or more, the rate drops by half to 5%.

Source: http://tax.state.nv.us.

Mustard and Brown Sugar Crusted Corned Beef (top) and Grilled, Stuffed Flank Steak (bottom).

Grilled, Stuffed Flank Steak

Whether you're serving lamb, beef or chicken, a stuffing of locally-grown greens, a little cheese and some sautéed shallots makes for a delicious, seasonal meal. This recipe has all my favorite flavors, but for those who prefer to use spinach in lieu of arugula, or a different kind of cheese—no problem—you can also have it your way! So, head to the market and fire up the grill.

INGREDIENTS

1 two-pound (approximately) beef flank steak
1 large or 2 small shallots, minced and sautéed in one or two tablespoons olive oil
1/4 cup chopped basil leaves
1/4 cup chopped arugula leaves
1 cup marinated artichoke hearts, drained and chopped
1/2 red bell pepper, seeded and chopped
1/4 cup drained and chopped sundried tomatoes
1/4 cup crumbled blue cheese
1/4 cup crumbled feta cheese
Kitchen string

DIRECTIONS

Lay flank steak on cutting board and pound to approximately 1/3-inch thickness with a meat pounder. Set aside.

Mix remaining ingredients in a bowl and stir to combine well. Spread filling over flank steak, leaving a 2-inch border without filling at the far long end. Roll steak, beginning from the long side with stuffing next to edge, toward long end with no stuffing at the edge. Tie with kitchen string in three or four places, and if necessary enclose each end by using wooden toothpicks, so that stuffing won't escape!

Grill over medium-low heat for approximately 20-24 minutes, total. Grill for six minutes and then turn one-quarter turn, repeating two more

Tax Bite

Wagering Tax

Speaking of gambling pastimes, perhaps you already know that you are required to declare your winnings from betting and card games on your tax returns. But, in several states (Pennsylvania, West Virginia, Illinois and Oklahoma) the government also exacts a "wagering" tax on casino and track owners. The cost of that tax can, and most likely is, passed onto customers through the cost of amusements at the facility.

Source: CNNMoney.com "America's Wackiest Taxes"

Tax Bite

Sure Bet Tax

In Minnesota you'll pay 6% on the value of bets recorded, accepted, forwarded or placed. This tax is due by the 20th day of the month following the month in which the bets were recorded, accepted, forwarded or placed.

Source: Minnesota Department of Revenue

times so that all four sides have cooked directly on the grill. This produces a medium-rare doneness to the meat. Remember, the meat in the center of the pinwheel will take longer to cook through. Remove from grill and slice into 3/4 inch slices.

Kiwifruit-Teriyaki Marinade for Skirt Steak (or Chicken)

(Enough for 4-5 pound skirt steak)

Kiwi is a natural tenderizer, so by marinating the skirt steak for a few hours in this marinade, the meat will be very tender and the flavor really seeps through the meat.

INGREDIENTS

4 kiwi fruit (peel and puree 2 of the kiwi fruit, and peel and slice the other two, set aside)
1/4 cup white wine
Juice of 1 whole lime
1/4 cup soy sauce
2 tablespoons brown sugar
1/4 cup chopped fresh cilantro leaves
1/2 teaspoon grated fresh ginger
1 small clove garlic, minced
2 tablespoons olive oil

DIRECTIONS

Place all ingredients except sliced kiwi, in a container with a tight-fitting lid. Shake well. Divide marinade in two, and pour half over the meat to marinate for at least several hours or overnight in refrigerator. Save remainder of marinade to serve over cooked meat.

To cook meat, remove from marinade and grill on barbecue to desired doneness. Serve with sliced kiwi and drizzle remaining marinade over top of both.

Tax Bite

Kansas "Where's the Beef?" Tax

Kansas has its own beef council as do 45 other states. It appears that the $1 per head cattle tax can be collected multiple times, whenever the head of cattle changes ownership. The only time the tax does not apply is if the owner sells the cow or calf within 10 days of purchase and files a "non-producer" status form to avoid paying an additional dollar. In Kansas, a portion of each $1 tax stays in state to support the Kansas Beef Council and the remainder goes to the National Beef Council.

Source: www.kansasbeef.org

Rib-Eye Steak with Dried Cherry-Balsamic Reduction Sauce

(Serves six)

Besides barbecue season, the holidays are the best time of year to entertain. Even in winter, you can throw a steak on the "barby" and enjoy a reduction sauce that's been brewing on the stove for hours or one that you just made five minutes ago. The most important thing is to make a meal that will afford you plenty of time for fun with your family and guests.

INGREDIENTS

6 rib-eye steaks
2-3 beef bones
5 tablespoons olive oil (2 to rub on bones, and 3 for sautéing veggies)
3 large shallots, finely chopped
1 clove garlic, crushed
1/2 carrot, finely chopped
1 tablespoon minced fresh thyme, or 1/2 teaspoon dried
1 cup dried sour cherries (Mariani packages these)
1 teaspoon Balsamic vinegar
1 tablespoon soy sauce
1/2 cup Pinot Noir
One 14-ounce can beef broth

DIRECTIONS

Steak preparation

Season the rib-eye steaks with salt and pepper. Grill on medium heat for approximately 3-4 minutes per side for medium-rare, depending upon thickness.

Serve steaks, spooning sauce with a generous portion of cherries atop each.

Tax Bite

Beefy Cattle Tax

By law, all producers selling cattle or calves must pay $1 per head to support beef/veal promotion, research and information through the National Beef Promotion and Research Act. Persons in non-compliance with the Act and Order are subject to a civil penalty of up to $5,500 per transaction, plus unremitted check-off dollars and interest. Generally, the buyer is considered the "collection point" however, if it's more convenient the seller may do so. It should be noted that both seller and buyer are equally liable to ensure the payment is made on time. Payments must be postmarked by the 15th of the month following the transaction. A 2% late charge is applied to any late payments.

Source: http://www.beefboard.org/compliance/compliance.asp

Dried Cherry-Balsamic Reduction Sauce

Prepare sauce at least several hours, or a day ahead, so flavors meld and sauce achieves a rich character.

Preheat oven to 450°F. Place beef bones in a roasting pan and rub each with olive oil; roast for approximately 45 minutes to an hour, or until the bones are nicely browned. Add bones and pan scrapings to saucepan for next step.

In a large skillet or saucepan, heat 2-3 tablespoons of olive oil over medium-high heat and add shallots, carrot and roasted beef bones. Sauté until the veggies brown and begin to get slightly crisp.

Add garlic, thyme and cherries and continue to sauté for another five minutes. Add Pinot Noir and beef broth and cook over medium-high heat until sauce is reduced to half, stirring occasionally. Remove and discard bones. Add Balsamic vinegar and soy sauce and cook for another 1-2 minutes over high heat. Can refrigerate sauce for several hours or a day, before reheating to serve.

Tax Bite

Tennessee Professional Tax

An annual $400 occupations tax is imposed on people who have an active Tennessee license or registration to practice any of the following professions: accounting, securities agent, architect, attorney, audiologist, broker-dealer, chiropractor, dentist, engineer, investment advisor, landscape architect, lobbyist, optometrist, osteopathic physician, pharmacist, physician, podiatrist, psychologist, real estate principal broker, speech pathologist, sports agent, or veterinarian. The fee is due June 1.

Source: Tennessee Department of Revenue

Lamb Burgers with Feta Cheese and Greek Olive Tapenade

(Serves 6)

When headed for Reno, Nevada we like to stop at one of our favorite places—the Silver Peak Restaurant and Brewery. Their lamb burger with feta cheese and Greek olive tapenade is so delicious I had to give it a try at home. Same story … delicious!

INGREDIENTS

2 pounds ground lamb

1 teaspoon dried oregano (or 1 tablespoon fresh minced)

1 teaspoon dried rosemary (or 1 tablespoon fresh, finely minced)

1 teaspoon sea salt

1 teaspoon ground black pepper

1 tablespoon finely minced fresh parsley

1 large shallot, finely chopped

1 cup crumbled feta cheese for topping

1 recipe Kalamata olive tapenade (recipe follows)

6 bakery buns

Tax Bite

Tennessee Bail Bond Tax

In case you are a Tennessee professional falling under the category above and fail to pay your professional tax, or if you're charged with any other crime, you may be interested in knowing about the Bail Bond Tax. This tax is collected by your friendly bail bondsman, who must collect it from the person who posts bail for you, before the bond is written. The cost is $12 per bond.

Source: Tennessee Department of Revenue

DIRECTIONS

Burgers

Mix all ingredients (except feta cheese) and form into six burger patties. Grill over medium heat for about 4- 5 minutes per side, for medium-rare, longer or shorter for desired doneness. Immediately after removing from grill, top each burger with approximately 2 tablespoons crumbled feta cheese so it begins to melt. When serving, spoon 1-2 tablespoons olive tapenade over cheese.

Greek olive tapenade

2 cups pitted green or black Greek olives, or both

1 tablespoons extra virgin olive oil

1/4 cup finely chopped sundried tomatoes (optional)

Place olives in a food processor and on pulse, process until chopped, but not pureed. If using sundried tomatoes, process first, then add olives and continue to process. Stir in olive oil and refrigerate until ready to use.

Moroccan Lamb Meatloaf

INGREDIENTS

1 pound ground lamb
1 pound ground turkey (can use ground chicken)
2-3 tablespoons olive oil
1 yellow onion, chopped
1/3 cup slivered almonds
1/4 cup currants
2 teaspoons Hungarian paprika
2 teaspoons cumin
2 teaspoons dried oregano
1 teaspoon turmeric
1/2 teaspoon cardamom
Pinch allspice
Salt and pepper to taste
1 slice whole wheat bread, torn into bite-sized pieces
1 egg, beaten
1/3 cup milk
3 slices cinnamon-raisin bread, whole (for bottom of pan)
1 cup crumbled feta cheese (for topping)

DIRECTIONS

For this recipe, sauté the onions until soft, add slivered almonds, currents, and spices and sauté for another five minutes, stirring constantly, until almonds are slightly browned and mixture becomes aromatic. Place cinnamon-raisin bread in bottom of loaf pan and lay meat mixture on top of the bread. Cook at 350°F for 30 minutes or so, and then sprinkle feta cheese evenly over top and finish cooking. This recipe is delicious served with pomegranate sauce or chutney.

Tax Bite

Bio-"Fool" Tax

The Congressional Budget Office (CBO) estimates the diversion of 3 billion bushels of corn from food production to fuel production accounted for about 10-15% of the increased cost of food between April 2007 and April 2008.

Source: Congressional Budget Office

Grilled Lamb Chops with Shallot Blue Cheese

(Serves 4)

Lamb makes for a festive meal, especially when served with red pepper and jalapeno jellies to give a Christmas flare. But, lamb chops are great any time of the year. This recipe calls for a slice of the shallot-blue cheese log (recipe below), which melts over the chop, creating a rich, elegant flavor for your special holiday occasion.

INGREDIENTS

8 lamb chops (approximately 1½ inch thick)
1/3 cup olive oil
2-3 tablespoons lemon juice or red wine vinegar
1/4 cup chopped shallots (2-3 medium shallots)
2 cloves garlic, crushed
2-4 teaspoons minced fresh rosemary
1/4 cup Dijon mustard
1/4 cup honey
1 teaspoon salt
1 teaspoon freshly ground pepper

DIRECTIONS

Place lamb chops on the bottom of a plastic container or glass baking dish. Mix remaining ingredients and pour over lamb chops. Marinate for several hours or overnight, turning at least once.

Tax Bite

Aircraft Excise Tax

This is an annual tax imposed for the privilege of using any aircraft in the state of Washington. Interstate commercial aircraft are exempt from the tax, so it primarily applies to private owners of small planes used for personal or business purposes. The tax is an annual fee based upon number of engines and type of aircraft. The rate ranges from $65 for a single engine, fixed wing to $140 for a turbojet multi-engine, fixed wing. Helicopters pay $90 and home built sailplanes pay $35.

Source: Washington Department of Revenue

Shallot-Blue Cheese Log

1 cup crumbled blue cheese
2 tablespoons extra virgin olive oil
2 medium shallots, finely chopped
1 clove garlic, minced
1 tablespoon lemon juice

Heat one tablespoon olive oil in small skillet and sauté shallots and garlic over medium-high heat until slightly browned. Remove from heat and set aside to cool. Meanwhile, using an electric beater, mix blue cheese, remaining tablespoon olive oil and lemon juice until mixture is fairly smooth and fluffy. Add shallots and garlic. Using plastic wrap form the bleu cheese mixture into a log (roughly 1 1/2 inch in diameter) and refrigerate until firm. Can be made several days ahead. When ready to use, remove from refrigerator and let sit at room temperature for about 30 minutes.

FINAL PREPARATION

Prepare grill. Slice shallot-bleu cheese log into slices between 1/4 and 1/2-inch thick. Grill lamb chops over medium flame for approximately 4-5 minutes per side, for medium-rare. (Depending upon thickness and desired doneness, you may wish to grill lamb slightly longer or slightly shorter.) When meat is cooked, place a slice of the bleu cheese log atop each chop. Serve with roasted baby potatoes and onions garnished with a sprig of fresh mint and a medley of jellies. Jalapeno, red pepper, mint or cranberry jellies provide nice Christmas colors.

Mother's Day Lamb with Herb Vinaigrette and Cherry Tomatoes

(Serves 4)

This is the dish I always ask for when my kids want to make dinner for Mother's Day. It is a variation on a recipe found in Bon Appetit magazine years ago. Something about the fresh basil and mint, with shallots and herbs, is just perfect for a festive spring meal.

INGREDIENTS

8 lamb chops, 1 1/2-inch thick

Marinade

1/4 cup extra virgin olive oil
1 clove garlic, crushed
1 teaspoon Dijon mustard
1 tablespoon balsamic vinegar
1/4 cup chopped fresh mint leaves
1/4 cup chopped fresh basil leaves
Salt and pepper to taste

Mint-basil vinaigrette

1/2 cup extra virgin olive oil
3 tablespoons red wine vinegar
2 tablespoons balsamic vinegar
1 tablespoon Dijon mustard
1/2 teaspoon sugar
1/2 teaspoon salt
1 small clove garlic, crushed
2 shallots, chopped and sautéed until slightly browned and cooled
1/3 cup chopped fresh mint leaves
1/2 cup chopped fresh basil leaves
1 cup cherry tomatoes, quartered
Fresh ground black pepper to taste

Tax Bite

A Little Income Tax History from the Library of Congress

1913: The income tax rate originated at one percent on incomes up to $20,000 and progressed to 7 percent on incomes greater than $500,000.

1917: Revenue Act of 1917 was passed, lowering exemptions and increasing tax rates. In 1916, a taxpayer needed $1.5 million in taxable income to face a 15 percent rate. After the Revenue Act of 1917, taxpayers making that same $1.5 million faced a tax rate of 67 percent.

1941: Taxpayers with taxable incomes of only $500 per year were taxed 23 percent, while incomes over $1 million were taxed at 94 percent.

1981: The Reagan Tax Cuts were passed, reducing individual tax brackets 25 percent and bringing the top tax bracket down to 50 percent.

(continued)

DIRECTIONS

Mix all marinade ingredients and pour over lamb chops in covered, airtight container. Marinate lamb chops for several hours or overnight, turning several times.

Mix all vinaigrette ingredients and refrigerate until ready to use.

When ready to grill, remove lamb chops from marinade and grill over medium flame for approximately 4-5 minutes per side, for medium-rare. (Depending upon thickness and desired doneness, you may wish to grill lamb slightly longer or slightly shorter.) Spoon Mint-Basil Vinaigrette over meat and serve with roasted boutique potatoes such as Sangria, Yukon Gold, Huck Finns, Peruvian Purples or baby New Potatoes. A Caprese salad of fresh mozzarella, sliced tomatoes and fresh basil leaves with a gentle vinaigrette is the perfect accompaniment to complete the meal.

Tax Bite

(continued)

1988: Perhaps illustrating the significance of taxes in politics, George H.W. Bush stated "Read my lips. No New Taxes" in the 1988 Presidential Election. Many cite the statement as the reason he won in 1988 and lost in 1992, after he broke the promise.

2001: President Bush signed a $1.35 trillion "tax-cut" bill, which lowered U.S. income taxes across the board

Tax Bite

FDR's Tall Tax Order

In 1941 President Franklin Roosevelt proposed a 99.5 percent marginal tax rate on all incomes over $100,000. After that proposal failed, he issued an executive order to tax all income over $25,000 at a rate of 100 percent! Before it was enacted, Congress repealed FDR's order.

Source: Viewpoint, Mackinac Center for Public Policy,

CHAPTER VI

Politicians Love Their Pork

Pork & Stimulus (Spending, Spending, and More Spending)

"Everything else is overshadowed by the stimulus spending—the most insidious tax on the dollar itself. It is robbing all future earnings and every dollar you have saved. It is like a death tax, except that they don't bother waiting for us to die."

—Marc Goldstone, Chairman Arizona Tax Revolt.

Pork is *obviously* the favorite dish of U.S. politicians. For most of them, the question that first comes to mind is, "How can I fill the trough so my constituents will re-elect me?" Our governmental representatives, hungry for power and consumed by starving egos, offer up a menu of bad policies. What is far less clear is why we Americans continue to toss them the feedbags, given how little good they actually get done for us.

Much of the $787 billion American Recovery and Reinvestment Act of 2009 (HR-1) was not really stimulus at all, but a huge spending bill with a large serving of "bailouts" for irresponsible state governments. Those states with the largest deficits are naturally the most egregious offenders of fiscal discipline. Collectively, states lined-up to request hundreds of billions in bailout money.

As a result, taxpayers from fiscally sound states with disciplined governing practices have been forced to transfer their wealth to states with feckless governance. Folks all over the nation blew their tax dollars to bailout bankrupt states like California, and as the stimulus rolls out the folly continues. Citizens of Arizona might be paying for the railway connecting Las Vegas to Los Angeles. Residents of Arkansas could be purchasing the new runway at the John Murtha Airport in Johnstown, Pennsylvania, and people of every state will funnel yet more money to failing schools across the country. How does this kind of stuff happen? And, more importantly, how does it stimulate the economy?

This 1,047-page bill, printed in the dead of the previous night, passed overwhelmingly by the House, before representatives had a chance to review it. Not a single Republican supported the bill, and seven Democrats voted against it. It was rushed to the President's desk where, with the emergency suddenly quelled, it waited for four days to be signed into law.

The passage of this bill, HR-1, set the stage for government intervention and control of healthcare, energy policies and education. It is the first step toward nationalization of these sectors. We had no idea, then, Obama would also takeover our nation's banks and auto companies, firing General Motors Chief Executive Officer on the spot.

According to Obama, the stimulus bill would create or save (whatever that means) 3.5 million jobs at a cost of $787 billion. Each of those jobs would be created or "saved" at an average cost of $224,857 per job. If you assume an average salary of $50,000, the cost to create these jobs if nearly five times the going wage—a rather inefficient way to create work and a waste of scarce financial resources. Ultimately, within six months of passage of the bill, the economy had shed another 2.5 million jobs, a far cry from the original claim of creating or "saving" jobs.

According the Recovery.ca.gov website, California stood to receive more than $80 billion in stimulus for various spending programs, more than one-tenth the value of the entire bill. The Golden State faced a $42 billion deficit for fiscal year 2009. Just five years ago, the citizens recalled former Governor Gray Davis for a comparably minor offense—a $4 billion budget deficit. The Governator dwarfed Davis' poor performance as CEO of the largest state in the union. He increased spending some 40 percent over the past five years, catapulting past the 3.2 percent inflation by a mere 36.8 percent!

While some $550 billion of the nearly $1 trillion "pork" package was earmarked for shoring up individual states' welfare—Medicaid, schools and unemployment programs—zero was allocated to reduce corporate taxes, which would have had the twin benefits of stimulating the economy while reducing consumer prices. Everyone should understand that corporations don't actually pay taxes, because they pass on the cost in the pricing structure of goods produced and services rendered. In a nutshell, when government drives the economy, it does so at the peril of crowding out private enterprise.

While we're at it, let's take a look at the 2009 Omnibus bill, a.k.a. "Porkulus" Bill. President Obama loved to chat up the fiscal irresponsibility of the past administration. I'd like to ask what exactly he meant by his remark: "Another manifestation of irresponsibility is the large budget deficits we are inheriting. These deficits, over time, will harm economic growth and impose burdens on our children and grandchildren." Was he actually talking about his own administration? Because that is where this man, who repeatedly blamed the past administration (did he forget he was a sitting U.S. senator in the majority for the last two years of the Bush Administration?) should focus, not on the former administration. He promised to look forward, and yet a good portion of his daily speeches continue to lay blame on the past. Inside of his first six weeks in the oval office, he dwarfed the deficit spending of the eight-year Bush administration (which was bad enough), by increasing the budget deficit from $482 billion to nearly $1.43 trillion by the end of 2009.

In this chapter you'll read about just a few of the pet pork projects the president approved by signing the 2009 American Recovery and Reinvestment Act and the 2009 Omnibus spending bill. These two bills alone combined for nearly $1.2 trillion in new spending. Imagine how much food we could put on America's dinner tables for this sum!

Stimulus spending is generally unfair and impractical. The "Pork Posse" lavishes spending on those who can keep them in office, in other words, the "political machine". It has nothing to do with who earns the money in the first place, and little to do with those indigent groups, most in need of a hand up.

In honor of "Porky" the congressional pig, I've presented some of my favorite pork dishes in the chapter.

Stilton-Stuffed Figs Wrapped in Prosciutto

(Makes 24)

This appetizer is really easy and quite impressive for your family or guests. The ginger-mango Stilton is available in the gourmet cheese section in most markets, and if you can't find it, just use regular Stilton.

INGREDIENTS

12 figs

12 slices prosciutto, each cut in half lengthwise

4-6 ounce package of Mango-Ginger Stilton cheese, cut into 24 bite-sized slices

24 fancy toothpicks

DIRECTIONS

Cut figs in half. Place a piece of cheese on top of each. Wrap with prosciutto and skewer with a toothpick. Place on a baking sheet and cook at 350°F for 10-15 minutes, until cheese is hot and prosciutto begins to brown. Serve hot.

*can use pork or turkey bacon in place of prosciutto

Tax Bite

Pigs Do Fly (By)

Taxpayers forked out a cool $328,835 for the publicity photo shoot of Air Force One flying low on the horizon in front of the Statue of Liberty in April, 2009. The flight was apparently unauthorized by the President, but somehow this fact does not magically refund the hundreds of thousands of taxpayer dollars the stunt cost in the first place. I can't vouch if this was stimulus money, but it did stimulate an uproar and intense anger amongst New Yorkers, who had no previous warning about the event. When they spotted the jumbo jet looming low on the horizon in the Big Apple, it instilled fear and panic à la September 11, 2001.

Sources: Bloomberg.com; Times Online

Hard Cider Grilled Baby Back Ribs

(Fox Barrel Cider)

(Serves 4)

INGREDIENTS

Four 6-rib baby back pork racks
One 22-ounce bottle hard apple cider
3/4 to 1 cup brown sugar
Coarse sea salt and pepper to taste

DIRECTIONS

Place ribs in one or two large Ziploc bags or plastic containers with lids. Season to taste with salt and pepper. Distribute cider evenly over ribs and seal bags. Marinate in refrigerator overnight.

Spray roasting pan with non-stick spray. Place ribs in pan and pour juices over. Sprinkle evenly with 1/2 cup brown sugar. Seal very tightly with aluminum foil. Cook ribs at 325°F for 2 1/2 hours or until very tender. Remove from oven and drain off 1/3 of the juices, keeping the ribs in the remaining juices. Cool, cover and chill until ready to grill.

Preheat grill or barbecue to medium heat. Spread gelled juices over ribs and sprinkle an additional 1/4 to1/2 cup brown sugar evenly over curved sides of rib racks. Grill for about 3-4 minutes per side, just until ribs are nicely browned and sugar begins to get crunchy. Serve hot.

Tax Bite

Congressional Pork Fest

The Congressional Pig Book reports that the number of pork barrel spending projects skyrocketed from 2,658 and $13.2 billion in 2007 to 11,610 and $17.2 billion in 2008, under the Bush Administration. Last year's (2009) Pig Book reports 10,160 projects earmarked for pork to the tune of a whopping $19.6 billion. As a means of comparison, in 1991, the first year for the Congressional Pig Book, pork projects numbered 546 and a cost of $3.1 billion.

Source: Citizens Against Government Waste, www.cagw.org

Pan-Glazed Pork Chops with Apples, Onions and Sage

(Serves 4)

INGREDIENTS

4 boneless pork chops (at least one-inch thick)
5 medium-sized apples (Empire, Fuji, Granny Smith), peeled, cored and cut into ¾ inch thick wedges
1 large yellow onion, chopped
1 bunch fresh sage (Remove several stems for garnish, and chop the remainder)
1 teaspoon dried thyme
1 teaspoon dried oregano
1 teaspoon dried sage
1 teaspoon ground black pepper
1 teaspoon sea salt
1/2 cup dry white wine
1/2-3/4 cup chicken broth
3 tablespoons olive oil

DIRECTIONS

Trim pork chops of any excess fat. In a small bowl, mix dried herbs, salt and pepper. Coat top and bottom of each chop with herb mixture.

Heat oil in large skillet and brown chops thoroughly on both sides. Remove from pan and tent with foil.

In same pan, add a little more oil, and cook onions over medium-high heat until translucent. Add apples and sage and continue to cook until apples are al dente and mixture begins to brown.

Add wine to deglaze the pan and then reduce heat to medium-low and add chicken broth. Replace pork chops into pan along with apples and onions, cover and cook until chops are cooked to desired doneness. This will depend upon the thickness of the chops.

Chops about 11/2 inch thick take approximately 15-20 minutes to cook over medium-low heat. Be careful to check chops occasionally, because overdone chops will become dry. Serve pork chop on plate with onion-apple mixture spooned over the top. Garnish with reserved sage leaves.

Tax Bite

The Four P's (Pesky Pork Pet Projects)

A few of the more egregious pork barrel projects to be paid for by the 2009 Stimulus bill include: $3.8 million for the Old Tiger Stadium Conservancy in Detroit; $1.9 million for the Pleasure Beach water taxi service in Connecticut; and $1.8 million for "swine odor and manure management" research in Ames, Iowa. The last one on this list won the "Porky Le Pew" award. And, finally we citizens will pitch in to pay $800,000 to repave an alternate runway at the John Murtha Johnstown in Johnstown, PA. There are exactly three daily flights from this airport and they all go to Washington D.C.

Source: Citizens Against Government Waste

Crown Roast of Pork with Caramelized Onion-Chicken Sausage Stuffing

This dish makes a wonderful party or holiday meal with an impressive presentation.

INGREDIENTS

Pork

1 8-pound crown pork roast

3 tablespoons minced fresh sage

2 cloves garlic, minced

1 teaspoon dried thyme

2 teaspoons poultry seasoning

Stuffing

1 1/2 cups chicken broth

1/2 cup calvados (French apple brandy from Normandy)

2 large onions, chopped

2 tablespoons butter

1 tablespoon olive oil

Six chicken apple sausages, casing removed and crumbled

1 tablespoon fresh sage, minced

1 batard loaf sourdough French bread, torn into bite-sized pieces

Salt and pepper to taste

DIRECTIONS

Place crown pork roast in roasting pan, with bones sticking up. Wrap tips of bones in foil. Mix herbs and garlic in small bowl and then rub all over meat. Roast pork for 1.5 hours at 350°F. Remove from oven, fill cavity with stuffing (recipe below) and continue to cook for another hour or so, until meat thermometer reaches between 155 and 170 degrees, depending on desired doneness.

Tax Bite

Off to the Pork Races

There's something to be said about coming in last. Hawaii and Alaska, the last two territories to gain statehood, finish in first and second place out of the 50 states plus the District of Columbia when it comes to "pork" per capita. Alaska wins top honors by a landslide with $322.34 for every one of its 686,293 residents, with Hawaii in hot pursuit bringing home $234.96 of federal bacon to each of the 1,288,198 citizens. Interesting to note, Washington D.C. climbed from 10th in 2008 to 4th in 2009, keeping $185.52 for each of its 591,833 people.

Source: Citizens Against Government Waste

While roast is first cooking, prepare stuffing. In a large skillet, melt butter with oil. Add chopped onions and cook until translucent. Add chopped apples and continue to cook over medium-high heat until onions and apples begin to caramelize, stirring often. Add Calvados or apple brandy, and cook until slightly reduced. Add crumbled sausage that has been removed from casing. Stir well.

In a large bowl, tear up bread and add onion-apple-sausage mixture, minced sage, and toss well. Season to taste with salt and pepper. Pour chicken broth over and toss to moisten stuffing. Set aside until ready to stuff roast.

Tax Bite

Swine Design

As part of the 2009 Stimulus bill, $200 million was allocated to "design and furnish" the Department of Homeland Security headquarters. This has very little to do with "stimulating" the economy, but I suppose it creates a pleasant atmosphere for hunting down terrorists!

Source: U.S. News and World Report, "Finding Pork in the Obama Stimulus Bill" February 26, 2009 by Matthew Bandyk

Pork Tenderloin with Currant Glaze

This recipe is a holiday favorite of former Mayor Severson of Orinda, California.

INGREDIENTS

2 pounds small pork tenderloin roast
2 tablespoons dry mustard
2 teaspoons dry thyme
1/2 cup pineapple juice
1/2 cup soy sauce
1 large clove garlic, minced
1 teaspoon dried ginger

Tax Bite

Forking Out Pork

The 2009 stimulus package (The American Recovery and Reinvestment Act of 2009) and the 2009 Omnibus spending combined for a total $301.2 billion increase over 2008 spending, resulting in a 79.6% increase, year over year.

Source: Congressman Chaffetz, http://chaffetz.house.gov

DIRECTIONS

Place tenderloin in shallow pan. Rub with dry mustard and thyme. Combine pineapple juice, soy sauce, garlic and ginger. Pour over meat. Cover and refrigerate overnight. Turn meat over frequently to marinate. Pour off marinade when ready to cook, reserving some to use as basting while roasting. Roast uncovered at 325°F for 1 hour. Slice pork into medallions and serve with currant glaze.

Currant Glaze

1 10-oz. jar currant jelly

1 tablespoon soy sauce

2 tablespoon pineapple juice

Over medium heat melt the jelly with added soy sauce and pineapple juice. Stir and simmer for 2 minutes. Serve over pork slices. Recipe serves 6 people (about 1/3 pound per person).

Tax Bite

Pork Posse to the Rescue

For the first time in history, as of April 2009, federal aid topped sales, property and income tax as the largest source of revenue for state and local governments. While state and municipal spending rose 1.5% in Q1 2009, state and local revenues declined by 2.9%. Yet total revenue rose 1.6%, thanks to the Pork Posse. There's no need for responsible belt-tightening when Uncle Sam comes riding in on his pork posse to "save the day!"

Source: USA Today "Federal Aid is top revenue for states" May 5 2009 by Dennis Cauchon

Hard Cider Grilled Baby Back Ribs (top) and Pork Tenderloin with Currant Glaze (bottom).

FOX
HARD CIDER
BARREL
REVOLUTIONARY CIDER
from California

CHAPTER VII

Tax Munches and Corporate Lunches

Sandwiches & Corporate Income Tax

Congressional legislators seem to enjoy the sport of browbeating America's corporations whenever they get the chance. As a professional pastime, they liken their crusade to Robinhood, thieving from Peter, but they forgot the part about paying Paul. In truth, by taxing corporate income, they're robbing Paul—twice.

Like it or not, corporate America provides jobs, health insurance and many other fringe benefits of employment. Big business is a reliable and sizeable customer, especially for the many small to medium enterprises hoping to get bigger. Corporations purchase everything from toilet paper to automobiles and everything in between, which enables operations to function. They hire janitorial and legal services, too. In addition, corporations are able to utilize economies of scale, bringing products and services to consumers efficiently and cost-effectively—unlike the thieving, thuggish government, which delivers products at a much higher cost to society.

Perhaps the most important thing to remember about American corporations is that not all are huge conglomerates, but often small operations that have opted to incorporate for a variety of reasons. These may range from legal protection and access to financial markets, to image in the marketplace. In my view, corporate income tax is the silliest tax of all, because it flows directly through to consumers in the guise of increased prices of goods and services. Why do it?

I'll tell you why, it's simple. The federal government derives 12 percent of its revenues ($300 billion) from corporate income tax, while the 50 states collectively earn 6.5 percent of revenues ($51 billion) from state corporate income tax. This is a lot of money, and it would be political suicide to extract these sums directly from taxpayers. It's more palatable to sneak it through the revolving doors of "evil" corporations. Keep in mind a politician's appetite for your dollars is insatiable.

The United States levies one of the highest corporate income tax rates in the developed world. Among OECD (Organization for Economic Cooperation and Development) we share top honors with Argentina, Morocco, Pakistan and Zambia, at a top rate of 35 percent. But, when combined with state levies, that average reaches 39.27 percent. India and Japan have higher rates, with top rates reaching 40 and 40.69 percent, respectively, and the UAE and Kuwait each charge 55 percent. The global average is 23.2 percent in the European Union, 26.6 percent in Latin America and 28.4 percent in Asia-Pacific.

America is on the wrong trajectory. In 2008, 23 countries cut their corporate tax rates, while the U.S. rate has been the same since 1994. Even in Sweden, where the top personal income tax rate is 57 percent, a new business-friendly approach includes cutting the corporate tax rate by 1.7 percent to 26.3 percent.

Meanwhile, back home on the range, Iowa takes top honors with a combined federal-state corporate tax of 47 percent, reduced to 41.6 percent when adjusted for federal tax deductions. Don't laugh, there may be some corn stuck in your teeth!

As corporations flee states with hostile business environments, including high corporate taxes, those states with sensible policies and low tax rates benefit. And so do their citizens. The states with the lowest tax munch, will rise up to host to the business lunch!

Deb's Smoked Gouda and Chicken Salad Pita Sandwiches

(Makes 6)

My son Joel arrived home one night raving about the dinner he'd had at his friend Scott's house. When my kids rave about someone's meal, I need the recipe. If they love it, then I want to make it. And, more importantly, I want my readers to learn about it, too!

INGREDIENTS

Dressing

1 clove garlic, minced
1/2 cup safflower or canola oil
2 tablespoons honey
2 tablespoons cider vinegar
4-5 teaspoons Dijon mustard
1 teaspoon dry mustard
3/4 teaspoon salt
3/4 teaspoon curry powder
3/4 teaspoon ground coriander
1/4 teaspoon ground allspice

Honey Pecans

2 tablespoons honey
2 teaspoons hot water
2 tablespoons brown sugar (optional)
1/2 teaspoon ground allspice
1/8 teaspoon salt
3/4 cup pecan halves

Tax Bite

"Take Me Out to the Ballpark" Tax

Businesses or persons in Washington D.C. that register more than $5 million in gross receipts and are subject to filing franchise tax returns, or employers required to make unemployment insurance contributions must pay a Ballpark Fee on or before June 15 of each year. The fee ranges from zero for businesses with less than $5 million in gross receipts and increases on a sliding scale from $5,500 to $16,500 per year.

Source: Government of the District of Columbia Office of Tax and Revenue

Salad Fixings

4 boneless skinless chicken breasts or turkey, cooked and cut into 1/2 inch strips, or small cubes

2 large stalks celery, strings removed and cut into 1/2 inch pieces

2 unpeeled tart green or red apples, or one of each, cored and coarsely chopped

6-8 ounces smoked Gouda cheese, cut into 1/2-inch cubes, or strips

6 pieces of Pita or flat bread

DIRECTIONS

Dressing

In a container with a tight-fitting lid, add all dressing ingredients and shake well. Can be made ahead of time and refrigerated.

Honey Pecans

Preheat oven to 400°F. Line a baking sheet with foil, and spray with cooking spray. Mix honey, hot water, allspice, brown sugar, and salt in a small bowl. Add pecans and toss to coat. Spread out on prepared baking sheet, spooning liquid over pecans. Bake for about five to seven minutes, or until pecans are well browned. Check after five minutes, and stir pecans around a bit on sheet. Remove from oven and transfer to a cutting board to cool, separating nuts. Allow to cool completely.

Sandwich Assembly

Place all ingredients in a large salad bowl, add pecans and dressing and toss to coat. Serve in pita bread, or on flat bread, or on a bed of Romaine lettuce.

Grilled Artichoke Heart Sandwiches

This recipe came about one summer, when we had just purchased a giant jar of marinated artichoke hearts from Costco. We also had a jar of sun dried tomatoes and feta cheese in the refrigerator, so this concoction just sort of came together. We have been making them ever since, and they are elegant enough to serve for a nice luncheon to guests.

INGREDIENTS

1 cup marinated artichoke hearts, drained and coarsely chopped

3 tablespoons sun-dried tomatoes, drained and chopped

1/4 cup crumbled feta cheese

4 ounces chèvre (goat cheese—can be herbed)

3/4 cup grated sharp cheddar, or Parmesan, or sliced fresh mozzarella

French bread, sliced or baguettes halved, or sliced whole wheat sandwich bread

DIRECTIONS

Mix artichokes, sun-dried tomatoes and feta in bowl. Spread goat cheese on bread slices. Spoon artichoke mixture over and sprinkle with cheese. Grill in a frying pan with a little cooking spray or olive oil, or bake open-faced at 425°F until cheese is melted and bubbly and bread is toasted. Or, grill close-faced, if using sliced bread. Serve with a side dish of mixed Mediterranean olives.

Tax Bite

Mixing Tax

The state of Tennessee charges gross receipts tax on the sale of any mixed drink or setups for mixed drinks or alcoholic beverages whether or not they're consumed on the premises of any country club, nightclub, private club, or fraternal society. The 15% tax is due the 20th of each month.

Source: Tennessee Dept. of Revenue

Barbecued Chicken-Cheddar English Muffins

(6 servings)

This dish is really easy if you have leftover barbecued chicken. My kids and their friends always loved this for an afterschool snack.

INGREDIENTS

6 English muffins, split and lightly toasted
3 cooked chicken breasts cut into bite-sized pieces
1/2 cup grated sharp cheddar cheese
1 cup Ultimate Barbecue Sauce (See Chapter X)

DIRECTIONS

Spread barbecue sauce on both sides of English muffin. Place a handful of chicken pieces on top and cover again with sauce. Top with grated cheese and place under the broiler for a couple of minutes, just until cheese is melted and bubbly.

Tax Bite

Touchdown Tax

The football stadium tax was created for the development of professional football stadium facilities in Wisconsin. The 0.5% football tax is levied on the sale, storage, use or other consumption of tangible personal property and taxable services in Brown County, home of the Green Bay Packers. This brings the total sales tax on such retail to 5.5% (5% state plus 0.5% football stadium tax.) If you're not a football fan, too bad!

Source: Wisconsin Department of Revenue

Grilled Asparagus-Prosciutto Sandwiches

(You can use your favorite seasonal vegetable in this recipe)

This sandwich calls for grilled asparagus and grilled green onions, prosciutto, Gorgonzola and Pecorino Romano cheese to create a light mid-week meal—served open-faced or closed. Of course, this sandwich can be made with any grilled seasonal vegetable, for example eggplant or bell peppers, when they come into season later in the summer.

INGREDIENTS

1 pound asparagus, trimmed and cleaned

2 bunches green onions, root tips removed

2 tablespoons olive oil

1 tablespoon white (or red) balsamic vinegar

1 teaspoon coarse sea salt

1 teaspoon ground pepper

12 slices of bread, whole wheat or white, crusts trimmed

3 ounces prosciutto, sliced, optional

3 ounces gorgonzola cheese, crumbled or thinly sliced

3 ounces Pecorino Romano cheese, grated, or very thinly sliced

Extra oil or butter for grilling sandwiches; or broil open-faced instead of grilling

DIRECTIONS

Clean and trim asparagus and green onions and place with oil, vinegar, salt and pepper in plastic container with tight-fitting lid. Shake well. Heat barbecue to medium heat and grill veggies for 1-2 minutes per side, until nicely browned, but al dente. Remove from grill and set aside.

Meanwhile, trim crust from bread and heat oil or butter in large skillet over medium heat and place each slice of bread in pan, (in several

Tax Bite

Sports Hero Tax

Professional athletes are required to pay state income taxes to the states where their games take place. This is a revenue grab for state legislators wanting to partake in super sports heroes' unimaginably awesome salaries. But, even those athletes who earn less than phenomenal figures are subject to this tax hassle. This rule applies to other "traveling" professionals such as performers or even corporate execs. The major drawback is the need to keep track of where income was earned and the need to file multiple state income tax returns. Filing just one return is enough to make most people crazy, let alone multiple returns!

Source: National Taxpayers Union

batches, depending on the size of the pan) and place Gorgonzola on half the bread slices and Pecorino Romano on the rest. Heat until cheese begins to melt. On the Romano halves, lay two to three slices prosciutto over cheese, then 4-5 grilled asparagus spears, trimmed to fit bread, and 2-3 onions. Place Gorgonzola bread slices on top and press down with spatula and continue to grill for one to two more minutes. Serve hot.

Tax Bite

"Etched in Concrete" Tax

Any person who manufactures or produces cement, imports cement, distributes or sells cement in intrastate commerce, or uses cement in Texas must pay 55¢ per ton or 2.75¢ per 100 pounds of taxable cement.

Source: Texas Window on State Government

Grilled Chicken with Avocado, Green Olives, Feta and Cheddar

(Serves 6)

INGREDIENTS

2 tablespoon oil

12 slices of your favorite bread

11/2 cups grated cheddar cheese

3 chicken breasts, pre-grilled and sliced

3 ripe avocados, peeled and sliced into 1/3-inche slices

11/2 cups crumbled feta cheese

1/2 cup Mediterranean green olives, pitted and thinly sliced

DIRECTIONS

Heat oil in skillet over medium heat. Sprinkle cheddar cheese on each piece of bread and cook until cheese begins to melt. Place chicken and olives on half of the slices, and lay crumbled feta and avocado over top. Cover bottom halves of sandwiches with top halves and grill until all cheeses are melted and bread is golden brown. Flip once to brown both sides.

Tax Bite

Oil Slick Tax

A tax of 4¢ per 42-gallon barrel is imposed on the transportation of crude oil or petroleum products by ship or barge into navigable waters of Washington State and off-loaded at an in-state terminal. There can also be an additional charge of 1¢ per barrel, depending on the fund balance in the oil spill response account.

Source: Washington Dept. of Revenue

Grilled Turkey Sandwiches with Ortega Chilies, Blue Cheese Dressing, and Grilled Onions

(Serves 6)

INGREDIENTS

12 slices of bread, (we suggest whole grain or sour dough)

6 tablespoons bottled blue cheese dressing

1 pound sliced deli salsa turkey

12 slices of sharp cheddar or Monterey Jack cheese

1/2 cup diced, fire-roasted Ortega chilies

1 medium onion, thinly sliced and sautéed until caramelized in 1-2 tablespoons olive oil.

DIRECTIONS

Spread one side of each slice of bread with blue cheese dressing. Place bread, dressing side up, in skillet. Layer turkey on six slices of the bread. Sprinkle Ortega chilies and onions evenly over turkey and layer cheddar or jack cheese on top. Place the remaining six slices of bread on top of halves with all the goodies. Grill on medium-high heat, flipping part way through, until cheese is melted and bread is golden-brown.

Tax Bite

Timber Tax

Washington State imposes a 5% Forest Excise tax based upon the stumpage value (market value of the lumber) of harvested timber. The owner of the timber is responsible for making sure the tax is paid. The tax is split between the State (1%) and the counties (4%) where the harvest occurred. Many states impose a timber tax.

Source: Washington Dept. of Revenue; National Timber Tax Web site

Grilled Asparagus-Prosciutto Sandwiches (top) and Café Vista Pulled Pork Sandwich (bottom).

Grilled Turkey, Cranberry, Goat Cheese Thanksgiving Sandwiches

(Serves 6)

There's only one meal that can possibly trump a traditional Thanksgiving feast, and that's leftovers the very next day. Having gorged on turkey and accoutrements the previous night, we begin to drool over the thought of a freshly carved turkey sandwich, with cranberry sauce and lettuce. Here is a little twist on the cold sandwich, a grilled turkey, cranberry, goat cheese sandwich with caramelized shallots. If you're one of those preferring to steer clear of goat cheese, (many are) simply use cream cheese.

INGREDIENTS

12 slices of bread, whole wheat, potato or French

Sliced leftover turkey (2-3 slices per sandwiches, depending on thickness)

6 tablespoons cranberry sauce (or use jalapeno pepper jelly, if you prefer spicy)

3 shallots, thinly sliced and caramelized

6 ounces Montrachet goat cheese or cream cheese (1 ounce per sandwich)

1/2 to 3/4 cup grated cheddar or white cheddar cheese

2-3 tablespoons butter or olive oil for pan grilling

DIRECTIONS

Place six slices of bread in skillet with olive oil or melted butter. Sprinkle grated cheddar cheese on top side of each slice and layer turkey on top of cheese. Place shallots over turkey. On remaining bread slices spread softened goat or cream cheese and right on top of that spread cranberry sauce or pepper jelly. Invert second slices on top of bread in pan and close to make a sandwich. Grill on first side until bread is golden brown and grated cheese begins to melt. With a wide spatula flip sandwiches over. Continue grilling until second side is golden brown.

Tax Bite

"Ditto the Privilege" Tax

In Arizona, certain classifications of businesses, including retail sales, must pay a tax for the "privilege of doing business" in the state. Some counties and most cities in the state also add a privilege tax of their own to the state rate, making the top rate in the state up to 10.7%. This tax is imposed in place of a sales tax. Food and prescription drugs are exempt from this tax.

Source: Arizona Dept. of Revenue

Turkey Sloppy Joes on French Bread

(Serves 4-5)

This was one of the first recipes I ever ran in my food column and though my mom made it for many a meal when we were young, many people have never tried making Sloppy Joes. These can be served on hamburger buns, but slices of French or Rustic Italian bread make the dish a wee bit fancier.

INGREDIENTS

2 tablespoons vegetable oil
1 large yellow onion, coarsely chopped
1 clove garlic, crushed
1 teaspoon sugar
1 tablespoon yellow mustard
1/2 teaspoon salt
1/2 teaspoon pepper
1 teaspoon soy sauce
3/4 cup ketchup
1 1/2 pounds ground turkey (can use ground beef)

DIRECTIONS

Heat oil in skillet and add onions and garlic. Sauté until well-browned. Add ground turkey and cook thoroughly until slightly browned. Add sugar and stir well. Then mix in mustard, salt, pepper, soy sauce and ketchup. Stir well and cook until heated all the way through.

Meanwhile slice bread into 3/4 inch slices and arrange on plate. Spoon sloppy Joe mixture over bread.

Tax Bite

Gun and Ammo Tax

Manufacturers of firearms and ammunition pay a federal excise tax on all firearms and ammunition manufactured. The tax rate on handguns is 10% while the rate for all other firearms and ammunition is 11%. According to the August 3, 2009 Firearms and Ammunition Excise Tax Collection Report, between January 1 and March 31, 2009, **$33.0 million** was collected in taxes for pistols and revolvers, **$38.9 million** for long guns and **$37.8 million** for ammunition. Compared to the same quarter in 2008, collections were up **65.5%** for handguns, **42.9%** for ammunition and **28.3%** for long guns

Source: Right Side News

Café Vista Pulled Pork Sandwich

(Serves 6-8)

This pulled pork sandwich recipe comes from the Vista Café in Meadow Vista, California. It is simple and satisfying!

INGREDIENTS

2 to 3 lb. boneless pork roast with the fat trimmed off (shoulder or loin will do, but the loin cooks faster and is not as moist)

1 cup ketchup

1/2 cup firmly packed brown sugar

1/2 cup cider vinegar

1/4 cup Dijon mustard

2 tablespoons melted butter

2 tablespoons Worcestershire sauce

1 teaspoon Tabasco sauce

Salt and pepper to taste

French Rolls (or baguettes)

DIRECTIONS

Place pork roast in slow cooker, salt and pepper to taste. Whisk together the rest of the ingredients and pour over the pork roast. Cook for approximately 4 hours until it pulls apart easily. (If you don't have a slow cooker, cut the roasts in half and place them in a roasting pan along with the sauce and cover tightly with foil. Bake at 300ºF for 3.5 hours for the shoulder roast and about 3 hours for the loin roast.)

Pull pork apart with two forks and serve on warm French rolls.

Tax Bite

Import Tax for Dummies

For $24.95 you can purchase the 199-page book, Importing into the United States, A beginner's Guide to Importing. This will give you all the information you need to pay the import taxes on goods brought in from another country. All goods entering the United States are subject to the same import procedure and the same tariff (tax) assessment, however every product has its own tax rate and some have a tax rate of zero. Import taxes are the second largest source of revenue for the United States behind the Internal Revenue Service and they are used to control domestic markets by raising or lowering taxes on particular goods in an effort to give domestic producers an edge over foreign imports. This does nothing for the American consumer, but it does protect domestic manufacturers … until the afflicted foreign country retaliates! For just $54.95 you can get the U.S. Harmonized Tariff Schedule and the Customs Valuation Encyclopedia, to complete your importing guide collection.

Source: Informed Trade International

CHAPTER VIII

Grocery Bill on Steroids

Veggies & Farm Subsidies

Many cooks don't know they've already paid for, yet never received, several food items before ever setting foot in a grocery store—in the form of taxpayer-funded farm subsidies. And, these subsidies are not used to keep prices in check, but rather to keep them artificially high! When competitive pricing is completely ignored, supply and demand have little impact on pricing to the detriment of the consumer.

As part of the 2008 Farm Bill, otherwise known as the Food, Conservation and Energy Act of 2008, certain qualified farmers are paid monies from the Federal Government (i.e. your tax dollars) to uphold minimum prices for a host of commodities. These are paid through the Direct and Counter-cyclical Payment Program (DCP) or subsidized loans. DCP consists of direct payments, which are tied to established base acres and yields, no matter what the farmer's effective price. Counter-cyclical payments, which serve as a safety net in the event of low crop prices, pay the farmer the difference between his effective price and the target price. Oil, wheat, corn, sugar, peanuts, barley, grain sorghum, oats, soybeans, rice, upland cotton and some dairy items including cheddar cheese, butter and milk have been allocated some amount of money from tax revenues as part of the USDA's Commodity Programs.

It is estimated by the Environmental Working Group (EWG), a nonprofit watchdog and environmental research organization, the amount of taxpayer dollars supporting farm subsidies is roughly $43.79 per person, or $175 for a family of four, per year. These programs are a waste of taxpayer money, and completely broken, according to EWG. The majority of farmers are unhappy with the results of the commodities program, too.

What I want to know as a taxpayer is why Congress doesn't fix these programs they know are broken. Why must we continue to spend our hard-earned tax dollars paying landowners *not* to farm their land? This makes absolutely no sense and is an insult to our collective intelligence.

In a Washington Post investigative series entitled "Harvesting Cash," authors Dan Morgan, Gilbert M. Gaul and Sarah Cohen state, 'The cash comes with so few restrictions that subdivision developers who buy farmland advertise that homeowners can collect farm subsidies on their new back yards.'

No crops required!

In some counties across the country, if the property owner receives a federal payment, the land is considered agricultural, even when there is no actual farming taking place on the land. Agricultural land is assessed at a lower rate, often considerably lower. According to Tylene Gamble, chief appraiser for Wharton County in Texas, a parcel assessed as "agricultural" might be charged $55 per acre, whereas the same parcel for regular use might be charged $3,000 per acre.

Though tax assessors in these counties would like to rectify this situation, the problem stems from the federal government's definition of "farming" which does not actually require any farming at all.

"Harvesting Cash" goes on to list several other cases where non-farming landowners still receive farm rice subsidy payments. In one particular case, the payouts have been $1.8 million over ten years, despite the fact not a single grain of rice was produced on the land for the same 10-year period.

"The problem you are referring to was happening here in Harris County," said Dr. Gary P. Underwood, Director of Agricultural Appraisal for Harris County (Texas) Appraisal District (HCAD**)**. "We have former rice land that was broken up for ranchettes," he explained."Rice base stays with the property even if converted to residential."

He cited examples of a five-acre tract on which the property owner built a 4,000 square-foot home. Because his property had been in rice production years ago, he still qualified for subsidy payments for the four acres surrounding his home. Underwood denied his application for an agriculture exemption, so the landowner took HCAD to District Court and the judge ruled in his favor, since he was in a federal government agriculture program.

In 2007, Underwood wrote legislation and a bill was passed to prevent this from continuing. Effective January 1, 2008, the landowner no longer qualified for the property tax break. Unfortunately, the USDA Farm Service Agency (FSA) said there was nothing they could do and property still receives a rice base payment.

In 2006 alone, taxpayers sent $13.4 billion in farm subsidies to more than 1.4 million recipients. In a 12 year period, the EWG tracked more than $177 billion in subsidy payments, with 75 percent of those subsidies going to just 10 percent of the beneficiaries! While some farmers really rake it in, others, usually those small farmers most in need, receive little or no assistance. Farmers with less than 10 acres, are not eligible, so the government discriminates on who has access to these funds, and apparently it isn't the small family farmer.

Wouldn't it be great, if the federal government guaranteed what your widgets would sell for? Actually, that is getting closer and closer to the truth for many industries, such as the banking and automobile industries. When they run out of money, Congress and the Administration reach deeper and deeper into our taxpaying pockets to take what they will.

So, you often go to the store to purchase goods that, unbeknownst to you, you've already purchased, but somehow never received. Then in order to take them home, you must buy them again. This time, you pay for them with your after tax dollars, and included in the purchase price is the corporate tax that was levied on the corporate farmers who produced the goods. Uncle Sam's gotcha again!

The Farm Bill is not all bad, but it is a lot bad. Of the entire USDA budget, 25 percent goes to farm subsidies, conservation and the like, while the balance goes toward the Food Stamp, WIC (Women Infants and Children's educational programs) and School Nutrition. These welfare programs are at least designed to provide education and proper nutrition to those citizens at risk.

The 2008 Farm Bill in its entirety has a price tag of $290 billion over a ten year period, small peanuts when compared to the spending approved by Congress in the first five months of 2009, but still a very hefty sum! Curtailing the U.S. farm subsidy program would lower food costs around the world. Protectionist moves to shield farmers from global competition is done at the risk of increased food costs and a higher cost of living.

VEGGIE ENTREES

Roasted Veggie Crêpes

(Makes 6 Crêpes)

This is one dish I could truly inhale. The roasted veggies combined with Gruyère cheese are indescribably delicious!

INGREDIENTS

1 eggplant

1 red bell pepper

1 carrot

2 zucchini

3 tomatoes

1 to 2 cloves garlic, peeled

2 medium red or yellow onions

1 1/2 cups grated Gruyère cheese

1 recipe crepe batter (recipe below)

DIRECTIONS

Clean all veggies and cut into large chunks. Toss with 2 teaspoons Italian herbs, salt and pepper and 1/4 cup extra virgin olive oil.

Place in large baking pan and roast at 425°F for 30-40 minutes, or until well-done and browned. Turn at least once during roasting.

Remove from oven. Cool completely and then coarsely chop all veggies together. Can be made a day ahead of time and refrigerated.

Crêpes

1 cup flour

2 large eggs

1 3/4 cup milk

1/2 teaspoon salt

1/2 stick butter for cooking crepes in frying pan

Beat eggs, milk and salt in a bowl. With wire whisk, stir in flour and blend until smooth.

Tax Bite

Handout Heaven

Farm subsidies totaled $177,589,000,000 from 1995 to 2006, equivalent to $580 for every man, woman and child in the United States. Over that 10-year period, 10 percent of the beneficiaries received 75 percent of all subsidy payments.

Source: Environmental Working Group

Batter should be rather thin. Cook crêpes in melted butter (like pancakes) in a frying pan with very shallow sides. Crêpes will be thin. Store in between sheets of waxed paper until ready to use. Can be made ahead up to two days ahead and refrigerated.

To assemble crêpes:

Lay a crêpe out flat on a cutting board. Spoon three heaping tablespoons of veggie mixture into the center of the crêpe. Sprinkle with one tablespoon grated Guyère cheese. Roll up and place in well-greased casserole dish, seam side down. Continue with remaining crêpes until filling is used up. Sprinkle extra grated cheese over the top of the crêpes. Heat through at 350 ºF until cheese on top melts.

Caramelized Onion-Walnut, Blue Cheese Tart

Here is a tart that is bursting with flavors of caramelized onion, walnuts and blue cheese—perfect for entertaining. It's very easy to prepare, and since walnuts are available year-round, this dish can be prepared almost any time of the year.

INGREDIENTS

1 cooked tart crust (recipe below)

1 large red onion, peeled and sliced

1 cup walnut halves

2 tablespoons olive oil

4-5 ounces blue cheese, crumbled

4 tablespoon half & half, or cream

DIRECTIONS

In a large frying pan heat olive oil and add onions. Cook until soft and beginning to brown. Add walnuts and continue cooking over medium-high heat until walnuts are browned and onions are caramelized. Place mixture in cooled tart shell and evenly distribute crumbled blue cheese over onion mixture. Drizzle half and half evenly over filling. Bake for 15-20 minutes at 350ºF.

Tax Bite

Unsavory Subsidies

In 2006 USDA subsidy payments were distributed to 1,446,280 farmers totaling $13.4 billion, averaging $9,571 per recipient. $11.2 billion of those subsidies went to commodity programs to prop up farmers' incomes.

Source: Environmental Working Group

Tart crust

11/2 cups all-purpose flour

1 teaspoon salt

1 cube unsalted butter, chilled and cut into small cubes

1 teaspoon cider vinegar

1/4 cup ice-cold water

In a large bowl, mix flour and salt. With fingertips or a pastry cutter, work butter into flour mixture until fine and crumbly. Sprinkle vinegar over mixture and stir in well with fork. Gradually add ice water, a little at a time, until dough can be rolled into a ball. Place ball in tart pan with a removable bottom and with fingers, pat into the pan, filling in up to the tops of the sides. (If using a pie dish, just push dough 3/4 of an inch up the sides of the pan, because tart filling will not fill the entire dish, as a pie would. With a fork, poke a bunch of holes into the bottom and sides of the crust and bake at 400ºF for 15 minutes, or until golden brown. Remove from oven and cool to room temperature.

Roasted Corn and Poblano White Cheddar Tart

INGREDIENTS

1 cooked tart crust (on prior page)

2 large poblano chilies

2 large ears of corn on the cob (if you can't find this, just use frozen corn; also Trader Joe's sells pre-roasted corn kernels in a bag)

11/2 cups grated sharp white cheddar cheese

3-4 tablespoons half & half, or cream

DIRECTIONS

Preheat oven to 450ºF. Remove husks from corn and brush corn and poblano chilies with olive oil and season with salt and pepper. Place corn and peppers on baking sheet and roast in for approximately 20 minutes, turning vegetables at least once while roasting. Veggies should become quite browned. Reduce oven temperature to 350ºF. Remove veggies from oven and place peppers in a small paper bag with top folded closed. Allow to cool.

Meanwhile cool corn to room temperature. Cut corn off cob and set aside. Remove skins and seeds from peppers and cut the meat of the pepper into thin strips or bite-sized pieces. Mix corn and chilies and place in bottom of precooked tart shell. Sprinkle grated cheddar over mixture and drizzle half and half evenly over all. Bake 15 to 20 minutes in 350 degree oven, or until cheese becomes golden brown. This dish is good hot or at room temperature.

Tax Bite

Cream of the Crop

There are three major Federal Dairy programs currently in place as part of the 2008 Farm Bill: milk price support, Federal milk marketing orders, and MILC (milk income loss contract) payment. Dairy price support is provided through the purchases of specific products at specific prices. Since this recipe calls for butter, cheddar cheese and cream, you may be interested to know that the Secretary of Agriculture must purchase cheddar cheese in blocks at not less than $1.13 per pound, butter at not less than $1.05 per pound and nonfat dry milk at not less than $0.80 per pound. Your tax dollars at work!

Source: USDA Economic Research Service

Eggplant "Crêpes" Sorrento

This is one of those dishes my mother-in-law introduced me to, and it is fabulous—one of my all-time favorite meals!

INGREDIENTS

4 medium eggplants cut into ¼-inch ovals
1 teaspoon sea salt
1/4 cup olive oil

Mushroom-Cheese Filling

1 tablespoon olive oil
1 large yellow onion, finely chopped
1 clove garlic, minced
3/4 pound fresh cremini mushrooms, sliced
3/4 pound fresh ricotta cheese
1/2 cup freshly grated Parmesan
1/2 cup freshly grated Romano
1 egg
1 tablespoon minced fresh basil
1/4 teaspoon dried oregano (or 1 teaspoon fresh)

Tomato-Basil Marinara Sauce

2 tablespoons olive oil
1 large yellow onion, minced
1 clove garlic, minced
1 tablespoon minced fresh basil
1/4 teaspoon dried oregano (or 1 teaspoon fresh)
3 cups tomato puree
1 tablespoon tomato paste
1/2 cup red wine
Salt and pepper to taste

Topping:

6 ounces fresh Mozzarella, or Scamorza thinly sliced

Tax Bite

Everlasting Losers … Us!

The biggest loser in the farm subsidy game is the American consumer. The USDA Commodity Assistance Program amounts to little more than protectionism by shielding the domestic market from global competition. Government farm subsidy programs raise the cost of food and with it the overall cost of living. According to the Organization for Economic Co-operation and Development, the higher domestic food prices caused by U.S. farm programs transferred $16.2 billion from American consumers to domestic agricultural producers in 2004. And, in 2005, direct agricultural subsidies amounted to $26 billion, or $234 per household. This consumer tax is paid over and above what we dole out to farmers through the federal budget.

Source: http://www.reason.com/news/show/36207.html

DIRECTIONS

Crepes

Lightly salt eggplant slices and set aside to release moisture. When ready, heat olive oil in large frying pan and sauté eggplant slices until just cooked through. Set aside.

In same pan, sauté onions in 1 tablespoon olive oil, just until soft and translucent. Add mushrooms and continue to cook, until mushrooms begin to brown. Remove and cool.

In a large bowl, mix remaining filling ingredients well and then stir in cooled onions and mushrooms.

Place one large spoonful of filling at one end of eggplant slices, and roll up so that the filling goes across the short span of the eggplant, like a short crepe. Place in casserole dish and if necessary, secure crepe with a toothpick.

Sauce

To make sauce, heat olive oil in a one-quart pot and cook onions until translucent. Add garlic and herbs and continue to cook for one to two minutes, just to release flavors and fragrance of herbs. Add wine and bring to boil, scraping any browned bits from the bottom of the pan. Cook down slightly, before adding tomato puree and paste. Season to taste with salt and pepper.

When ready to serve, pour sauce over eggplant "crêpes" in casserole and top evenly with slices of cheese. Bake at 350ºF for 20 minutes, or until heated through and cheese begins to bubble.

Stuffed Acorn Squash

(Serves six)

Keep in mind that you can alter the ingredients and quantities to suit your own tastes, for example a squash stuffed with nothing but caramelized onions is also quite nice. We like this combination and it offers up nice fall colors with the squash, nuts and cranberries.

INGREDIENTS

3 medium to large acorn squash
2 tablespoons olive oil
1/2 large onion, chopped
1 1/2 cloves garlic, pressed
2 tablespoon minced fresh sage, or ½ teaspoon dried
1/2 cup chopped walnuts
1/2 cup dried cranberries
3 large pre-cooked chicken apple sausages, skinned and crumbled
1/2 cup dry sherry
1/2 cup grated sharp cheddar, gruyere or smoked gouda cheese
4 slices of whole wheat bread, dried out or toasted, broken into breadcrumbs or small pieces.

DIRECTIONS

Cut acorn squash in half length-wise. Remove seeds and stringy stuff and season cavities with salt and pepper. Place cut side down in greased baking dish. Bake in at 350°F for approximately 20-25 minutes, or until a knife easily pierces the skin and meat of squash. Remove squash from oven, turn right side up, and set aside in baking dish.

Meanwhile, sauté onion and garlic in olive oil. Cook over medium high heat until onion is soft. Add sage, walnuts, cranberries, crumbled sausage and breadcrumbs (or pieces) and

Tax Bite

It's Nuts! (Or is it?)

Fruits, vegetables and nuts are generally not covered by the USDA Commodity Subsidy programs.

Source: American Farmland Trust

Tax Bite

Kernels for Brains

Producing Ethanol for use in motor fuels increases the demand for corn, which ultimately raises the prices that consumers pay for a wide variety of foods at the grocery store, ranging from corn syrup sweeteners found in soft drinks to meat, dairy, and poultry products. The increased use of corn increases overall food prices by increasing the price of meat, because corn is used as animal feed, and it also indirectly increases the costs of other food crops, because the land is diverted from them to corn, rendering the other crops more scarce, hence more expensive.

Source: Congressional Budget Office

continue to cook over medium-high heat until mixture begins to brown slightly—10 minutes or so. Add sherry and cook until liquid is almost evaporated. Remove pan from heat, add cheese and gently toss to mix. Spoon stuffing mixture into squash cavities. Bake at 350ºF until heated through, approximately 15 minutes.

Polenta Alla Contadina

(Serves 4)

This recipe comes from Jeff Assadi, owner of La Finestra Restaurant in Lafayette, California. When I tasted this dish of grilled polenta and wild mushrooms at dinner one night, I knew it would have to find a way to my cookbook. Jeff was more than happy to share the recipe with all of us.

INGREDIENTS

Polenta

1 cup polenta (enriched cornmeal)

3 cups water

1/4 cup heavy cream

1 tablespoon crumbled "sweet" gorgonzola cheese (gorgonzola aged approximately 3 months)

Pinch salt and pepper

Wild Mushroom Sauce

1-2 tablespoons oil (7/8 canola oil, and 1/8 olive oil)

3 cups mushrooms, thinly sliced (combination of fresh shitake and oyster mushrooms and a little bit of dried porcini)

1-2 cloves garlic, pressed

Tax Bite

Ethanol Update

As farmers devote more land to corn to fulfill the Ethanol Mandate, they must devote fewer acres to other crops, such as soybeans. This reduces the soybean crop and increases soybean prices. Even for crops that have nothing to do with corn, prices rise because of the competition for farmland. And, the increased cost of corn, which is a huge component of farm animal feed, increases food prices across the board.

Source: Institute for Energy Research

Tax Bite

I-owe-A

Iowa was the single largest state recipient of direct farm payments in 2007 (latest available data) garnering a total of $500 million, or 9.9% of the total. A total of 82,567 recipients received a combined $399 million in direct payments for corn.

Source: Environmental Working Group

1/4-1/3 cup julienned sun dried tomatoes, packed in oil, drained

1/4 cup fresh parsley, chopped

Salt and pepper to taste

1/2 -3/4 cup heavy cream (more or less, adjust as you see fit for your family)

DIRECTIONS

To make polenta, heat water to boiling, add cream and gorgonzola cheese. Slowly add polenta, stirring or whisking all the while. Reduce heat to low and continue to cook for 30 to 40 minutes, stirring often. When very thick, turn into greased dish, such as a bread pan, until set. Chill until ready to use. Then slice into ¾ inch slices, approximately 3 inches square. Set aside, or refrigerate until ready to use.

For sauce, preheat a frying pan to very hot. Add oil, then garlic and mushrooms. Cook until mushrooms begin to brown, stirring or tossing occasionally. Add sun dried tomatoes, heat and toss together. Season to taste with salt and pepper. Add parsley and cream. Cook until just until slightly thickened.

Spoon over grilled polenta and garnish with freshly grated Parmesan cheese. Serve immediately.

Tax Bite

Corn is King

Over the past 12 years, corn has been the top crop for federal assistance, receiving $56 billion. In 2007 alone 755,358 corn growers received a total of $2.04 billion in direct subsidy payments.

Source: Environmental Working Group

VEGGIE SIDES

Roasted Sweet Peppers with Grated Cheddar

Sweet "pickle" peppers are about two inches in length and normally come in an assortment of red, yellow and orange. These peppers are really quite sweet and, as the name suggests, they are perfect for pickling and make a beautiful presentation in a clear jar. This recipe calls for roasting the peppers with pearl onions and grated cheese. It is a perfect side dish to accompany grilled marinated chicken or flank steak, or a nice main course for those who prefer not to eat meat.

INGREDIENTS

2 pounds sweet miniature peppers–tri-color if possible

2 cups pearl onions (tri-color or all white are fine)

2-3 tablespoons extra virgin olive oil

1/2 cup grated cheddar

1/2 cup grated Monterey Jack cheese (can use pepper jack)

1/2 cup crumbled feta

Salt and pepper, to taste

DIRECTIONS

Bring a large pot of water to boil and add pearl onions to boiling water. Boil for approximately 3-4 minutes. Drain in a colander or strainer and cool to room temperature. Peel onions with a sharp paring knife, beginning at the fringy end and pulling towards the opposite end. This process will pull off the tough exterior skins. Place the skinned onions in a large roasting pan.

Tax Bite

CO2 Crackpots

The U.S. bio-fuels industry receives a 45¢ tax credit for every gallon of ethanol produced, or about $3 billion each year, while there is a 54¢ per gallon import tariff on top of the 4-7¢ ad valorem tariff imposed on sugar-based ethanol from Brazil and the Caribbean. The Obama Administration is pushing for a mandate to increase the amount of corn-based ethanol in gasoline from 10% to 15% despite the fact an EPA study shows, through a series of alternative scenarios over a 30-100 year period, that corn-based ethanol is just as likely to produce a net increase as it is to produce a decrease in CO_2 emissions when compared to burning fossil fuels.

Source: "Ethanol's Grocery Bill" Wall Street Journal editorial, June 2, 2009;

Wash sweet peppers and place in same roasting pan, stems intact. Toss onions and peppers with olive oil and season with salt and pepper. Roast in hot oven, 400°F, for approximately 20-25 minutes. Remove from oven and sprinkle cheese over top. Continue to cook for another 5-10 minutes until cheese is melted and bubbly.

Tax Bite

Sizing Up Farmers

Since this recipe uses mini-peppers, it's a good time to notify you that if a farm is "mini" (10 acres or less) the farmer is not eligible to receive farm subsidies unless the owner is socially disadvantaged (those subjected to racial or ethnic prejudice), or a limited-resource farmer with gross farm sales not more than $116,800 in each of the previous 2 years in 2005 dollars, (adjusted for inflation each year) with a total household income at or below the national poverty level for a family of four, or less than 50 percent of county median household income in each of the previous 2 years.

Source: USDA Economic Research Service

Baked Stuffed Poblano Peppers

Poblanos chilies are mild to medium hot, heart-shaped peppers that are large and have very thick walls, making them great for stuffing. Chile rellenos are often made with poblano peppers. Poblanos are usually roasted and peeled before use. Poblanos, when dried, are called ancho or mulato chiles.

INGREDIENTS

6 poblano chile peppers
1 1/2 cups ricotta cheese
2 cups grated cheddar, Monterey jack, pepper jack or mozzarella cheese
1 large yellow onion, peeled and coarsely chopped
1-2 tablespoons olive oil
1 cup corn kernels (frozen or straight off the cob)
2 tablespoons finely chopped cilantro
Salt and Pepper to taste
Dash of cayenne pepper

DIRECTIONS

Oil peppers with olive oil and place in a shallow baking dish. Bake in 450-degree oven for approximately 15 minutes, or until soft and pliable. Remove from heat and set aside. When cool, remove stems and seeds from chilies, leaving body intact.

Sauté onions in olive oil, over medium-high heat, until softened. Remove from heat. In a separate bowl, mix ricotta cheese, 11/2 cups of the grated cheese, (reserving the other 1/2 cup to sprinkle over tops of stuffed chilies), corn, cilantro, cayenne pepper, salt and pepper. Add onions and stir to mix.

Make a two-inch slit down the length on one side of each pepper. Remove any remaining seeds. Through this opening, spoon 1/3 cup of the cheese mixture into each pepper. Close the gap and lay with seam side up in greased baking dish. Chiles can be prepared several hours ahead and refrigerated until ready to bake. For final baking, sprinkle remaining 1/2 cup of grated cheese over tops of stuffed chilies and cook at 400°F for 15 minutes, or until heated through and cheese is bubbly. Serve piping hot.

Tax Bite

Congressional Fat Cats

Of the 435 U.S. Congressional districts, just 22 of them receive more than 50% of all farm bill subsidies. During 1995-2006, the 1st District of Kansas won top honors, with 4.2 % of all payments, followed by the "At Large" District of North Dakota also with 4.2% and in third with 4.1% was the 3rd District of Nebraska.

Source: Environmental Working Group

Tax Bite

"Break" for Horses

The 2008 Farm Bill includes $126 million in tax breaks over 10 years for the thoroughbred horseracing industry. Apparently, horses are Kentucky's largest agricultural product and the industry contributes some $3.5 billion to the state's economy, $39 billion to the U.S. economy and directly employs 50,000 Kentuckians.

Source: McClatchy Washington Bureau "Farm Bill includes tax breaks for horse racing industry" May 9, 2008, by Halimah Abdullah

Creamed Spinach (or Arugula)

We love to add the goat cheese and shallot twist to the traditional version of this dish.

INGREDIENTS

20 ounces of fresh spinach (or arugula)
4 shallots, finely chopped
2 cloves garlic, minced
2 tablespoons olive oil
2 ounces Montrachet goat cheese (or cream cheese)
1 tablespoon Dijon mustard

DIRECTIONS

Sautee garlic and shallots in olive oil. Stir in Dijon. Add spinach (or arugula) a bit at a time. As it cooks down, you can add more leaves. When all spinach is sautéed, add goat cheese and cook until spinach is creamy.

Curling Ribbon Carrots

12 large carrots, peeled
2 tablespoons extra virgin olive oil
Salt and Pepper to taste

Shave carrots into long, wide ribbons by using a potato peeler. Preheat oil in a large frying pan and add carrots, salt and pepper. Cook until carrots become browned on the outside edges and curled, stirring often. Serve plain, or over a bed of creamed arugula.

Tax Bite

Supersized Subsidies

In 2007, the top 10% of direct farm payment recipients collected about 60 percent of the subsidy funding. While direct payments are limited to $40,000 per person ($80,000 per married couple), large subsidized farming operations with complex, interlocking business organizations and multiple owners routinely enable individuals to collect up to $80,000 apiece each year in direct payment subsidies under USDA rules governing subsidies for partnerships, corporations, joint ventures and trusts. If the House version of the direct payment provision is adopted, the maximum payment will be increased from $40,000 to $60,000 per person per year ($120,000 per married couple).

Source: Environmental Working Group

Poached Fennel with Gorgonzola Crust

(Serves 4 as a side dish, or 2 for an entrée)

INGREDIENTS

2 fennel bulbs, sliced in half horizontally (save a few leaves for garnish)
1 cup chicken broth
1/2 cup crumbled Gorgonzola or bleu cheese
1/4 cup breadcrumbs

DIRECTIONS

Trim bottom edge and tops of fennel bulbs and slice bulbs in half horizontally. In a large frying pan with lid, place halved fennel bulbs cut side down. Pour chicken broth over fennel and cover pan. Bring to boil and simmer over low heat for approximately 20-25 minutes, or until fennel is easily pierced with a knife. Remove fennel from broth and set aside. Boil broth until reduced to 1/4 cup and set aside.

Place cooked fennel bulbs, cut side up this time, in a shallow casserole large enough to hold them. Pour reduced broth over fennel. Mix breadcrumbs with Gorgonzola to make a paste. Spread paste evenly over each fennel half and bake, uncovered, at 375°F until cheese mixture is beginning to brown, about 25 minutes. Serve piping hot with a sprig of fennel leaves as garnish.

Tax Bite

Got MILC?

The USDA's Milk Income Loss Contract Program (MILC) is administered by the Farm Services Agency and compensates dairy producers when domestic milk prices fall below a specified level. The 10-year projected cost of the program according to the CBO is $4.2 billion. In order to qualify, dairy farmers must commercially produce and market cow milk in the U.S. or produce milk in the U.S. and market it abroad. They must also be in compliance with Highly Erodible Land and Wetland conservation provisions.

Source: USDA Farm Services Agency; US Senate Budget Bulletin

Baked Stuffed Poblano Peppers (top) and Roasted Green Beans with Shallots and Walnuts (bottom).

Roasted Green Beans with Shallots and Walnuts

INGREDIENTS

2 pounds green beans, trimmed
8-10 shallots, peeled and quarterd
1 cup walnut halves
3 tablespoons extra-virgin olive oil
1 teaspoon sea salt
1 teaspoon fresh cracked pepper

DIRECTIONS

Preheat oven to 400ºF. Clean beans and set aside. Prepare shallots and coat with 1-2 tablespoons olive oil. Spread out on baking sheet and bake at 400ºF for approximately 8-10 minutes. Remove from oven. About 15 minutes before serving, toss beans with walnuts and pre-roasted shallots with remaining olive oil and sprinkle with sea salt and pepper. Roast at 400ºF for another 10 minutes or so, until beans are just cooked and walnuts begin to brown. Serve at once.

Tax Bite

Protectionism Push-Back

The U.S. reintroduced dairy export subsidies in May 2009, following a similar move by the European Union. The subsidies apply to roughly 91,000 tons of mainly powdered milk, butter and cheese. Twenty-nine World Trade Organization (WTO) members have criticized the move as protectionist and particularly damaging to unsubsidized farmers in developing countries. The common perception is that subsidies undermine the spirit of free trade and drive commodity prices even lower.

Source: MercoPress and AOL News Australia

Zucchini Pancakes

The fact that our gardens are plentiful doesn't always translate to, "Oh, Mom, can we *please* have zucchini for dinner tonight!" I have discovered over the years, that no matter how enthusiastic I may be about our homegrown zucchini, it mostly finds its way into the compost pile. Luckily, there is one way most kids will eat this prolific vegetable and that is in pancakes—zucchini pancakes. These little treasures make a delicious side dish to accompany any meat. No need for syrup, they are best with a little sprinkle of Parmesan cheese.

Tax Bite

Unquenchable Thirst

The federal government has subsidized California and Arizona farmers to the tune of nearly $700 million in 2007 and 2008 to plant thirsty crops like alfalfa, rice and cotton on arid land. Subsidies do more than promote wasteful water use. Cotton demands vast quantities of insecticides, herbicides and fertilizers that end up polluting our rivers and streams. Taxpayers subsidized this environmental damage, paying out more than $600 million in cotton subsidies from 2003 to 2005. That's 10 times what the federal government spent during that period to help farmers improve their conservation practices in California.

Source: Organic Consumers Association; Associated Press

INGREDIENTS

5 cups zucchini, grated (approx. six medium-sized zucchini)
1 small red onion, grated
1 clove garlic, minced
1 teaspoon salt
1/2 teaspoon pepper
1/2 teaspoon paprika
1 teaspoon baking powder
1/2 cup flour (white or whole wheat)
1/2 cup seasoned breadcrumbs
3 eggs
1/2 to 3/4 cup milk
2-3 tablespoons butter or olive oil for frying

DIRECTIONS

Grate zucchini on the larger side of hand-held grater, or use grating tool on food processor. Wrap zucchini in cheesecloth or a kitchen towel and ring out the excess liquid. Peel and grate onion. Place both zucchini and onion in large mixing bowl. Add garlic, salt, pepper, baking powder and paprika. Mix well. Stir in flour and breadcrumbs to integrate with zucchini. In a small separate bowl, beat eggs with fork, and add milk. Pour liquids into dries and mix well.

Drop by large spoonful onto greased frying pan. Pancakes should be roughly 3-4 inches in diameter. Sauté at medium-high heat until cooked through and golden-brown on both sides. Serve warm as side dish or as a meatless entrée, garnished with freshly grated Parmesan or a dollop of sour cream or crème fraîche.

CHAPTER IX

Uncle Sam's "Mini Me"

Potatoes, Rice, Stuffing & State Income Tax

Every main course needs a sidekick, because all by itself, an entrée is not quite enough to satisfy the appetite. This same philosophy holds true for government operations in the United States. It's been proven that the vast sums of money citizens send to the federal government each year do not come close to filling the enormous appetite of the Federal government, let alone individual state bodies and their legislators. Just like Dr. Evil, Uncle Sam has a "Mini Me" with a monstrous appetite in every state.

Of course there are a handful of states that do not levy income tax, but they make up for it in "oh so many" ways, from sales tax, excise taxes, license fees, property taxes, estate and inheritance taxes and even illegal drug stamps! States also collect taxes from nonresidents in the form of hotel, restaurant and tourism taxes, hunting and fishing licenses and in some cases, on income earned by nonresidents temporarily working in the state. This happens to sports stars and entertainers on a regular basis, but even corporate executives can be stung.

The state of Washington does not impose state income tax, but it does levy a four percent excise tax on the selling price of any home. This is crazy! A homeowner in Washington must account for 10 percent of the selling price in added expenses— six percent for Realtors and four percent for Mini Me—in addition to capital gains tax on the appreciated value.

Each state has its own tax code and many states have a taxpayer's bill of rights. But, somehow taxpayers' rights are overlooked when the state is in financial crisis, as is the case with many states today.

For example in my state, California, the Governator browbeat enough votes from the legislature to pass his budget in July 2009. But many residents remain unaware of two "trailer" bills tacked onto the budget. Among other things, these trailers increase personal income tax withholding and accelerate installment payments for personal income and corporation franchise taxes by 10 percent! Most folks were clueless until their first paycheck after October 31, 2009, the effective date of trailers.

Isn't that just like the government to slip something devastating into a bill, under the radar? It's exactly how the House of Representatives snuck F-22 defense aircraft business into the Cap and Trade bill.

The states that miraculously survive without imposing personal income tax are: Alaska, Florida, Nevada, South Dakota, Texas, Washington, and Wyoming. Residents of Tennessee and New Hampshire get a little pass because they're taxed only on income from interest and dividends, but not normal wages.

More than half the states recommended or attempted to raise a collective $24 billion in taxes and fees in 2009/2010 to fill deficits caused by runaway government spending and lower tax revenues. California, accounts for a huge portion of the total, but Illinois and New York each proposed close to $4 billion in tax increases. The proposed increases would affect personal income tax, sales tax and excise taxes on cigarettes and alcohol.

The five states with the highest marginal income tax rate for single filers for 2009 were: Hawaii and Oregon at 11 percent, New Jersey at 10.75 percent, California at 10.55 percent and Vermont at 9.4 percent. These rates, however, are applied at different levels of income and varying standard deductions and personal exemptions. The highest rate for a taxpayer with a $50K income is California at 9.55 percent.

The states with the lowest marginal income tax rate excluding those that impose no personal income tax are: Illinois, Indiana, Pennsylvania, Michigan and Arizona.

Now, for a look at the states with the highest overall tax burden: New Jersey (11.8%), New York (11.7%), Connecticut (11.1%), Maryland (10.8%) and Hawaii (10.6%). California ranks sixth overall at 10.5 percent while the U.S. average hovers right at 9.7 percent.

Despite giving nearly one-tenth of our salaries to the State after forking out somewhere between one-quarter and slightly more than a third to the federal government, the hunger for more taxpayer dollars is still not satisfied! These political pigs have devised another new way to grab more of the dough—"borrowing" from municipal governments.

Until just recently, I had no idea that our California State government was entitled to "borrow" money from city and county property tax revenues when certain conditions exist. I still don't know how many other states may be utilizing these tactics, but it might be worth a call to your governor or state comptroller to find out.

According to California's 2004 Proposition 1A, the State Legislature can "borrow" up to 8 percent of the revenues (in California that is approximately $2 billion) if the Governor issues a proclamation of "severe fiscal hardship," the Legislature enacts an urgency statute suspending the Prop1A property tax protection clause with a 2/3 vote of each house, and if the legislature enacts a law providing for full repayment of the "borrowed funds" plus interest, within three years. The State may invoke this clause no more than twice in any 10-year period, and may only do so if any previous borrowing under this provision was repaid. But, once the loan is paid back, the State can turn around and "re-borrow" it immediately, thereby extending the loan period to six years. For one of our local towns, that "loan" to the State of California could amount to $353K or 4.2 percent of the general fund annual revenue budget of $8.425 million. In the case of incremental property tax revenue accounts such as redevelopment funds, the State can simply take 8 percent without the added burden of having to pay it back!

While the nation's population grew a mere 12.6 percent in the 10-year period 1998 to 2008, aggregate state tax revenues increased 65 percent over the same period. The personal income tax component, comprising 35 percent of total state revenues, increased 74 percent, far outpacing population growth.

Arm thyself from Mini Me!

Sources: Original data from the US Census Bureau; other statistics: Tax Foundation and RetirementLiving.com

Tax Bite

Car Tax Take-Two

The California State Legislature passed a budget for 2009 which increased costs for residents, including an across the board 1% sales tax increase and the doubling of the vehicle license fee. A new $25K car purchase will cost an additional $2,311 total in taxes and fees.

The breakdown:

Sales Tax $2,063

Registration $31

Vehicle license fee $163

CHP fee $22

Fingerprint ID fee $1

Smog High Polluter Repair Fee $6

Original Smog Abatement $6

Alternate Fuel Tech Smog Fee $8

Auto Theft or DUI Crime Deterrence Program fee $1

Air Quality Management Fee $6

Alternate Fuel/Tech Registration Fee $3

Reflectorized License Plate Fee $1

Source: California Dept. of Motor Vehicles

Barley Pilaf

Every year, my mom made barley pilaf along with barbecued chicken for my birthday. Nowadays, I still make it for my own birthday celebration! It's that good.

INGREDIENTS

13/4 cup pearl barley
1/2 cube butter
2 medium onions, chopped
1 cup sliced fresh mushrooms
5 cups chicken broth

DIRECTIONS

Preheat oven to 350°F. In a Dutch oven, or pot with a tight-fitting lid, sauté onions in half of the butter until soft and translucent. Add remaining butter and barley and continue to cook over medium heat until barley is golden brown. Add mushrooms and cook for two minutes longer. Add 2 cups of chicken broth and stir. Cover pot and bake for about 45 minutes. Remove from oven and stir in 2 additional cups of broth. Bake again for another 45 minutes. Finally add last cup of broth and continue to bake for 30 minutes longer.

To leftover barley pilaf, add sundried tomatoes, Greek olives, toasted pine nuts and feta cheese for a yummy lunch treat the next day!

Tax Bite

Tax Dollars Stealing Private Jobs

From 2000 to 2007, the state of New Jersey created 6,800 private sector jobs compared with 55,800 public sector jobs for the same period.

Source: WSJ, "Main Street" July 28, 2009 by William McGurn

Tax Bite

Minnesota Cares

MinnesotaCare is a 2% tax imposed on healthcare providers, hospitals, surgical centers and wholesale drug distributors. The tax is charged on gross receipts from patient services and from pharmaceutical sales made by wholesalers. The tax is paid monthly and deposited into the State's Healthcare Access Fund, which is used in part to pay for state-subsidized health insurance for low-income residents who are otherwise uninsured.

Source: Minnesota Dept. of Revenue

Portobello Multi-Grain Pilaf

(Serves 6+)

The good thing about potluck gatherings is that you have the occasion to try lots of great food without having to cook every dish. Our good friend Kathe Beadle, brought this wonderful pilaf dish to our house for dinner many years ago. It is made with a variety of grains, each with a different texture and bite.

INGREDIENTS

1 tablespoon butter
1 tablespoon olive oil
1 clove garlic, crushed
1 medium onion, finely chopped
2 cups baby Portobello, or cremini mushrooms, sliced
1 cup pearl barley
1/4 cup brown rice
*1/2 cup soft winter wheat berries**
1/2 cup wild rice
3 cups chicken broth
Salt and pepper to taste

DIRECTIONS

Using a large, ovenproof dish with a tight-fitting lid (such as cast iron or glass) melt butter over low heat. Add olive oil, garlic and onion and cook until translucent, approximately 10 minutes. Add mushrooms and cook over medium-high heat until soft and beginning to brown on the edges. Add all of the grains and cook, stirring often, over medium-high heat for about 10 more minutes. Add chicken broth and bring to boil. Cover dish and bake at 350ºF for 40 minutes or until all grains are cooked, but still slightly al dente. Season to taste with salt and pepper.

Tax Bite

I.O.U. State Refunds

Instead of tax refunds, the State of California handed out IOU's in 2009. Most banks did not accept them for deposit, so the unfortunate Californians who over-withheld taxes waited in a long queue to claim their rightful money.

Source: California State Franchise Tax Board

Tax Bite

Idaho Potato Tax

Idaho imposes a mandatory potato tax of between 7 and 15 cents per hundredweight. The first handler pays 60% of this fee, while the second handler pays the balance. Every August the Board of the Idaho Potato Commission determines the hundredweight levy for the next year. The tax funds a variety of Idaho Potato Commission operations.

Source: Idaho Potato Commission

J-Dog's People Fries

Try as we might to raise civilized children, they still end up with names like "J-dog" or just plain "Dog." While I don't pretend to understand the "dog" thing, it's actually kind of funny. With a little good grooming, this generation of "dogs" can be inspired to prepare some excellent people treats, like these homemade, oven-baked fries that my son likes to make. This recipe calls for approximately one medium-large russet potato, or 1 1/2 large new potatoes per person. If your family really loves fries, you may want to consider preparing two potatoes per person.

INGREDIENTS

6 medium to large russet potatoes (or 12 new potatoes)

2 tablespoons olive or canola oil, either one is fine

**Seasoning options–this is totally up to your own taste, use any of those listed, or come up with your own favorite seasoning, and please adjust seasoning quantities by experimenting to suit your taste. (Options: 1 packet dried French onion soup mix, or 1 teaspoon each: salt and pepper, or 2 teaspoons Montreal steak seasoning, or 2 teaspoons, or more Cajun seasoning, or 2 teaspoons, or more Lemon pepper.)*

Tax Bite

FDIC Bank Heist

As of April 1, 2009 banks wishing to issue FDIC-insured debt (Federal Deposit Insurance Corporation) must pay a surcharge for this service if the debt has a maturity of one year or longer from date of issuance. Due to the 2009 recession and the fear of bank runs, the FDIC guarantee coverage was increased from $100,000 to $250,000. In order to pay for this service, banks must pay a surcharge of between 10 and 50 basis points, depending upon the whether it is an insured or uninsured depository institution and depending upon when the original debt was issued.

Source: Morrison and Foerster LLP

DIRECTIONS

Peel potatoes and slice into strips 1/2 inch wide by 1/4 inch deep and the full length of the potato. Place potato strips onto a large baking sheet.

Drizzle oil over potatoes and with hands coat potatoes. Sprinkle seasoning over potatoes and again with hands, toss well to distribute seasoning over all potatoes.

Bake at 400ºF for 20-30 minutes, or until potatoes are easily pierced, but beginning to get a bit crunchy on the outside. You should turn potatoes with a spatula at least once or twice during baking to make sure all edges get a little crispy. Serve immediately, piping hot.

Sweet Potatoes and Yams Roasted with Red Onion and Sage

Just like Congress, we have a divided family when it comes to certain issues and around Thanksgiving, one of those issues is certain to be sweet potatoes. I love them, but my husband doesn't, simply because they are ... sweet. I'd like to ask what he expects from "sweet" potatoes and he'd like to filibuster the motion of serving them at all. In the end, we usually reach across the aisle ... I serve them and he politely abstains.

INGREDIENTS

2 large sweet potatoes, peeled and cut into 1 1/2 to 2-inch chunks

2 large yams, peeled and cut into same large chunks

1 large red onion, peeled and sliced

2 tablespoon olive oil

2 teaspoons dried sage, or 1/4 cup chopped fresh sage

2 teaspoons poultry seasoning

1 teaspoon salt

1 teaspoon black pepper

DIRECTIONS

Preheat oven to 350ºF. Grease a 9x13 inch baking dish.

In a large bowl, toss sweet potatoes, yams and onions with olive oil. Sprinkle seasoning over all and toss until well distributed. Place mixture in casserole or baking dish and bake, uncovered for at least one hour, until edges of sweet potatoes and yams become well browned and begin to get crunchy.

Tax Bite

Unwise, Unhealthy-Wealthy Surtax

The wealthy are bound to suffer under ObamaCare, but it won't just be the wealthy who will suffer unhealthy tax increases. The surtaxes floated to underwrite this monstrous piece of legislation will affect millions of non-corporate businesses in America that pay their taxes on individual tax returns. This tax increase will affect individuals (or small businesses) with adjusted gross incomes above $200K and joint filers above $250K. The surtax will increase the current 2.9% Medicare Tax to 3.8%. In addition, for those in this earnings group, this tax will now be levied on all "passive" income, from dollar one. Passive income includes royalties, rents, interest, annuities, dividends and capital gains, formerly not subjected to Medicare Tax.

Sources: The Tax Foundation; ObamaCare's Worst Tax Hike, WSJ 3/17/2010

Portobello Multi-Grain Pilaf (top) and J-Dog's People Fries (bottom).

Joseph's Table Risotto Cakes with Parmesan, Portobello Mushroom Caps and Portobello Syrup

(Serves 4 as entrée or 8 for a side dish)

One night, after a torrential downpour in Taos, New Mexico, we settled in for dinner at Joseph's Table, a cozy spot with phenomenal food. My eyes wandered directly to the Risotto Cakes with Prosciutto and Parmigiano Reggiano in Portobello Syrup. Oh my goodness. This was one exceptional dish! Of course, I emailed the chef, who politely parted with his recipe for me to try at home and, if successful, pass along to my readers. His original recipe calls for twice the amount of both molasses and honey, and no port, but we added this touch to see what would happen and it worked quite well.

Tax Bite

Reduced Raffle Tax

Effective July 1, 2009, the New Mexico Bingo and Raffle Act was enacted and the former Bingo and Raffle Act repealed. I'll bet you were just wondering how the government could take advantage of your after dinner bingo game. The new legislation enacted comprehensive reform, which included a change from 3% tax on net receipts to 0.5% tax on gross receipts from bingo and raffle activities and a shift from monthly reporting and payment to quarterly reporting and payment. Now, you know and I'd bet you're pleased.

Source: New Mexico Taxation and Revenue Department

Risotto Cakes

2 tablespoons virgin olive oil
2 tablespoons unsalted butter
1 cup finely diced red onion
2 cups raw Arborio rice
6 cups beef broth
1/4 cup freshly grated Parmesan cheese
1 teaspoon kosher salt
1 teaspoon red pepper flakes

Preheat a 3-quart sauce pan over medium heat. Add oil and butter and cook until butter melts and begins to brown. Add onion and cook until translucent.

Add rice and sauté until it has a sheen, stirring often. Add beef broth, one cup at a time, letting broth absorb each time while stirring constantly to prevent rice from sticking to the pan. Once rice becomes creamy, about 15 minutes, stir in Parmesan, salt and red pepper flakes.

Pour rice into a greased 8-inch square baking dish with at least one-inch sides, and spread to 3/4-inch thickness. Cool to room temperature. Cover with plastic wrap and refrigerate for at least one hour. This is important so the cakes can be cut and transferred to sauté pan later.

When ready to serve, cut risotto into 2-inch squares. Heat two sauté pans with 3-4 tablespoons olive oil in each. When oil is hot, place half of cakes into each pan, searing until golden brown on each side, approximately two to three minutes per side.

Portobello Mushroom Syrup

2 packages baby Portobello mushrooms, cleaned and finely chopped
2 tablespoons virgin olive oil
1-2 tablespoon diced onion
1 clove garlic, crushed
1 sprig fresh thyme, minced
2 fresh sage leaves, minced
1 teaspoon minced fresh rosemary
1 tablespoon honey
1 tablespoon light molasses
1/4 cup vintage port
1 1/2 cups beef broth

Finely chop mushrooms. Heat a large sauté pan over high heat. Add enough of the oil to coat bottom of pan. Add mushrooms, onions, garlic and herbs. Sauté and stir until mushrooms and herbs begin to stick to bottom of pan. Add beef broth and stir. Add port, honey and molasses and cook until liquid is reduced by half. Strain into a bowl, pressing mushrooms with the back of a spoon to extract the liquid. (I don't strain, preferring to keep the mushrooms in the sauce.)

Tax Bite

North Dakota Talking Tax

The North Dakota State Board of Equalization assesses telecommunications carriers 2.5% tax on their adjusted gross income receipts. Of the revenues, $8.4 million is distributed to counties and local taxing districts each year, while any surplus heads for the state general fund.

Source: Office of State Tax Commissioner

Baked Portobello Mushrooms Caps

4 Portobello mushrooms caps (large size) stems removed
Olive oil to brush over caps

Preheat oven to 300ºF. Brush caps with olive oil. Place them stem side up on a baking sheet, not touching one another. Roast for 25 minutes, until mushrooms look meaty and moist. Set aside.

TO FINISH AND SERVE

1/2 pound thinly sliced prosciutto
1/2 pound shaved Parmesan
4-6 tablespoons unsalted butter
1-2 cloves garlic, diced
2 teaspoons fresh chives, finely snipped
Salt and fresh-cracked pepper to taste

Place equal amounts of prosciutto and Parmesan around each plate.

Heat butter in large skillet. Add diced garlic and cook until slightly browned. Add Portobello mushroom caps and mushroom syrup and reduce again by half. Remove Portobello caps and place over seared risotto cakes and pour sauce evenly over cakes. Sprinkle with salt and pepper, and chives.

Wild Mushroom Risotto with Port Reduction Sauce

INGREDIENTS

Soffrito and Rice

11/2 cups Arborio rice
2 tablespoons olive oil
1 tablespoon butter
2 shallots, finely chopped
1/2 pound mushrooms, pureed
1 cup white wine
1 cup beef broth, heated
3 cups chicken broth, heated
1/8 cup heavy cream
1/4 cup grated parmesan

Condimenti

1 tablespoon butter
2 cups wild mushrooms (combination of morels, cepes, porcini or chanterelles)

Port Reduction Sauce

4 cups chicken or beef stock
Chicken bones or beef bones (your choice)
2 carrots, cut into large chunks
1 yellow onion, coarsely chopped
1/2 teaspoon whole black peppercorns
1 bay leaf
1 cup port

DIRECTIONS

Melt butter with oil in large pot over medium-high heat. Add shallots and cook until translucent. Add rice and cook for one to two minutes, until rice is coated with oil. Add wine and cook until evaporated, stirring constantly. Add mushroom puree and stir well. Mix broths and add, one soup ladle at a time, until all is used up, making sure each addition is absorbed before adding the next. Stir occasionally during this

Tax Bite

Milwaukee Exposed

The City of Milwaukee created a Local Exposition District called the Wisconsin Center Tax for the purpose of acquiring and managing exposition center facilities. These facilities are funded by an exposition tax levy of 2% for basic hotel rooms, 7% additional room tax in the city of Milwaukee, 3% rental car tax and a 0.25% food and beverage tax applied to any persons selling or renting any of these items anywhere within Milwaukee County.

Source: Wisconsin Department of Revenue

Ultimate Best Barbecue Sauce

My sister and I used to call this "secret sauce #1" because we loved snitching it so much. Secret sauce #2 was the beginning of brownie batter before the eggs were added. We couldn't seem to get enough of the either one. Nowadays, many people mix the two for a chocolate barbecue sauce. This one, however, is just the basic, but still the best!

INGREDIENTS

3/4 cup yellow onion, chopped
3 tablespoons vegetable oil
1 cup ketchup
1 tablespoon soy sauce
1 cup water
1 tablespoon brown sugar
2 tablespoons Worcestershire sauce
2 tablespoons French's mustard
1/2 teaspoon ground pepper
2-3 tablespoons fresh or bottled lemon juice

DIRECTIONS

In medium sauce pan, heat oil and cook onions until just beginning to brown. Add remaining ingredients and stir well. Bring to a boil and boil for one full minute, stirring constantly. Can store for weeks in the refrigerator!

Tax Bite

New York's Impending iPod tax

In an effort to fill a growing budget gap, the state of New York is considering several tax measures. One of the proposed taxes is a 4% tax on the sale of downloaded music and other digitally delivered entertainment services.

Source: blog.syracuse.com; New York Daily News

Tax Bite

San Francisco "Butt" Tax

I know it sounds worse than it is, but the City of San Francisco has imposed a 20¢ per pack surcharge on cigarettes for an education fund and to cover the cost of cleaning up tobacco litter. This is in addition to the State's 87¢ per pack excise tax, on top of the federal $1.01 tax per pack. It really doesn't pay to smoke.

Source: cigarettereviews.com

Lenny's Thanksgiving Turkey Gravy

I have to say, my husband makes the best gravy I've ever tasted. He uses hearty red wine for part of the liquid and he browns the pan drippings well, before adding herbs.

INGREDIENTS

Turkey roasting juices

Pan drippings

3-4 tablespoons gravy flour (regular flour will do, but whisk really well to avoid lumps)

1 large clove garlic, crushed

1 teaspoon dried or powdered sage (or ½ teaspoon fresh, minced)

1 sprig fresh Rosemary, minced

1 cup red wine

1-2 cups chicken broth

DIRECTIONS

When preparing turkey, place neck in roasting pan alongside turkey and bake with turkey the entire cooking time. When turkey is done, remove neck and place in a saucepot. Cover neck with water and bring to a boil. Continue on a slow boil for about 15 minutes. Set aside for gravy.

Remove turkey from roaster onto carving board. From turkey roaster pour juices into a fat separator or a bowl and allow fat and juices to separate. Pour fat off, retaining as much of the meat juices as possible. Keep turkey scrapings in roasting pan and use same pan for gravy.

Heat pan over medium high heat and with a spatula, scrape sides and bottom to loosen contents. Add herbs and garlic and with a wire whisk stir together. Sprinkle 3-4 tablespoons flour evenly over pan and whisk, creating a paste-like mixture—over medium-high heat, browning the mixture in the process. Add 1 cup red wine, and bring to boil, stirring all the while, and

Tax Bite

Government Motors Tax Twist

On the other hand, some industries get a tax break. Despite the fact Americans' tax bills are bound to increase in order to pay for the phenomenal 2009 spending programs, GM has been given a tax break unlike any other corporation in America. The new GM has been authorized to carry forward $16 billion of net operating losses from the old company, thereby avoiding taxes on future profits for years. Although this practice is common and is known as "tax loss carried forward" what makes this case so unusual, is the fact that under normal circumstances, when a business undergoes a change in ownership, the old company's operating losses are forfeited. Since the government (aka taxpayers) owns 60.8% of the new GM, why should we care? Because the United Auto Workers retiree health-care trust fund has a 17.5% stake, and this illustrious group stands to benefit handsomely.

Source: Wall Street Journal, "GM's Tax Shelter" July 31, 2009.

reduce slightly. Add reserved meat juices, and neck broth and stir well on a low boil. As gravy reduces slightly, add 1-2 cups chicken broth and boil again. Continue to boil and stir until desired consistency. Season to taste with salt and pepper and serve hot!

Marilyn Greco's Enchilada Sauce

If you haven't tried homemade enchilada sauce before, you'll be surprised at how easy it is. I had always wondered how to make it, when one day Marilyn told me she makes a great enchilada sauce. She was right. This is heads and tails above the canned version.

INGREDIENTS

2 tablespoons canola oil
3-4 tablespoons chili powder
2 tablespoons flour
3/4 teaspoon salt
1/2 teaspoon garlic powder
1/4 teaspoon dried oregano
1/4 teaspoon cumin powder
2 teaspoons cider vinegar
2 cups water

DIRECTIONS

In a medium pot, heat oil and with a wire whisk add chili powder, flour, seasonings and spices and brown slightly over medium heat. Slowly add hot water, stirring all the while with a whisk to keep from clumping. Bring to a boil and continue on low boil for about 10 minutes, adding more water as necessary for desired thickness. Stir in vinegar. Cool and refrigerate until ready to use. Can store for several weeks in the refrigerator.

Tax Bite

Tax Advance Team

Coming to a state near you … Governor Schwarzenegger signed two budget trailer bills tacked on to the 2009/10 State budget that increase personal income tax withholding and accelerate the installment payments for personal income and corporation franchise and income taxes beginning October 2009. This does not actually increase the amount of taxes owed, but it does allow the government to take a larger piece of your pie, quicker, and hold onto it longer – interest free. And, to top it off, when you submit your tax return for a refund … you'll likely be issued an IOU.

Source: www.HRTools.com

Cranberry Port Dijon Sauce

This sauce is wonderful served over chicken, turkey or roast pork.

INGREDIENTS

3 large shallots, finely chopped
2 tablespoons olive oil
2 cloves garlic
1 cup dried cranberries
1 teaspoon Dijon mustard
Salt and pepper to taste
1/2 cup port
1 tablespoon fresh rosemary, finely minced
1 tablespoon brown sugar
1/2 cup orange juice
2 cups chicken broth

DIRECTIONS

Heat oil in medium pan and sauté shallots and garlic until soft and translucent. Add cranberries and sauté a few minutes longer. Add remaining ingredients and bring to a boil. Boil until sauce is reduced by half.

Tax Bite

Inheritance Tax

This tax is levied on the portion of an estate received by an individual and is strictly a state tax. Inheritance tax is different than estate tax, which is levied on the entire estate before it is distributed to individuals. There are 11 states that currently collect an inheritance tax: Connecticut, Indiana, Iowa, Kansas, Kentucky, Maryland, Nebraska, New Jersey, Oregon, Pennsylvania and Tennessee. In all of these states, assets transferred to a spouse are exempt. In some states, transfers made to children and close relatives are also exempt.

Source: Retirement Living Information Center

Cranberry Sauce (Made with Port)

However you decide to make your cranberry sauce, it is a simple and easy process and tastes worlds better than the canned variety. All it takes is less than 10 minutes and voila, you have a homemade cranberry sauce to match the nature of your feast.

INGREDIENTS

One 12-ounce bag fresh cranberries (or frozen)
1 cup light brown sugar
1 cup orange juice
2 tablespoons port (we used Zinfandel port, but any port will do)
1 cinnamon stick

DIRECTIONS

Mix orange juice, port and sugar in medium saucepan. Toss in cinnamon stick and bring mixture to boil. Add berries and continue to boil over medium-high heat, stirring constantly, until mixture thickens, approximately five minutes or so. Remove from heat and cool. Can make ahead and refrigerate for several weeks. When ready to serve, remove cinnamon stick.

Tax Bite

Texas Coin-Op Amusement Tax

A multi-faceted tax is imposed on any person engaged in any business dealing with coin-operated amusement machines or in the business of owning or operating coin-operated amusement machines exclusively on premises occupied by and in connection with the business. There is the registration certificate for $150, the occupation tax permit for $60, the general business license of between $200 and $500 depending upon the number of coin-operated machines, a $500 import license, and a $50 repair license. These rates also vary by the postmark date of the payment, with increasing costs according to postmark date. And, to top it off, an annual $60 occupation tax is imposed on each and every machine!

Source: Texas Window on State Government

Lisa Loe's Pepper-Cot Sauce

Our friends Lisa and Eric Loe keep us in jam! They send a wonderful assortment of olallaberry, apricot and strawberry jams almost every year. In addition to this great assortment, they send Lisa's original Pepper-Cot sauce, which is made with red chili pepper flakes and apricots and is a wonderful accompaniment to meats, or mixed with cream cheese makes a great dip for pita chips.

INGREDIENTS

7 cups pureed apricots (25-27, need to be either Patterson or Blenheim varietal)

7 cups sugar

1/3 cup lemon juice

1/4 cup red chili flakes

1 package Certo liquid fruit pectin

6-7 pint-sized glass jars with self-sealing lids and rings

DIRECTIONS

In a large stock pot, place apricots, sugar, lemon juice and chili flakes. Over high heat, stirring constantly, bring to a rolling boil. Once the mixture reaches a full boil, stir in pectin and set the timer to 1 minute and continue to stir. Remove from heat, skim off any foam that may have formed, pour into hot jars and seal according to glass jar manufacturing directions. Invert jars for 2 hours and then set upright. Sauce may not completely set for 2 weeks. Store in the pantry (or in any cool, dry place.)

Note* for best results, place jam jars onto a cookie sheet and into a 250-degree oven before pouring the hot sauce into the jars. This helps prevent breakage and will create a better environment for sealing the jars.

Tax Bite

ObamaCare Cops

Under the recently enacted ObamaCare law, the federal government will hire more than 16,000 new IRS employees to enforce compliance, at a cost of roughly $1 billion annually in salaries alone. The new law will also create some 159 new federal bureaucracies. This dizzying chart of organizations would comprise assorted new boards, agencies, commissions and programs.

Sources: Stephen Moore, Fox News analyst; Traditional Values Coalition; Human Events

Tax Bite

Pennsylvania "Sucking" Tax

The sales from compressed air vending machines and vacuuming vending machines are subject to Pennsylvania Sales and Use Tax, which is currently 6%.

Source: Pennsylvania Department of Revenue

Olive Salad for Muffaletta Sandwiches

We really had the "muffuletta" experience when we visited New Orleans for a national basketball tournament. The cuisine in this city is amazing anyway, but if you love olives and good bread, you'll really enjoy the muffaletta sandwich comprised of cold cuts, sliced cheese, Sicilian bread and olive salad. This olive salad is also a wonderful accompaniment for grilled meats.

INGREDIENTS

1 cup chopped pimiento-stuffed green olives
1/2 cup chopped pitted Kalamata olives
1/2 cup pickled pearl onions, chopped (see recipe below)
2 tablespoons capers, drained
1/2 cup chopped marinated artichoke hearts
2 tablespoons chopped sun-dried tomatoes packed in olive oil and drained
1/4 cup chopped mild pepperoncini
1 tablespoon virgin olive oil
1/2 teaspoon freshly ground pepper

DIRECTIONS

Mix all and store in airtight container. Can be stored for several weeks in the refrigerator.

Tax Bite

Coal Severance Tax

In North Dakota a coal severance tax of 37.5¢ per ton is imposed on all coal severed for sale or industrial purposes, except coal used for heating buildings, coal used by the state or any political subdivision of the state and coal used in agricultural processing and sugar beet refining plants in the state or adjacent states. The tax is in lieu of sales and use taxes on coal and property tax on minerals in the earth. A 50% reduction in the tax is allowed for coal burned in a cogeneration facility designed to use renewable resources to generate 10% or more of its energy output.

Source: North Dakota Tax

Kate's Pickled Pearl Onions

(Makes approximately 2 pints)

These make a great holiday, hostess or stocking gift.

INGREDIENTS

Two 10-ounce bags of pearl onions (white, brown or red–a combination is colorful)

2 cups water

1 to 2 teaspoons sea salt (your choice, depending on desired saltiness)

2 tablespoon sugar

11/2 cups white vinegar

1 tablespoon pickling spice (available at your local grocers in the spice section)

DIRECTIONS

Place onions in pot of boiling water and cook for approximately two to three minutes. Remove from heat, drain and rinse with cold water immediately. When cool, remove skins with a small paring knife. Start by slicing off root end and carefully peeling back skin. Save as much of the onion as possible. Place onions in sterilized jars. (For this recipe you should need about four half-pint jars.)

In a small pot, combine vinegar, sugar, salt and spices and bring to a boil. Stir until sugar and salt are dissolved. Remove from heat and pour liquid over onions in jars, leaving 1/2-inch of space at the top. To seal jars, cover closed jars with water and place in boiling water bath for several minutes. Follow manufacturer's directions for sealing jars properly.

Tax Bite

Watercraft Tax

Washington State imposes a tax of 0.005 on the fair market value of non-commercial boats that are 16 feet and over, and used on Washington waters. This tax is imposed in lieu of a property tax on the boat!

Source: Washington Dept. of Revenue

Cranberry Sauce made with Port (top) and Kate's Pickled Pearl Onions (bottom).

Port-Glazed Onions and Shallots

INGREDIENTS

One 10-ounce package red pearl onions
One 10-ounce package golden pearl onions
10 ounces small (1 inch diameter) shallots
2 tablespoons butter
1 cup ruby port wine
1/3 cup low-salt chicken broth
2 teaspoons red wine vinegar

DIRECTIONS

Blanch all onions and shallots in a large pot of boiling salted water 2 minutes. Drain. Peel onions and shallots, trimming any roots off ends.

Melt butter in heavy medium skillet over medium-high heat. Add onions and shallots. Stir to coat. Sprinkle with salt and pepper. Add Port, broth, and vinegar and bring to simmer. Reduce heat to medium; cover and simmer until onions and shallots are tender, about 15-20 minutes. Uncover and simmer until liquids are reduced to a glaze, stirring occasionally, about 20 minutes. Season to taste with salt and pepper. Can be made 1 day ahead. Cover and chill. Warm over low heat before serving. Serve with any meat.

Tax Bite

Alaska Commercial Passenger Vessel Tax

This tax is an assessment of $46 per passenger per voyage on commercial passenger vessels. The tax is to be collected by the person providing travel to the passenger. The tax return is due the last day of the month following the month the travel took place.

Source: Alaska Dept. of Revenue

Tax Bite

Vehicle Rental Tax

The state of Alaska levies an excise tax on total costs and fees charged for the lease or rental of passenger or recreational vehicles for a period of less than 90 days. The rate on passenger vehicles is a whopping 10% while the rate for recreational vehicles is far less at 3%. Naturally, the tax is waived for leases or rentals for official federal, state, or local government business!

Source: Alaska Department of Revenue

CHAPTER XI

Breadwinners vs. Boondogglers

Breakfast 'n Bread & Bailout Boondoggle

There seems to be a new trend in the U.S. banking industry. Instead of banks lending money to Americans for homes, cars, business inventories and consumer purchases, fiscally responsible citizens now finance banks in the form of taxpayer bailouts. Nowadays, we taxpayers give banks all the money they need, so they can turn around and lend it back to us, at a premium!

When Congress generously doled out $700 billion of our tax dollars through the Troubled Asset Relief Program (TARP), otherwise known as "Taxing Americans Ridiculous Proportions" or "Thieves and Recalcitrant Politicians" they naively thought these banks would write off toxic assets with the funding, but, instead, they used our money to pay executive bonuses, buy up smaller failing banks, and in the case of Citibank, attempt to purchase a brand new, $50 million, French-made corporate jet.

Then, after the first $350 billion vanished, these same banks came crawling back to Congress for more. And, they got it, but under a new name—2009 Financial Stability Plan (FSP) with an initial amount of $500 billion in assets, growing to $1, maybe $2 trillion. Moral hazard is irrelevant. Lost is the concept of fiscal responsibility and the need to balance risk and reward. When the government bails everyone out, regardless of their behavior, who cares about risks?

Financial institutions didn't get into this bind all by themselves. They had a lot of help from Congress and oddly, Congress wants the banks to continue the very business practice that got them into trouble in the first place—making questionable loans at a low rate of return, in a very bad economy.

In 1977, Congress passed into law the Community Reinvestment Act, (CRA) which was intended to encourage depository institutions to help meet the credit needs of the communities in which they operated, including low and moderate-income neighborhoods, consistent with "safe and sound" banking operations. In other words, make risky loans. Somehow Congress failed to connect the dots between "safe and sound" and "low-income" loans.

In 1996, Congress revised the act to "strongly encourage" large banks to have a program of ongoing "qualified" investment activity in their communities and regions in order to meet their obligations under CRA. Though a bank was not absolutely required to meet its obligations, it was highly motivated to do so, as regulatory agencies were expressly authorized by the CRA to take a bank's CRA performance into account when reviewing the bank's application for acquisitions, new branches, and the like.

In 2009, CRA obligations still dictate whether a bank's investments (i.e. loans) qualify under the act. In order to qualify, "investments" must satisfy the act's definition of *"Community Development"* and *"Primary Purpose."* Until 2004, "primary purpose" went undefined, but since the latest CRA rendition (thank goodness Congress stayed on task) "primary purpose" is now defined as an investment "designed for the express purpose" of accomplishing a community development activity if a majority of the dollars invested are identifiable as a community development activity, or if the investment has the express intent, specific structure or accomplishment of a community development purpose. (We actually pay politicians to create this stuff.)

CRA defines "Community Development" as loans for: affordable housing and community services for low and moderate-income people; activities that promote economic development by financing businesses or farms that meet the size eligibility standards of the Small Business Administration's Development Company or Small Business Investment Company programs; and activities which revitalize or stabilize low and moderate-income communities. (I'm sure glad we got that out in the open!)

Because many of these loans are high risk, banks only make them under the guarantee of two hybrid organizations, the Federal National Mortgage Association, better known as Fannie Mae, and the Federal Home Loan Mortgage Corporation, or Freddie Mac. "Fannie" was chartered by Congress in 1968 to purchase and securitize mortgages, while her heavy-weight baby brother "Freddie" came along in 1970 to expand the secondary market for mortgages. Both are stockholder-owned corporations insured by the federal government. And, what do you know, our tax dollars at work again!

This brings us back to 2008 when Fannie and Freddie, bankrupt as beggars, continued to buy up bad loans from issuing banks, re-package them into stock shares, and sell them off as securities and ultimately derivatives of securities (otherwise known as thin air) to investors. This was, and continues to be, a house built of [recipe] cards. When the real estate bubble burst, and housing prices spiraled into the abyss, underlying collateral deteriorated and credit markets basically shut down as a result.

In a hasty response, Congress shoveled $400 billion at Fannie and Freddie to keep them afloat and enacted TARP with the idea of re-opening credit to the American public in the form of business, mortgage and consumer loans and lines of credit. Billed as a miracle cure to ease the credit crunch, TARP was designed to help banks offset "under-water" mortgages. But financial institutions saw more "profitable" uses for the money and bought up $250 billion worth of stocks. TARP was basically a decision to hand over $700 billion of our tax money to rescue financial institutions negatively impacted by the system Congress construed in the first place! And, in keeping with a free lunch, there were NO strings attached to these handouts—billions of dollars doled out without as much as a single performance benchmark required.

You'd think our politicians, who are usually verbose, could write a page or two outlining bailout restrictions. After all, they authored the 668-page 2008 Farm Bill, the 1,100 page 2009 stimulus package, the 2000+ page ObamaCare bill, and the best yet, our 67,000 page tax code.

Put simply, TARP was just another avenue to transfer tax dollars from Americans to entities Congress deemed worthy. Recipients spent the money on non-lending activities that offered zero economic relief.

In addition to the $350 TARP and $500 FSP billions, it will end up costing taxpayers close to $238 billion just to rescue Fan and Fred—more than the entire federal budget deficit for fiscal year 2007. There are a lot of zeroes in $1.088 trillion ($1,088,000,000,000) and that is a lot of tax money from each and every one of us, regular citizens. If the government wrote a check to every man, woman and child in the country, instead of throwing $1.088 trillion at failed financial institutions, each would receive $3,567.21, and that is before even considering the taxpayer cost of Obama's $787 billion American Pork Act of 2009, which would put another $2,580.33 into each of our pockets. What would you do with $6147.54?

Our tax dollars also pay the annual $191,300 salary for United States Treasury Secretary Timothy Geithner. From 2003 to 2009, we paid him $398,200 annually for his role as President of the Federal Reserve Bank of New York. In this capacity, he presided over Wall Street during what has been one of the worst financial crises in our nation's history. And, from 2001 to 2003, while employed by the International Monetary Fund, he ignored his payroll tax obligation until forced to come clean when running for Treasury Top Dog. Ironically, he is now head honcho at the IRS. When most of us *forget* to pay our taxes the tax man cometh ... and he's not after milk and cookies.

In addition, Giethner is one of the masterminds behind TARP. The program that, in theory, would open credit markets so Americans could borrow for things like kitchen remodels, restocking grocery store shelves, or putting food on the table, but instead it became a game called "Who can lobby the loudest?"

TARP resulted in a massive dereliction of duty as congressmen like Barney Frank doled out millions in political payback to groups like Boston's OneUnited Bank, a small Internet bank in his home state of Massachusetts, a bank that, due to its small size and scope, would have no impact on rectifying the nation's financial crisis, no matter how many millions Barney threw at it. He was not alone. A USA

Today article dated February 23, 2009 indicated that some two dozen members of Congress had substantial ties to the banks and other companies getting a piece of the TARP rescue package.

And it turns out the bailout bug is contagious. U.S. automakers took $17 billion, before Hollywood movie makers and even Penthouse Magazine travelled to Washington for handouts. And, no surprise, within a few short months, the automakers were back in line for seconds.

So, this is how our hard-earned tax dollars are spent.

Meanwhile, favorite stores such as Linens and Things, Mervyns and Circuit City, places where home chefs once purchased pots and pans, blenders, dishes, kitchen towels and microwaves, have closed their doors, unable to survive the financial crisis and ensuing credit crunch. But, hey Barney's friends have some cash, Geithner finally paid his back taxes, and Citibank returned the jet, so I guess we should all be happy. Except that we aren't.

Tax Bite

Wrap that Tax, Please!

Back for some more Texas holiday cheer. Charges for gift wrapping are taxable if the store that sold the item also wraps the item. If, on the other hand, the gift is taken to another store to be wrapped, the wrapping is tax-free.

Source: Texas Window on State Government http://www.window.state.tx.us/taxinfo/taxpubs/tx96_237_3_06.html

Hoping no one would notice due to the 2009 Christmas Eve news about the Senate passage of the health care bill, the U.S. Treasury Department gave Fannie Mae and Freddie Mac a little Christmas present, courtesy of the American taxpayer. On December 24, 2009 Geithner lifted the $400 billion cap on potential losses for Fannie Mae and Freddie Mac and he even tucked in a stocking stuffer by eliminating the limits on what the two behemoths can borrow.

Merry Christmas America!

Poppa Willie's Sassy and Spicy Cornbread

Although this is my mom's recipe, it's my dad who has taken over making it. My parents still love to entertain, and since Pops is now retired, mom has enlisted his help in the kitchen. This is one of his specialties.

INGREDIENTS

1 3/4 cups yellow cornmeal
1 1/4 cups flour
1 tablespoon baking powder
1 teaspoon salt
2 1/2 cups milk
1/2 cup canola oil
3 eggs, beaten
1/2 large onion, chopped
1/4 cup chopped jalapenos
1 1/2 cups grated sharp cheddar cheese
3 strips bacon, cooked crisp and crumbled
1/2 cup chopped pimiento, or red bell pepper
1 clove garlic, pressed

DIRECTIONS

Mix dries. Add remaining ingredients and mix well. Pour into greased 9x13 inch pan. Bake at 400ºF for 25-35 minutes, or until toothpick comes out clean and top of bread is browned. Cool and cut into serving sizes.

Tax Bite

Mississippi Salt Tax

In Mississippi there is a 3% tax imposed on the value of the production of salt severed or produced from the land or water within Mississippi.

Source: Mississippi Tax Commission

Yankee Pier Dill Drop Biscuits

Brad Odgen, founder of the Lark Creek Restaurant Group in Northern California, created this recipe that is now served with clam chowder at the company's Yankee Pier Restaurants.

INGREDIENTS

1 cup all-purpose flour
1 tablespoon sugar
11/2 teaspoon baking powder
1/2 teaspoon salt
1/4 cup shortening
1/4 cup buttermilk
1/2 cup sour cream
2 tablespoons fresh dill
1/4 teaspoon fresh ground black pepper
Egg wash or melted butter

DIRECTIONS

Preheat oven to 425°F. In a large bowl, sift together the dry ingredients. Using a pastry cutter, cut in the shortening until the mix resembles coarse meal. In another bowl mix the buttermilk, sour cream, dill and black pepper. Make a hole in the center of the dry ingredients and pour in the liquid. Fold in the dry ingredients and mix till just moistened. Using a teaspoon, drop the batter onto a buttered sheet pan. Brush with the egg wash and bake for 8 minutes. Rotate the pan and cook for 4 more minutes.

Tax Bite

New York Nonresident Partnership Tax Trap

Recently enacted New York state legislation has amended the Tax Law to expand the definition of a sales tax vendor to include, under certain conditions, out-of-state sellers (remote affiliates) of taxable tangible personal property or services that are affiliated with businesses in New York. Partnerships and New York "S" corporations filing group personal income tax returns on behalf of their electing nonresident partners and shareholders must compute the New York State personal income tax due for each nonresident partner or shareholder based on the highest effective rate of tax. Recent tax law changes have increased the highest effective rate of tax from 6.85% to 8.97% for tax year 2009.This amendment is effective June 1, 2009, and applies to sales made or uses occurring on or after that date.

Source: New York State Dept. of Taxation and Finance

Cheesy (Smile) "Beer Summit" Bread

Everyone needs a little something to munch on at a "Beer Summit" and maybe this is just the thing to satisfy hunger pangs if you're ever summoned to a White House Beer Summit.

INGREDIENTS

*3 cups self-rising flour**

2+ tablespoons sugar

One 12 oz. bottle of beer (your choice)

1 cup grated sharp cheddar cheese

1/2 cup grated Parmesan cheese

Optional: To customize your bread fold diced items into batter such as Ortega chilies, olives or onions. *If you don't have self-rising flour, sift regular flour with 3 teaspoons of baking powder and 1 teaspoon sea salt.

DIRECTIONS

Mix dry ingredients and half of each cheese in a bowl. Make a well in the center and slowly pour in the beer. With a wooden spoon or a large fork mix just until combined—17 to 20 strokes or so. Put in a greased 9x5 loaf pan and sprinkle remaining cheese on top. Bake at 350ºF for about 50 minutes, or until done. Check with a tester at about 45 minutes.

Tax Bite

Barry "The King of Brew" Beer Summit Tax

What the heck? Now our President is holding beer summits? And undoubtedly the taxpayer is footing the bill. I wonder if he served Kenya's Tusker Lager, Kona's Longboard or Sam Adams Light. Whatever the case, it was not cheap payback for the President's slip of the tongue, when you consider transportation and security costs for the attendees!

Speaking of beer, Oregon has floated the idea of a 1,900% percent increase in the tax on beer. The current tax rate is $2.60 per barrel, but would go up to $49.61 per barrel or between $2 and $4 per six-pack if the bill passes. This would amount to the single largest tax hike on beer in the nation's history.

Source: slashfood.com; Oregon News.

Pumpkin Bread with Caramel Glaze

(Makes two 9x5 loaves)

My friend Michelle Steinman has one of the best pumpkin bread recipes I've ever tasted! It is pure decadence, brushed with a caramel glaze, and, though we intend to eat it for breakfast, just as often we have it for dessert.

INGREDIENTS

Bread

3 1/3 cups all purpose flour
3 cups granulated sugar
2 teaspoons baking soda
1 1/2 teaspoons salt
1 teaspoon cinnamon
1 teaspoon nutmeg
1 can (15 oz.) pumpkin
1 cup vegetable oil
4 eggs, lightly beaten
2/3 cup water

Caramel Glaze

1/4 cup butter
1/4 cup granulated sugar
1/4 cup brown sugar
1/4 cup heavy cream
2/3 cup powdered sugar
1 teaspoon vanilla

DIRECTIONS

In a large bowl combine the first six ingredients. In another bowl combine the pumpkin, oil, eggs and water. Mix well with a whisk. Stir egg mixture into dry ingredients and mix well with whisk or wooden spoon. Pour evenly into two greased 9x5 loaf pans. Bake at 350ºF for 60 to 65 minutes or until a toothpick tests clean. Cool for 10 minutes in the pans. Remove pans to a

Tax Bite

Turkey Taxes

Because anything baked with pumpkin reminds me of Thanksgiving, this tax bite involves hunting for turkeys. For those interested in bringing home a Montana turkey for the feast, there are costs involved. For residents, the cost to hunt one turkey will be $24 ($8 for the conservation license, $7.50 for the upland game bird license, $2 for the hunting access enhancement fee and $6.50 for the turkey tag.) For non-residents, the same turkey will cost between $135 and $185 in license fees.

Source: Montana Fish Wildlife and Parks

wire rack to finish cooling. (When making mini loaves, cook for 30-40 minutes, or until tester is clean.)

For glaze, combine in a saucepan butter, sugar, brown sugar and whipping cream. Cook until sugars are dissolved and mixture starts bubbling. Cool for 20 minutes. Stir in powdered sugar and vanilla until smooth. Drizzle over cooled loaves.

"No More Bad Bananas" Bread

(Makes one loaf)

Do you ever get the brown banana blues? Well, at our house we do. It seems that whenever I stock up on bananas, no one is in a 'banana' mood and all the bananas turn brown. So one day, I got kind of smart. I decided to freeze the bananas in their peels as they began to turn. Through some experimenting, I discovered that thawed frozen bananas are perfect for making bread. Freezing stops the browning process and they stay nice and yellow inside the peel. No more bad, brown bananas chez moi.

INGREDIENTS

8 tablespoons butter or margarine
3/4 cup sugar
2 eggs
2 cups flour (can use half whole wheat flour, if desired)
1 teaspoon baking soda
1/2 teaspoon salt

Tax Bite

The Great Pumpkin Strikes Again

In 2006, the state of Iowa implemented a 6% sales tax to be charged on pumpkins for decorative use rather than edible use. Pumpkins were exempt from the sales tax only if the buyer completed an exemption certificate stating they'd be used exclusively for food; the pumpkins were a certain variety used in making pies; or the pumpkins were purchased with food stamps. The outcry over this policy forced the State to rapidly retreat from the Great Pumpkin Tax and the tax was repealed within the year.

Sources: About.com; Foxnews.com "New Iowa Pumpkin Tax Puts Damper on Growers' Halloween Spirit"

2-3 large, ripe bananas, mashed (if frozen, defrost before adding)
1 teaspoon vanilla extract
1/2 cup coarsely chopped walnuts or pecans

DIRECTIONS

Grease or spray one 9x5x3 inch loaf pan. Preheat oven to 350°F.

Cream butter and sugar until light a fluffy. Add eggs and beat well. Add vanilla and bananas and mix until integrated. Sift baking soda, salt and flour right into mixture. Stir. Add nuts (optional).

Bake for 55 minutes, or until cake tester inserted into the center of loaf comes out clean. Cool in pan on baking rack. Recipe can be doubled. This bread can also be made ahead and frozen.

Tax Bite

Happy Hunting in California—*If* You're Californian

For those who want to hunt in California, it's expensive for both residents and non-residents, but non-residents really get the shaft. If you're out to hunt Elk, the resident will pay $41.20 for the basic license plus $376 for the elk tag for a total of $417.20. The same excursion will cost a non-resident $1,305.80. But, don't worry you won't be spending any of it, if your name is not picked from the lottery drawing to hunt elk in the first place!

Source: California Dept. of Fish and Game.

Rose's Famous Zucchini Bread

Rose Mornin has been making this bread for years. I think she's famous for it all across Northern California! If you're lucky enough to be counted among her many friends, you may have already received a loaf as a gift.

INGREDIENTS

3 eggs, beaten
1 cup oil
3 teaspoons vanilla
2 cups granulated sugar
2 cups shredded zucchini, squeeze in cheesecloth or towel to remove excess liquid
1/2 cup chopped nuts (pecans or walnuts)
1/2 teaspoon baking powder
1 teaspoon baking soda
2 teaspoons cinnamon
1 teaspoon salt
3 cups flour
Optional: 1/2 cup raisins soaked in one cup brandy for at least 30 minutes or overnight, and drained before putting in batter.

DIRECTIONS

In a large bowl, mix the first six ingredients in the order given. Mix dries together. Add to batter. If using raisins, add last. Bake in two 9 x 5 inch loaf pans, greased and dusted with flour. Bake in 325ºF for 11/4 to 11/2 hours. Test with cake tester for doneness.

*Can be wrapped in plastic wrap and frozen for several months in preparation for holiday gifts!

Tax Bite

"When the Rubber Hits the Road" Tax

I recently purchased two new tires for my son's 1999 Honda Civic. Naturally, I was curious to see the tax impositions listed at the bottom of the bill. Here is what I discovered:

$140 Tires ($70 each), $3.50 California Tire Fee, $4.25 Hazardous Waste Disposal, $6.50 TD-Tire Disposal to 16.5", $13.51 Sales Tax. The total in taxes and fees was $27.76, or 19.8% on a purchase of $140.

Source: Plaza Tire & Auto Service Invoice

Carrot Bran Muffins

These are wonderfully moist, fairly healthy, and absolutely delicious muffins!

INGREDIENTS

11/4 cups milk
2 cups whole bran cereal
1/4 cup canola oil
2 eggs, beaten
13/4 cups shredded carrots
1/2 cup raisins or currants
1/2 cup coarsely chopped walnuts
1/2 cup baking coconut
11/4 cups flour
1/3 cup brown sugar, packed
1/4 cup white sugar
2 teaspoons baking powder
1 teaspoon baking soda
2 teaspoon cinnamon
1/2 teaspoon salt

DIRECTIONS

Combine cereal, eggs, milk and oil in a large bowl and let soak about 10 minutes. Then add carrots, raisins and coconut.

In a large bowl, mix together the dry ingredients. Add the cereal mixture and stir just until combined. Grease mini Bundt pans or line muffin pans with paper cups. Fill about 2/3 full and bake in 350ºF 20 to 25 minutes or until toothpick comes out clean when inserted. The baby Bundt pans allow the muffin to cook in the middle more evenly.

Tax Bite

Excise Tax

You may wonder what an excise tax is, exactly. It is a tax imposed when certain acts are performed, for engaging in particular occupations, for obtaining certain licenses, and for the enjoyment of certain privileges granted by the government. There are a variety of excise taxes which arise in all sorts of activities from manufacturing to retailing, wagering, environmental activities, qualified investment entities, "golden parachute" arrangements and certain group health plans just to name a few. In addition, anytime you are required to pay license or permit fees or even parking meters, these payments can be considered excise taxes.

Source: FreeAdvice.com

Mumsie's Scones

Whether you find some long lost relatives on your doorstep one Sunday morning, or you've planned a brunch or tea, you can be sure these scones will come together quickly and easily. You can use any fruit you like—fresh or dried—so you don't need much in the way of advanced planning. White corn meal makes these scones light and airy, and most of the other ingredients should be readily available in your cupboards.

INGREDIENTS

2 cups sifted flour
2 1/2 tablespoons sugar
2 1/2 teaspoons baking powder
1/2 teaspoon baking soda
1/4 teaspoon salt
2 tablespoons white corn meal
1/2 cup butter, melted
1 egg, beaten
1/3 cup milk
2 tablespoons sour cream
3/4 cup fruit (we use tart apples cut into small chunks, but currants, raisins, dried cranberries, fresh berries, apricots, etc. are all delicious.) The orchard is your palette!

DIRECTIONS

Mix all dries in a large mixing bowl. Mix butter, egg, milk and sour cream in another small bowl. With a large fork, blend liquid mixture into dries. Finally mix in fruit. Shape into 6 large, 8 medium, or 10 small round scones, or roll into large circle and cut into pie wedge shapes.

Bake on lightly greased baking sheet at 400°F for 9 minutes. Reduce heat to 350°F and bake an additional 8 minutes. Serve warm with jam, apple butter, crème fraîche), or clotted cream.

Tax Bite

Unions' Excise Tax Exemption

Though it has been shelved for several years, possibly until 2018, ObamaCare calls for a 40% excise tax on premium health care plans—those with an annual value of more than $24K. Before it was delayed due to enormous public pressure, Obama met behind closed doors with labor union leaders to exempt union members from this tax. This was presumably a Washington-as- usual "pay to play" deal for union support in his 2008 presidential election. Fortunately, that language was eventually omitted from the health care bill … so far!

Source: Heritage Foundation, Morning Bell

Tax Bite

Tax, Inc.

The U.S. is tied with Argentina, Malta, Morocco, Pakistan and Zambia with a 35% corporate tax rate. All of these nations are out-taxed by the world leader, India, where corporate taxes can be as high as 40%.

Source: Worldwide-Tax.com

Rosalie's Coffee Cake

I never met Rosalie, but she was one of my grandmother's bridesmaids and she sure made a delicious coffee cake. The recipe is very easy to make and reminds me quite a bit of Starbuck's Classic Coffeecake, which I've always enjoyed precisely because it reminds me of good old Rosalie's!

INGREDIENTS

3/4 cup brown sugar
1/4 cup white sugar
2 cups flour, sifted
1 teaspoon salt
1 teaspoon cinnamon
2/3 cup canola oil
1/2 cup finely chopped walnuts or pecans
2 beaten eggs
1 cup sour milk (milk with 1 teaspoon vinegar mixed into it)
1 teaspoon baking soda

DIRECTIONS

Mix all dries together with oil. Set aside one cup of mixture along with the nuts for topping.

To main batter, add 2 beaten eggs, 1cup sour milk and 1 teaspoon baking soda. Mix well. Spread batter in 9x9 inch glass baking dish. Sprinkle topping generously over top.

Bake at 350ºF for 35-40 minutes, or until cake tester comes out of center clean.

Tax Bite

Giddy-up Horseracing Tax

Ever since 1933 Ohio has imposed a tax on pari-mutuel wagering on horse racing. The tax is based upon the amount wagered each day and the permit holder must remit the taxes the day after collecting them. Tax rates progress as wagers increase, sliding from 1% on the first $200,000 of bets wagered, to 4% on total bets amounting to more than $400,000. In addition there is an "exotic" wagering tax of 3% over and above the pari-mutuel tax for bets on anything other than pari-mutuel outcomes of "win, place or show." This extra tax is for "daily double," perfecta, quinella and trifecta etc.

Source: taxohio.gov

Holiday Sugar and Spice Pull-Apart Rolls

Yes you can! If you're afraid of yeast breads, don't be. This recipe is as easy as pie, actually easier. All you need is a little patience to let the dough rise—twice. Once you get past the dough, let the family chip in. Form a little assembly line, and the rolls will be done in no time. While you make the balls, let the little munchkins roll them in the butter and sugar mixture. This breakfast treat is so tasty you'll wish every weekend was a holiday. This recipe is a take-off on an old Better Homes & Gardens *Plaid* Cookbook recipe for Golden Bubble Ring.

INGREDIENTS

Dough

4-4 1/2 cups all-purpose flour
2 packages active dry yeast
1/2 cup butter or margarine (1 stick)
1 cup milk
1/2 cup sugar
1 teaspoon salt
2 eggs

Toppings

1 cube butter, melted
11/2 cups finely chopped walnuts or pecans, or both
11/2 cups currants

Sugar and spice filling

1/2 cup granulated sugar
1/2 cup brown sugar
1 1/2 teaspoons cinnamon
1 teaspoon cardamom

Tax Bite

Hotel Double-Take

The state of Massachusetts imposes an excise tax on the transfer of occupancy, for $15 or more, of any room in a bed and breakfast establishment, hotel, lodging house, or motel for a period of ninety days or less. The tax is required to be collected by the operator of such establishments at the rate of 5.7% of the total amount of rent for each such occupancy. In addition, each Massachusetts city or town is permitted to levy a local room occupancy excise tax of up to 4%. In the cities of Boston, Worcester, Cambridge, Springfield, West Springfield, and Chicopee, an additional 2.75% tax is levied for convention center funding.

Source: www.mass.gov General Laws of Massachusetts, Title IX Chapter 64G

DIRECTIONS

In a large bowl combine 2 1/2 cups of the flour and yeast and mix well. Heat butter, milk, sugar and salt in a small saucepan, stirring all the while until butter almost melts and mixture reaches approximately 115ºF. (Do NOT boil.) Add milk mixture to dries. Add eggs and beat with electric mixer on low speed for about 30 seconds. Beat for another three minutes on high speed, scraping down sides of bowl with a rubber spatula.

Add enough of the remaining flour (half cup at a time) and mix by hand to form soft dough. Place dough on lightly floured surface and knead for about 5-8 minutes. You may need to add a little bit of flour as you knead dough, and you'll need to sprinkle the work surface with extra flour, too. The dough should be slightly elastic, and bounce back when you pull at it.

Shape dough into a smooth ball and place in a large greased bowl, turning once to lightly grease top of dough. Cover top of bowl with a slightly damp clean kitchen towel, and place in a warm, or sunny spot (*not* in a heated oven) for about 11/4 hours, or until dough has doubled in size.

Meanwhile grease a 10-inch tube or Bundt pan. Melt the butter and let cool slightly. Mix sugars and spices in a medium bowl. Finely chop nuts. When dough has risen, punch a little hole in it to let it deflate.

Divide dough into approximately 36 balls, each 1-11/2 inch in diameter. Roll balls in butter and transfer into sugar mixture. Roll in sugars and place in bottom of tube pan. When you have a full layer, sprinkle 1/3 of the nuts and currants over the dough balls. Repeat for two more layers, ending with nuts and currants. Cover with damp kitchen towel and let rise again until doubled, approximately 1 hour.

Bake at 350ºF for 35-40 minutes. Remove from oven and cool in pan for 10-15 minutes. Invert onto plate, removing tube pan. Serve warm. Can be made ahead and refrigerated or frozen. Wrap in foil and reheat before serving.

Tax Bite

Cable's Un-Tax

If you were hoping to watch the Buckeyes and the Wolverines square off on the gridiron over your holiday break, you might be disappointed to see a match between the cable and satellite broadcast providers instead. Ohio is among six states that currently levy a special tax on satellite companies. The 5.5% tax is designed to level the playing field, because cable companies must pay franchise fees. Satellite companies argue these fees are a cost of doing business, just as investments in satellites are a necessary budget item for satellite providers. The Ohio law, passed in 2003 has garnered more than $100 million in just five years. One thing is certain … customers are not winning this battle.

Source: Joshua Culling, National Taxpayers Union

Yogurt Pecan Coffee Cake

I think nearly every family has a sour cream coffee cake recipe. This is an alternate version using plain yogurt in place of the sour cream.

INGREDIENTS

Cake

1/2 cup margarine or butter, softened
1 1/2 cups granulated sugar
3 eggs
1 1/2 teaspoons vanilla
3 cups all-purpose flour
1 1/2 teaspoons baking powder
1 1/2 teaspoons baking soda
1/4 teaspoon salt
1 1/2 cups plain low-fat yogurt

Cinnamon-Pecan Filling

1 cup brown sugar
1/4 cup granulated sugar
3/4 cup coarsely chopped toasted pecans
1/2 teaspoon cinnamon

DIRECTIONS

In a medium bowl, sift together flour, baking soda, baking powder, and salt. In a larger bowl, cream butter (or margarine) and sugar with electric beater. Add eggs, one at a time, beating well after each (this is really important for this recipe.) Blend in vanilla. Add flour mixture alternately with yogurt, beginning and ending with dries. Mix well.

To Assemble Coffee Cake

Grease either a 10-inch tube pan or 10-inch Bundt pan with cooking spray. Sprinkle 1/4 of the filling on the bottom of pan. Spread 1/3 of the cake batter over filling, taking care not to mix with topping. Repeat process two times, ending with final 1/4 filling. Bake at 35°F for 45 minutes or until a cake tester inserted in center of coffee cake comes out clean. Cool in pan and when cool, turn out upside down onto plate. Store in airtight container until ready to use.

Tax Bite

Lodging Tax

In 2003, the Oregon State Legislature passed a bill to establish a 1% state lodging tax to promote statewide tourism. Proceeds fund the Oregon Tourism Commission. This tax is above and beyond any local municipal hotel taxes, which fund local programs.

Source: Oregon Dept. of Revenue

Tax Bite

Burn Notice

There is a tax on solid fuel burning devices in the state of Washington. The tax of $30 per device is collected by the retail seller and applies to wood, pellet, and coal stoves; manufactured fireplaces; masonry heaters or any other device burning a solid fuel.

Source: Washington Dept. of Revenue

Virgil's Vanilla Pancakes

(Makes approximately 24 5-inch pancakes)

Virgil is a retired veteran who was the favorite customer at our local kitchen shop. He was the willing subject of one of my newspaper articles, "Gourmet Parade" and as a favor he shared a few of his tried and true recipes. His pancake recipe is so unusual made with olive oil and lots of vanilla. It's a real winner.

INGREDIENTS

2 cups all-purpose flour

1 heaping tablespoon baking powder

1/4 cup sugar

1/8 teaspoon salt

2 eggs

6 tablespoons olive oil

2+ cups milk

2 tablespoons vanilla extract (Virgil said, "Be very generous with the vanilla—don't worry to over burden batter with vanilla, as it excites the palate and induces air bubbles to the batter making the pancakes very light.")

DIRECTIONS

Combine dries in a large bowl. Add eggs, oil, vanilla and milk and mix with power mixer until smooth and the consistency of thin paste. Allow to proof (sit and bubble) for 10 minutes. Cook on hot griddle (375°F) until browned. Two tablespoons batter makes a five-inch pancake.

Tax Bite

Top Tax Dog

The U.S. has highest federal corporate tax rate of all OECD nations. The U.S. tax rate is 35% for incomes greater than $18.3 million. Ireland takes bottom honors at 12.5%. When combined with state levies, the U.S. average for all states is 39.27, second only to Japan's combined rate of 39.54. Iowa leads the entire pack with a combined rate of 47%, reduced to 41.6% when adjusted for federal tax deductions.

Source: The Tax Foundation

Holiday Sugar and Spice Pull-Apart Rolls (top) and Yogurt Pecan Coffee Cake (bottom).

Nutty Granola

It's not that granola is so low-cal, because it really isn't, but rather that it's a delicious energy food, chock-full of nuts, brown sugar and healthy oats! This actually makes a great topping for frozen yogurt or ice cream, and a Dixie-cup size settles hunger pangs that can arise in the middle of the afternoon.

INGREDIENTS

8 cups quick oats
3/4 cup light brown sugar
1 teaspoon salt
1 teaspoon ground cardamom
1 teaspoon ground cinnamon
1 cup pecan halves
1 cup walnut halves
1/2 cup slivered almonds
1/2 cup honey or agave syrup
1/2 cup canola oil
1 tablespoon vanilla extract

DIRECTIONS

Mix first five ingredients in a large mixing bowl. Stir in nuts. Add oil and toss thoroughly to coat as many of the oats and nuts as possible. Add vanilla to the syrup, or honey if you prefer, and mix well, then add to granola ingredients and stir to mix the syrup very well over nuts and oats. Turn granola onto two greased baking sheets with at least one-inch high sides, and bake at 325ºF for 20 minutes. Remove from oven and with a spatula or large spoon, stir granola to mix the granola on the edge of the baking sheet into the center. Reduce oven temperature to 180ºF and continue to bake for another 45 minutes to one hour, until granola is slightly browned and crunchy. Cool completely on baking sheet before storing in airtight containers.

Tax Bite

Nutty Millionaire Tax

California's 1% Mental Health Services Tax applies to individual California taxable income over $1 million. The Mental Health Services Tax was approved by voters on November 2, 2004 via Proposition 63. It took effect beginning with the 2005 taxable year.

Source: Gina Rodriquez, Sacramento Editor Spidell Publishing, Inc.,

CHAPTER XII

Un-Just Desserts, The Government's Final Helping

Desserts & Death Tax

No meal is complete without dessert. Unfortunately Uncle Sam feels the same way about our lives and his final helping of our money. Even in death, the tax man cometh. While a sweet morsel at the end of the meal is rather satisfying, this final serving of taxes is not!

The lifelong bonus for hard work and effort is an enormous Death (Estate) Tax on accumulated wealth. Of course, we are dead, so what do we care? We care, precisely because it's our money, born of blood, sweat and tears. Uncle Red, White and Blue did nothing to earn it, and furthermore, every penny of income that went into the estate, has been taxed already. If any tax is necessary, the only reasonable one would be a capital gains tax on appreciated value, not a 45 percent tax on the whole pie.

The Estate Tax rate varies depending upon the value of the estate. The tax has been on a phase-out schedule since 2001 and is thus far repealed in 2010. But, barring a literal act of Congress, the estate tax reverts to the 2001 rate of 55 percent in 2011 and only a $1 million exemption. The older generation would be well-advised to sleep with one eye open in 2010!

The Estate Tax, originally instituted in 1916, is a tax on the act of transferring property at death. Lest you depart unaware, the estate includes any real estate (both foreign and domestic) bank deposits, securities (stocks and bonds) and personal property such as vehicles, art objects, insurance policies, the deceased's interest in trusts or jointly held property, as well as interest in other estates.

The Death Tax can impose particular hardship for family-run businesses or farms. Unlike the super-wealthy who have foundations and other vehicles to shield them from huge tax liabilities, the estate tax can cripple family-run operations that are unlikely to have sufficient liquid assets to meet estate tax liabilities. Often families are forced to sell a business or property just to pay the tax.

I found it interesting that in a little hand book named *10 Excellent Reasons Not To Hate Taxes* (what a joke!) the proponents of maintaining the Estate Tax believe "a tax on inherited wealth enables society to recapture its investment in individuals and recycle it for future generations." (Not your future generation however!) The author goes on to state "Rather than punishing successful people, progressive taxation recognizes that some individuals have disproportionately benefited from society's investments and have a special obligation to pay them back." Even Microsoft grandpa, Bill Gates, Sr. is quoted in the book as saying the Estate Tax is an "opportunity recycling program."

It has been estimated that the Estate Tax has reduced the capital stock in America by $800 billion. How's that for "opportunity recycling?"

Estate Tax is imposed at both federal and state levels. Not every state levies an Estate Tax, but many do. States are not required to follow federal estate tax policy and may chart their own course by "decoupling" from the federal tax code, enabling them to protect the revenue generated from this tax.

Currently, five states are permanently decoupled from federal tax code including Kansas, New York, Ohio, Oregon, and Virginia plus the District of Columbia. (D.C. decoupled from the Feds? That's kind of funny!) Without legislative action, they will retain their own estate tax policy. In addition to these five, 12 other states impose some form of estate tax: Illinois, Maine, Maryland, Massachusetts, Minnesota, Nebraska, New Jersey, N. Carolina, Rhode Island, Vermont, Washington and Wisconsin.

There are several ways to reduce the Estate Tax obligation of the deceased by donating conservation easements* under the authorization of the Pension Protection Act of 2006, or giving property directly to grandchildren, thereby keeping property out of their children's taxable estates. Congress caught on to this scheme quickly, however, and enacted the Generation-Skipping Tax (GST) imposed at the same rate as regular gift and estate tax. For surviving spouses there is the "marital deduction," which may serve to postpone the inevitable. The transfer of property for spouses is generally free from estate tax because the marital deduction is unlimited. Spouses who are not citizens may not claim this deduction unless their share is in a qualifying domestic trust (QDOT). Another common way to reduce the estate tax liability is to gift portions of the estate throughout one's life.

This brings us to the Gift Tax, which is applied in the exact same way as the Estate Tax, but offers an annual per capita exemption of $13,000 ($26,000 for couples) and a lifetime exemption of $1 million. Gifts to spouses are completely exempt under the gift tax marital deduction as long as the spouse is a U.S. citizen at the time of the gifting. Other rules apply to non-citizen recipients.

Any gifts that exceed the maximum annual exclusion, or are not otherwise exempt, must be reported and are subject to the same rates that apply to Estate Tax. After 2010, the Gift Tax reverts to the top rate for personal income tax, currently 35 percent, but likely going up as soon as the Bush tax cuts expire in 2011.

So much for having our cake, and eating it too. It appears only Uncle Sam gets to do that!

*For more information on Conservation Easements *http://forestry.msu.edu/extension/ExtDocs/easemnt.htm#What Is A Conservation Easement?*

CAKES

Tax Bite

Playing Card Tax

In case you decide to have friends over for a game of bridge and dessert, keep in mind that the state of Alabama levies a 10¢ tax on the purchase of a deck of playing cards that contains "no more than 54 cards." In addition, the retailer must pay an annual license tax of $3 and a fee of $1, according to the Alabama Department of Revenue.

Source: CNNMoney.com "America's Wackiest Taxes"

Ponds Picnic Chocolate-Cinnamon Cake

We grew up with a "pond" view in a Michigan neighborhood aptly named "The Ponds." In winter, we skated for hours playing games like pom-pom pull away and ice hockey, coming inside only to defrost the toes. By summer we spent the twilight hours searching for Big Foot.

In August, the families gathered for the annual Ponds Picnic, where each brought their favorite summer fare. Our next door neighbor, Betty, brought this cake every time. The cake comes with a warning that you can't leave an uneven edge. For that reason, we dubbed it the "even-off cake" and were compelled to eat an entire row once it had been started.

INGREDIENTS

In a large bowl mix well:

2 cups of flour

2 cups of granulated sugar

1 teaspoon cinnamon

1 teaspoon baking soda

In a medium-sized pan, melt:

1 stick butter

1 cup water

1/2 cup oil

4 tablespoons unsweetened cocoa powder

Stir until well blended and pour over flour mixture, mixing well. Add:

1/2 cup buttermilk

2 eggs

1 teaspoon vanilla

Bake in a jelly roll tin at 400ºF for approximately 20-25 minutes, or until cake tester comes out clean.

Frosting

1 cube butter or margarine
6 tablespoons milk
5 tablespoons unsweetened cocoa powder
4 cups powdered sugar
1 cup pecan halves

Melt above ingredients in pan. Slowly pour over four cups powdered sugar and 1 cup pecan halves. Mix until all powdered sugar is integrated and frosting is rather thick, but spreadable. Carefully spread over hot cake as soon as cake is removed from oven. Cool. Cake can be refrigerated for several days, but you'll probably find that it won't last too long.

Mississippi Fun Tax

In Mississippi you'll pay a 7% tax on all amusements, unless you are going to hear an amusement operation run by a religious, charitable, educational or non-profit civic club or fraternal organization.

Source: Mississippi Department of Revenue

Cocoa Chocolate Chip Cake

This cake has become our go-to chocolate cake for birthdays or to take to a friend's house when we've been elected to bring dessert! It's easy to prepare and requires no eggs.

INGREDIENTS

Cake

3 cups all purpose flour
2 cups granulated sugar
1/2 cup unsweetened cocoa powder
2 teaspoons baking soda
1 teaspoon salt
2 cups cold water
1 cup vegetable oil
2 teaspoons vanilla extract
1 cup semi-sweet or bittersweet chocolate chips

Cocoa Frosting

1/2 cup unsalted butter softened to room temperature
1/2 cup cocoa powder
3-4 cups powdered sugar
2 teaspoons vanilla
1/2 cup milk (plus or minus for desired consistency)

DIRECTIONS

Cake

Place all dries in a large mixing bowl and blend well with a wire whisk. In a large measuring cup, mix oil, water and vanilla and add to dries, mixing thoroughly with a whisk or wooden spoon. Divide batter into three 9-inch diameter cake pans, prepared with cooking spray. Sprinkle chocolate chips evenly over batter in each pan. Bake at 350ºF for about 20-25 minutes, or until cake tester comes out clean. Cool completely and remove from pan. Split cake layers and spread frosting in between each layer, and on top of cake.

Frosting

With an electric mixer, beat butter until creamy. Sift cocoa powder into butter and cream together. Add powdered sugar and milk a little at a time, beating well after each addition, until you have a desired consistency. Finally, stir in vanilla.

Grandma's Chocolate Toffee Cake

Some recipes are just bigger than life. This cake is one of those. My husband's mom used to make this cake for every family birthday. Everyone anticipated its arrival to the celebration. The tricky part of the cake was keeping predators from snitching the toffee off the top before it was served. Rising to the challenge, and being the good sport she always was, Grandma indulged in the game, and began bringing a little side bag of toffee, then a larger one—for the purpose of replacing the toffee snitched from the top of the cake before dinner.

INGREDIENTS

Cake

1 cup cocoa powder
1 cup boiling water
1/2 cup sour cream
2 teaspoons vanilla
1/2 pound (2 sticks) unsalted butter, softened to room temperature
1 3/4 cup sugar
2 large eggs, room temperature
1 1/4 cups all-purpose flour
3/4 teaspoon baking soda
1/2 teaspoon salt

Frosting

8 ounces cream cheese
1 cube unsalted butter, softened to room temperature
2 teaspoons vanilla extract
4 cups powdered sugar
1/3 cup cocoa powder
1/4 cup milk
1 pound English toffee, broken into bite-sized pieces for topping

Tax Bite

Sugar-Sweet Beverage Tax

On May 18, 2009 the U.S. Senate Finance Committee released a proposal with ideas on how to finance health care reform. One of the ideas put forth is a special tax just for beverages sweetened with sugar or high-fructose corn syrup. If this is enacted into law, not only sodas, but energy drinks, sports drinks, iced teas, some juices and chocolate milk will be taxed. This tax would not apply to artificially-sweetened beverages. Seems Congress prefers chemical substitutes to natural ingredients!

Source: http://finance.senate.gov/press/Bpress/2009press/prb051809.pdf

DIRECTIONS

Cake

Grease a 9 x 13 inch baking pan. Preheat oven to 350°F.

Place cocoa powder in a small bowl. Add boiling water and mix until smooth. Cool to room temperature. Then stir in vanilla and sour cream. Set aside.

Beat butter and sugar in a large bowl on medium speed until fluffy, about 3-4 minutes. Add eggs, one at a time, and beat well after each addition, approximately one minute.

Whisk dries (flour, baking soda, salt) in a separate bowl. With beater on low speed, add 1/3 of the dry ingredients to the egg/butter batter, followed by 1/3 of the chocolate mixture. Beat just until blended. Repeat this process two more times, until all ingredients have been incorporated. Scrape down bowl with spatula and beat one final time for about 20 seconds.

Pour batter into prepared pan and bake at 350°F for 35 minutes, or until cake tester comes out of center of cake clean. Cool. Frost the cake with chocolate-cream cheese frosting and top with chopped toffee. Refrigerate cake until ready to serve.

Frosting

In a large bowl, beat butter and cream cheese with an electric mixer until blended and fluffy. Beat in vanilla. Sift powdered sugar and cocoa powder together. Add to butter mixture about 1/3 at a time and beat on slow speed of mixer until incorporated. Add milk a little at a time to arrive at desired consistency. Beat all until smooth and creamy. Spread on cake and distribute toffee evenly on top of frosted cake. Then hide the cake in a secret spot!

King of Coconut Cake (with Cream of Coco Cream Cheese Frosting)

Tax Bite

Chicago Soda Fountain Tax

Speaking of sweet drinks, if you buy a fountain soda drink in Chicago, you will be charged a 9% tax. If, on the other hand, you buy the very same drink in a bottle or can, you'll see your tax levy drop to 3%.

Source: CNNMoney.com

INGREDIENTS

Cake

2 3/4 cup all-purpose flour
1 teaspoon baking powder
1/2 teaspoon baking soda
1/2 teaspoon salt
1 3/4 cups granulated sugar
1 cup unsalted butter, at room temperature
1 cup canned, sweetened cream of coconut, such as Coco Casa Coconut Cream
4 large eggs, separated
2 teaspoons vanilla
1 cup buttermilk
Pinch of salt
Cream Cheese Frosting (recipe below)
4 cups sweetened, shredded coconut

Cream of Coco Cream Cheese Frosting

1 8-oz. package cream cheese, softened to room temperature
1 stick unsalted butter, at room temperature
3 cups powdered sugar
1/2 cup canned, sweetened cream of coconut plus extra 1/2 cup for between cake layers
1 teaspoon pure vanilla extract

DIRECTIONS

Cake

Preheat oven to 350°F. Line three 9-inch cake pans with waxed paper. Lightly spray paper with cooking spray.

In a medium bowl, mix flour, baking powder, baking soda and salt to blend. In a large bowl, cream butter together with sugar and coconut cream until light and fluffy. Beat in egg yolks and vanilla. On low speed beat in dry ingredients alternately with buttermilk, starting and ending with dries.

Using clean, dry beaters, beat egg whites with a pinch of salt in another bowl until stiff, but not too dry. Gently fold into cake batter.

Divide cake batter evenly between the three pans. Bake cakes until tester inserted into cakes comes out clean. About 30-40 minutes. Cool cakes on rack for about 10 minutes. Then run a sharp knife around the edges to loosen cakes. Remove cakes from pans to racks, and cool completely.

Frosting

In a large bowl, beat cream cheese with butter until fluffy. Add powdered sugar, alternately with cream of coconut and beat until well-blended. Add vanilla and beat once more.

To Assemble

With a long bread knife, cut each cake layer in half horizontally. Place first half layer on plate. Spread plain coconut cream over layer and lay other half layer on top. Spread cream cheese frosting on top of this first whole layer. Then sprinkle ¼ cup of shredded coconut over frosting. Repeat the process with each half layer, ending with cream cheese frosting on top of cake. Spread remaining frosting all around sides of cake. Completely cover cake with shredded coconut and pat gently into frosting with the palm of your hands.

Tax Bite

Syrup Tax

This Washington State special tax is levied on the wholesale or retail sale of syrup used in making carbonated beverages. The fee is $1.00 per gallon and is collected by the syrup wholesaler.

Source: Washington Department of Revenue

Fresh-Squeezed Orange Juice Cake (with Orange Curd Filling and Butter Cream Frosting)

This cake, made with fresh-squeezed orange juice, makes a beautiful presentation for a party dessert.

INGREDIENTS

Cake

2 1/4 cups all-purpose flour
2 teaspoons baking powder
1/4 teaspoon baking soda
1/2 teaspoon salt
4 large egg whites
3/4 cup water
1/4 cup fresh-squeezed orange juice
1/2 cup butter, softened to room temperature
1 1/2 cups granulate sugar
1-2 tablespoons orange zest

Orange Curd Filling

2 large eggs
6 tablespoons sugar
6 tablespoons fresh-squeezed orange juice
1 teaspoon grated orange zest
Dash salt
1 tablespoon unsalted butter, chilled

Fresh Orange Buttercream Frosting

1 cube butter, softened to room temperature (1/2 cup)
4 cups powdered sugar
Pinch of salt
1/4 cup fresh-squeezed orange juice
Orange slices for garnish

Tax Bite

Florida Citrus Commission Tax

This tax isn't applied just to oranges, but to all citrus grown in the state, for publicity and marketing efforts of the Florida Citrus Commission. The tax is levied at different rates for processed citrus and fresh citrus. The rates for fresh citrus are: 11¢ per box for oranges, 35¢ per box for grapefruit, and 10¢ per box for all other citrus. For processed, which is fruit that has been juiced, the levy is 24¢ per box for oranges, 35¢ (the same as for fresh) for grapefruit, and 24¢ for all others. This tax is mandatory for all growers.

Source: Florida Department of Revenue

DIRECTIONS

Cake

Place dries (flour, baking powder, baking soda, salt) in a bowl, stir well and set aside. In a large bowl, beat egg whites on high-speed of an electric beater until stiff peaks form; set aside.

Combine water and fresh-squeezed orange juice in a separate bowl. Set aside.

In a large bowl, cream butter and sugar together until light and fluffy. Add orange zest and mix well. Alternately add flour mixture and juice mixture, beginning and ending with dries.

Gently fold in beaten egg whites and spread into two, well-greased, 8-inch cake pans. Bake at 350ºF for approximately 25 minutes, or until center springs back when touched. Cool completely, and cut each layer in half horizontally. Can make a day ahead and refrigerate.

Filling

Mix eggs and sugar well. Add orange juice, orange zest and salt. Heat over medium-high heat, stirring constantly, until mixture thickens. Remove from heat and stir in butter. Cool before spreading over half-layers of cake.

Frosting

In a large bowl, cream butter with salt and half of the powdered sugar. Add orange juice a little at a time, adding remaining sugar to get to desired spreading consistency. Spread between whole layers and on top of cake. If you're good at it, and you have enough frosting, spread remaining frosting on sides of cake! (I'm not that good, so I just frost in between layers and on top!) Garnish with fresh orange slices.

Lemon Cake with Lemon Curd and Lemon Cream Cheese Frosting

This lemon cake says "spring" especially when served with a complement of fresh strawberries. I make this cake with the tart Lisbon lemons (or Eureka) but if you happen to have Meyers lemons, give it a try. The lemon flavor would be a bit more subtle.

INGREDIENTS

Cake

1 cup unsalted butter (2 sticks)
2 cups granulated sugar
4 large eggs, beaten
1 teaspoon pure vanilla extract
4 cups all-purpose flour
1 1/2 teaspoons baking soda
1 teaspoon salt
1 cup milk
4 tablespoons fresh squeezed lemon juice
1 pint fresh strawberries for garnish

DIRECTIONS

Line three 8-inch diameter cake pans with waxed paper. Set aside. Preheat oven to 350 degrees.

Beat sugar and butter in a large bowl until light and fluffy. Add the beaten eggs and beat well, for 2-3 minutes, until light yellow in color. Stir in vanilla. Sift dries: flour, baking soda and salt into a separate bowl. Stir flour mixture into batter alternately with milk, beginning and ending with dry ingredients. Stir in lemon juice. Divide batter evenly into the prepared pans and bake about 25-30 minutes or until cake tester comes out clean. Cool cakes completely on cake racks and remove waxed paper.

Tax Bite

Florida Admission Tax

While we're on the subject of Florida, let's say you had an especially nice lemon grove and you wanted to charge entrance for folks to see your beautiful trees. Well, you would have to charge a 6% tax on admission fees to those who entered. This tax not only applies to lemon grove gardens, but to any charged admission fee in the state.

Source: Florida Tax Watch

To Assemble

Using a long serrated knife, cut each layer into horizontal halves and spread lemon curd over each half layer and frosting between whole layers and on top of cake. Garnish cake or cake plate with whole or sliced strawberries. *If you like frosting the sides, you can make 1.5 frosting recipes and frost the entire cake.

Lemon curd

2 large eggs

6 tablespoons sugar

6 tablespoons fresh lemon juice

2 teaspoons grated lemon peel

2 tablespoons unsalted butter, chilled and cut into small pieces

Whisk eggs and sugar in medium sauce pan. Add lemon juice, butter and lemon peel. Cook over medium-low heat, stirring all the while, until mixture begins to thicken and thermometer temperature reaches 165 degrees. Sauce will be thick enough to coat the back of a spoon. Remove from heat and transfer lemon curd to a clean bowl and cool. If the curd is lumpy, strain before chilling. When cooled, cover with plastic wrap directly on surface and chill until cold in refrigerator.

Lemon Cream Cheese Frosting

8 ounces cream cheese, at room temperature

1/2 cup (1 stick) unsalted butter, at room temperature

3+ cups powdered sugar

1-2 tablespoons lemon juice

Beat cream cheese and butter until light and fluffy and thoroughly mixed. Add half of the powdered sugar and beat well. Add lemon juice and beat well. Add remaining powdered sugar, enough to make frosting the desired consistency.

Fresh-Squeezed Orange Juice Cake with Orange Curd Filling and Butter Cream Frosting (top) and Lemon Cake with Lemon Curd and Lemon Cream Cheese Frosting (bottom).

Carrot Cake with Cream Cheese Frosting

Sometimes nothing satisfies the old sweet tooth better than a spicy carrot cake with walnut chunks and cream cheese frosting. This cake holds very well for a week or more in the refrigerator and makes a "too-spexcellent" snack for the mid-afternoon munchies!

INGREDIENTS

Cake

3 cups all purpose flour
2 teaspoons baking soda
1/2 teaspoon salt
3 teaspoons cinnamon
11/2 cup canola oil (or vegetable oil)
2 cups sugar
3 eggs
2 cups grated carrots (can use grater on food processor or hand-held grater)
1 flat can (8 oz.) crushed pineapple, drained
1/2 cup walnuts, quartered, not chopped
2 teaspoons vanilla

Frosting

1 8-oz. package cream cheese
1/2 cube butter, softened to room temperature
4 cups powdered sugar, sifted
2 teaspoons vanilla

DIRECTIONS

Cake

Place first six ingredients in a large mixing bowl and blend with a large fork or wooden spoon to mix well. Add eggs, one at a time, beating after each with the wooden spoon. Add pineapple, carrots, nuts and vanilla and stir well. Batter will be very thick. Spoon batter into a well-greased 9x13 inch baking pan and bake in a

Tax Bite

Satellite Tax

The Massachusetts State Legislature recently enacted a 5% excise tax on gross revenues of any provider of direct broadcast satellite service to customers in the state. The tax took effect on August 1, 2009. Of course, as with any tax on a business, the tax will ultimately be paid by satellite customers, and will be listed as a separate item on the monthly bill. This tax will create a level playing field, as cable companies may be assessed a franchise fee of up to 5% of gross revenues in the community. This is considered a type of rent, if you will, for using public rights of way to run their cables. The satellite tax is more or less designed to even out the playing field, and to bring the state much-needed revenue. According to some reports, the new tax will add about $3.40 to a typical customer's monthly bill and will generate $11 million in new tax revenue to the state. Currently there are an estimated 275,000 satellite television customers and 2 million cable users.

Source: Massachusetts Department of Revenue: TIR 09-14

350ºF for approximately one hour, or until tooth pick inserted in center comes out clean. Cool completely before frosting.

Frosting

Beat butter and cream cheese until fluffy. Add vanilla and sugar and beat until smooth. Frost in between layers and top and sides of cooled carrot cake.

COOKIES

Gram's Pecan Shortbread

For shortbread and pecan lovers.

INGREDIENTS

2 cubes unsalted butter
1/2 cup powdered sugar
2 cups all-purpose flour
1/2 teaspoon salt
1 teaspoon vanilla
1/2 cup finely chopped pecans

DIRECTIONS

In a large mixing bowl, beat butter and powdered sugar until well-blended. Add flour and salt and mix in. Stir in vanilla and pecans.

Line a 9-inch square pan with parchment paper and preheat oven to 325ºF. Press dough into the bottom of pan and bake for 30 minutes. Reduce heat to 275ºF and bake another 15 minutes. Turn off heat and leave cookies in oven for another 10-15 minutes. Cool completely and cut into squares.

Tax Bite

Kentucky Fiduciary Tax

Fiduciaries in Kentucky must pay income tax on the portion of income from an estate or trust not distributed or distributable to beneficiaries. The tax is calculated using a graduated rate from 2% to 6%. Even non-resident estates and trusts are subject to tax on income from Kentucky sources or from activities carried on in the state.

Source: Kentucky Dept. of Revenue

Coconut Chocolate Chip Shortbread Cookies

(Makes about 6 dozen mini cookies)

These cookies just might be the very best cookies on earth, especially for coconut lovers! They are based upon a recipe from Michelle Steinman, who has a way of baking sweet treats that will have you begging for more. I added coconut for a Hawaiian-themed fundraiser for the Food Bank of Contra Costa and Solano Counties in California, and I must say, I love the addition! These are made in tiny little rounds, so beware—it is not possible to eat just one.

INGREDIENTS

1 cup (2 sticks) butter, softened to room temperature

1/2 cup powdered sugar

2 cups flour

1/4 teaspoon sea salt

1/2 teaspoon vanilla

1 cup baking coconut, finely grated or chopped

1/2 cup mini chocolate chips (If you prefer bittersweet, which I do, then chop larger chips in a wooden bowl until much smaller in size)

DIRECTIONS

In a mixing bowl, blend butter and powdered sugar on low speed of electric mixer until well integrated. Stir in vanilla and coconut, and mix until blended. Add flour and salt and beat on low speed, just until mixed. Stir in chocolate chips. Gather dough into two balls and roll each into a log, approximately 1 1/4-inches in diameter. Wrap in plastic wrap and refrigerate until chilled, about 30 minutes. When ready to bake, preheat oven to 350 degrees, slice dough with a sharp knife into 1/4-inch slices and place on ungreased baking sheet or Silpat mat. Bake for 15-18 minutes, or until just beginning to brown. Remove from oven and cool. These should freeze quite well.

Tax Bite

Kansas Sand Tax

In Kansas, a compensation of 15¢ per ton must be paid to the State for sand (or other materials) removed from rivers owned by the State or from any land in such rivers.

Source: Kansas Department of Revenue

Tax Bite

Enhanced 911 Tax

Several states impose a 911 tax on phone lines. In Washington, the State imposes a monthly tax on switched access lines (hard) and radio access lines (wireless telephone numbers). The tax is collected from the consumer by the provider at a rate of 20¢ per month for each switched or radio access line and reported on the excise tax return.

Source: Washington Department of Revenue

Grammie's Marzipan Brownies

No one really knows the origin of brownies, but every family seems to have a favorite recipe handed down from generation to generation. We had one in our family, too, but one day my mom (decidedly the chocolate champion in our family) felt ours didn't have nearly enough chocolate. So, off she went in search of the perfectly chocolate, perfectly rich, perfectly decadent brownies. When she came up short, she began concocting with different ingredients and landed the perfect chocolate combination. The addition of almond paste offers an extra rich texture and taste.

INGREDIENTS

3 1/2 ounces bittersweet chocolate
2 tablespoons cocoa powder
1" slice of almond paste (Odense makes one that can be found in the baking section of most markets and comes in a tooth paste shaped box)
1 cube unsalted butter
Dash of salt
1/2 cup granulated sugar
2 eggs
1 teaspoon vanilla extract
1/2 cup unbleached flour
1/2 cup sliced almonds (optional) for top of brownies
1/2 cup slivered almonds, or pecans, coarsely chopped (optional)

DIRECTIONS

Line metal 8x8 inch baking pan with buttered foil. Melt bittersweet chocolate, cocoa powder, butter and almond paste in medium-sized pot over low heat on stovetop and stir until well blended. Remove from heat. Add salt and sugar

Tax Bite

South Dakota's Air Ambulance Tax

The air ambulance is given a special tax in South Dakota that is not applied to ground ambulance rides. Air ambulance services are levied a 4% sales tax, unless the trip begins and ends in the same city, and then the additional city sales tax is also added. Ground ambulances are specifically exempted from sales tax by state law!

Source: South Dakota Department of Revenue

and stir until both are dissolved into chocolate-butter mixture. Add two eggs, one at a top, beating well after each—so that the egg and chocolate mixture form a spiral effect in pot. Add vanilla and flour and mix well. Stir in slivered almonds or chopped pecans at this time, if you wish to have nuts in the brownies.

Pour batter into prepared pan and sprinkle sliced almonds over top of batter. Bake at 350ºF for 18 minutes. Test with cake tester and if brownies still seem too wet, bake for one minute longer. If they seem just right, turn off oven and leave them in the oven for another minute. The brownies should be just slightly wet in the center when they are done baking.

Remove from oven and cool on rack. Cut into one-inch bite-sized brownies (36) or if you prefer a "big" bite of chocolate richness, cut slightly larger. Can be stored in freezer for several weeks.

Waioli Oat-Date Bars

This cookie recipe with origins in Hawaii, was handed down from my mom and grandmother. The oatmeal crust with the gooey brown sugar-date topping can satisfy any sweet tooth!

Be sure to let the cookies cool completely before cutting into squares. Once the date topping sets up, they're easy to cut.

INGREDIENTS

Filling

2 cups pitted dates
1/2 cup brown sugar
1 cup water
1 tablespoon flour
2 teaspoons vanilla

Crust

1 1/8 cups all-purpose flour
1 teaspoon baking powder
2 1/2 cups quick oats
1 cup melted butter (use salted butter in this recipe)

DIRECTIONS

Mix crust ingredients together and press into the bottom of a greased, 8-inch square baking dish.

For filling, combine all of the filling ingredients in a medium saucepot. Cook over medium heat five minutes, stirring frequently. Pour filling over crust and spread evenly. Bake at 350°F for 20 minutes. Cool completely and cut into squares.

Tax Bite

"Make-Up" Tax Break

In Ohio, applying makeup in a beauty salon is taxable, but applying makeup to dead people in a mortuary is tax-free. At least the recently departed get some breaks!

Source: http://www.accountingweb.com/item/102009

Wilma's Oatmeal Chocolate Chips

(Makes 3-4 dozen)

We have this ongoing debate in our household whether chocolate chips have a rightful place in oatmeal cookies. I say they do, while my husband thinks it's a crime to associate one with the other. I've tried fooling him, but something about the texture of oatmeal cookies is a dead giveaway. Anyway, if you're like me, you'll find these delicious.

INGREDIENTS

11/4 cups butter (2 1/2 sticks)
3/4 cup brown sugar
1/2 cup granulated sugar
1 egg
1 teaspoon vanilla
11/2 cups flour
1 teaspoon baking soda
1/2 teaspoon salt
3 cups quick oats
1 cup bittersweet chocolate chips

DIRECTIONS

With an electric mixer, beat butter and sugars until fluffy. Add egg and vanilla and beat well. Add flour, baking soda and salt and stir to mix. Stir in oats and chocolate chips. Drop by rounded teaspoons onto greased baking sheet. Bake at 375°F 8-9 minutes for chewy or 11-12 minutes for crispy cookies.

Tax Bite

"Take It to the Bank" Tax

Nevada imposes a $1,750 quarterly excise tax on each branch of a bank that operates more than one bank branch office in the state.

Source: Nevada Department of Revenue

Tax Bite

Diaper Dilemma

Disposable diapers are charged sales tax in Wisconsin, while the cloth versions are exempt from sales tax by State law. The general sales tax on disposables is 5%, in addition to the stadium taxes for baseball and football and any additional county sales taxes.

Source: Wisconsin Department of Revenue

Dolores' Mandelbrodt (Biscotti)

This recipe of Grandma Dolores is a favorite at our house. They keep very well in the freezer and last for several days at room temperature in an airtight container.

INGREDIENTS

3 cups flour
1 cup sugar
2 teaspoons baking powder
3 eggs
1 cup canola or vegetable oil
1 teaspoon vanilla
1 cup coarsely chopped almonds (or pecans)
1 1/2 cups bittersweet (not unsweetened) chocolate chips

DIRECTIONS

Mix dries in a large bowl. In a separate bowl, combine eggs, oil and vanilla and mix well. Add egg mixture, nuts and chocolate chips to dries and mix well. Place dough on floured board and knead until smooth and no longer sticky. Divide dough in equal thirds and shape each into a log about 10 to 12 inches long and 2-3 inches in diameter. Press down on log to flatten just slightly into an oval. Can bake immediately or refrigerate until ready to bake.

Bake at 350°F for 35 minutes, until lightly browned. Remove from oven and cut each log into 1/2–inch slices on the diagonal. Sprinkle with cinnamon sugar and bake for 10 minutes longer. Cool on pan before separating slices. Store or freeze in airtight container.

Tax Bite

Handicap Tax

This tax is the saddest tax I've come across in all my research. The state of Washington imposes a 6% excise tax on the gross receipts of intermediate care facilities for services provided to mentally retarded persons. The proceeds are used for the state's share of the cost of the facilities. I should think they could come up with a better funding source than taxing the very services designed to help the mentally handicapped. This is a classic example of how the government works!

Source: Washington Department of Revenue

Cardamom Currant Oatmeal Cookies

This recipe is adapted from one found in the August 2002 issue of Bon Appetit Magazine. The flavors are unbeatable! The original called for old-fashioned oats and dark brown sugar, but I prefer using quick oats in cookies and light brown sugar in place of the dark.

INGREDIENTS

2 cubes butter, at room temperature
1 1/2 cups light brown sugar
1 teaspoon vanilla
2 large eggs
1 2/3 cup flour
1 teaspoon baking soda
1/2 teaspoon salt
1 teaspoon cardamom
1/2 teaspoon cinnamon
1/4 teaspoon allspice
2 cups instant oats
1/2 cup currants
1/2 coarsely chopped walnuts

DIRECTIONS

Beat butter and sugar until mixed. Add vanilla and eggs and beat until thoroughly blended. Sift dries (flour, soda, salt, cinnamon, cardamom, allspice) and add to butter mixture. Mix well. Add currants, oatmeal and nuts.

Drop by large spoonful onto greased baking sheet. Bake at 350°F for 8 to 10 minutes or until golden brown. Cool on baking rack.

Tax Bite

"Holy Smokes!"

Smoking is certainly not one of my favorite activities. In fact, I really hate the smell of nasty cigarette smoke. But the cigarette has definitely become a favorite target of the tax man. Pretty soon, the tobacco industry will be forced underground and the government will have a gaping revenue hole to fill. Several states continue to raise excise taxes on cigarettes and other tobacco products in order to increase revenue. There is a federal excise tax of $1.01 per pack in addition to individual state and city levies. New York City is the most expensive place to buy cigarettes at $5.26 per pack just in taxes alone. The New York state tax is $2.75 and New York City adds another $1.50, on top of the federal $1.01 levy. After New York the top 12 states with the highest state tax on cigarettes are: New Jersey ($2.575), Massachusetts ($2.51), Rhode Island ($2.46), Washington ($2.025), tied for sixth place at $2.00 are Alaska, Arizona, Connecticut, Washington D. C., Hawaii, Maine, Maryland, and Michigan). Counties

(continued)

Mrs. Hab's Peanut Butter Cup Cookies

(Makes four dozen)

I'm not sure if it's just a coincidence or if all Michelles make good cookies, but I have another good friend named Michelle, who has yet another really great cookie recipe. Michelle Habenicht's Reese's peanut butter cup cookies just remind me of Halloween, even though they aren't decorated with any sort of scary creatures—just chocolate-peanut butter centers. They are the perfect cookie to take to class or costume parties, because the recipe makes four dozen and they are easy to bake. The only time-consuming part of this recipe is unwrapping the foil and paper wrappers from the Reese's peanut butter cups. Now, that's a good job for the kids, but do be sure to buy extra. You know how it goes ... one for the cookie and one for me!

INGREDIENTS

1/2 cup butter, softened
1/2 cup sugar
1/2 cup brown sugar
1/2 cup peanut butter (Michelle uses crunchy)
1 egg
1/2 teaspoon vanilla
11/4 cup all-purpose flour
3/4 teaspoon baking soda
1/4 teaspoon salt
48+ Reese's mini peanut butter cups

DIRECTIONS

* Note the recipe calls for baking in a mini-muffin tin, with cup diameter 1 1/2 to 1 3/4-inch at the top.

Preheat oven to 350°F. With an electric mixer, beat butter, sugars and peanut butter until creamy. Add egg and vanilla and beat again until

Tax Bite

(continued)

and cities may impose an additional tax ranging from 1 cent to $2.00 on a pack of cigarettes. About 82% of what consumers pay for a pack of cigarettes (average cost $4.32 - including statewide sales taxes, but not local cigarette or sales taxes) ends up going to the government in taxes and other payments rather than for the cigarettes.

Source: Retirement Living Center; NY City Dept. of Health and Mental Hygiene

well-blended. Add flour, baking soda and salt and mix on slow speed until blended.

Spoon 1-inch balls of dough, or rounded teaspoonful, into a mini muffin tin, prepared with "no-stick" cooking spray. Bake 8-10 minutes, or until lightly browned. Remove from oven and immediately press a peanut butter cup in the center of each cookie. Cool completely before removing from tin. During baking the cookies naturally indent a little bit, making a perfect space for the peanut butter cup.

Tax Bite

Motor Sport Tax Heaven

Members of racing teams and motor-sport sanctioning bodies in North Carolina are entitled to refunds on aviation fuel sales tax (when the aviation fuel was used to get to a motor sport event) because the state is a tax-free zone for motor sports! In addition, since February 2002, the State no longer assesses motor fuel tax on leaded racing fuel.

Source: North Carolina Department of Revenue; and http://www.accountingweb.com/item/102009

Christmas Snowballs

(Makes about 30 cookies)

These old-fashioned traditional holiday cookies are so simple, but they somehow seem to say "Christmas!"

INGREDIENTS

1 cup unsalted butter at room temperature
8 tablespoons granulated sugar
1/2 teaspoon vanilla
1 teaspoon bourbon
2 cups flour
1 cup finely chopped pecans or walnuts
1 1/2 cups powdered sugar

DIRECTIONS

In a large mixing bowl, beat butter and sugar with electric mixer. Add vanilla and bourbon and mix well. Add flour and beat until well mixed and add nuts. If dough is a bit crumbly, not to worry, it will clump together as you form the dough into 1-inch balls. Place two inches apart on sprayed baking sheet and bake at 325°F for approximately 20 minutes, or until bottoms are golden brown and cookie feels done to the touch. Remove from oven and immediately roll in either red or green powdered sugar. Let cool completely and roll again in the same colored sugar.

To mix the sugar, add about 1 teaspoon of food coloring for ¾ cup powdered sugar. Fluff with fork and let sit for half hour or longer. Sugar won't look very colorful yet. When ready to use, crumble clumps of sugar between fingers and the color will soon become apparent.

Tax Bite

Yuletide Texas Taxes

Charges to decorate a Christmas tree are not taxed in Texas if the customer provides the decorations. It the decorator both sells the decorations and decorates the tree, the total charge is taxable. The same rules apply to home decorating services. If the decorator provides the decorations, the total charge for materials and labor is taxable to the customer! Charges to paint holiday pictures and messages on windows are also taxable.

Source: Texas Window on State Government http://www.window.state.tx.us/taxinfo/taxpubs/tx96_237_3_06.html

PIES, COBBLERS AND FRUIT DESSERTS

Pie Crusts

There are really just two types of pie crust that I use for my desserts: My Aunt Clara's Pie Crust and Emily Stewart's oil-based crust. I use Aunt Clara's for everything from apple pie to mixed berry pie, and Emily Stewart's for strawberry pie and cream pies.

Aunt Clara's Pie Crust

INGREDIENTS

2 cups flour

1/2 teaspoon salt

1 1/2 cubes unsalted butter, chilled and cut into small cubes

2 teaspoons cider vinegar

1/4-1/2 cup ice water

DIRECTIONS

Mix flour and salt in a large bowl. With a pastry cutter, or fingers, crumble butter into flour until well integrated. Sprinkle cider vinegar over mixture and stir in well with a fork. Add ice-cold water, a little at a time and blend with fork until dough is moist enough to roll into a ball, but not too wet. Roll into one large ball for the pie crust and a smaller ball to use for patching your crust, or cinnamon roll ups for snacking!

Tax Bite

The Life Cycle of California's Beverage Container Tax

As part of the California Beverage Container Recycling and Litter Reduction Act, fees are assessed at multiple points along the lifecycle of aluminum, plastic and glass beverage containers. The money kind of goes full circle, starting with a processing fee imposed on the manufacturer, based upon the material and the quantity involved. The distributor is then charged a CRV (California Redemption Value) fee strictly based on container volume. For containers holding less than 24 ounces, the fee is 5¢ each and for those that hold 24 or more ounces, the fee is 10¢ per unit. In addition, the distributor pays an administrative fee of 1.5%. The distributor passes this cost onto the retailer, who in turn, passes the buck to the consumer. Finally, the consumer can take the empty containers to the nearest recycling center for a refund value. The refund at my local recycling center is based on per pound weight and offers $1.60 for aluminum, 90¢ for plastic and 10¢ per pound for glass.

Source: California Department of Conservation

Emily Stewart's Pie Crust

INGREDIENTS

2 cups flour
1 teaspoon salt
2 teaspoon sugar
2/3 cup vegetable oil
3 tablespoons milk

DIRECTIONS

Sift dries into medium-sized mixing bowl. Mix milk and oil together with fork and add to dries, mixing well. Pat this mixture into a 9-inch pie pan to form crust. Bake at 350ºF for 15 minutes, or until golden brown. Cool.

Tax Bite

Sweet Wheat Tax

The Kansas Wheat Commission is a farmer-funded agency charged with the task for promoting Kansas wheat. The commission is funded through a 1¢ per bushel assessment at the first point of sale on all wheat sold in Kansas—even if the farmer promotes his own wheat!

Source: Kansas Wheat Commission

French Apple Crumb Pie

INGREDIENTS

Pie

8 tart apples (Granny Smith, Pipin, Empire)
1 recipe Aunt Clara's Pie Crust
1/2 cup brown sugar
1/4 cup white sugar
1 1/2 teaspoons cinnamon
1/2 teaspoon cardamom

Crumb topping

1 cube butter, cut into small bits
3/4 cup flour
2/3 cup brown sugar
1 teaspoon cinnamon
1/4 teaspoon cardamom
1/4 teaspoon nutmeg

Place all dry ingredients in bowl and mix well. Add butter and using finger tips, work dries into butter until crumbly.

DIRECTIONS

Peel, core and slice apples into 1/2-inch slices. Toss with sugar and spices. Dump into prepared, unbaked pie crust and top with crumb topping. Bake at 400ºF for 45-50 minutes, or until top is golden brown and apples are al dente, but a knife easily pierces.

Tax Bite

Blueberry Taxes

Maine imposes a 15¢ per pound tax on the production, sale and purchase of blueberries. California is considering the creation of a "Blueberry Commission" to promote California's growing blueberry industry. The commission's $1.2 million annual budget, if passed, would be funded from a surcharge on blueberries.

Sources: Maine Revenue Services; California Assembly Bill 606

Very Berry Pie

I love to make mixed berry pies and one time I made one for our friend's birthday dessert. He's never forgotten it, and now every time we get together, he hints about a berry pie. Since it's not always berry season when he's in town, I've learned to make them from fresh or frozen berries, too.

INGREDIENTS

1 recipe Aunt Clara's Pie Crust

1 recipe crumb topping (see recipe below)

8-10 cups fruit (I use a combination of blackberries, blueberries and raspberries, but you can use just one, if you prefer)

3/4 cup brown sugar

1/2 -2/3 cup flour (depending upon how juicy the fruit appears to be … use a little more if fruit is extra-juicy)

1 teaspoon cinnamon

1/2 teaspoon cardamom

1/4 teaspoon nutmeg

Juice of one-half lemon

DIRECTIONS

Place washed berries in a large bowl. Mix all dries and gently toss with berries. Sprinkle with lemon juice and toss again. Dump into a prepared, unbaked 10-inch pie shell and pat crumb topping on top. Bake at 400ºF for 45 minutes, or until crust is golden brown and crumb topping is crunchy. Serve with a dollop of whipped cream, vanilla ice cream or frozen yogurt.

Crumb Topping

1 cube chilled butter cut into small pieces
3/4 cup flour
1/2 cup brown sugar
1/4 cup white sugar
1 teaspoon cinnamon
1/4 teaspoon nutmeg
1/4 teaspoon cardamom

In a medium bowl, mix all dries. With finger tips, or pastry cutter, cut butter into dries until crumbly and well integrated. Pat on top of fruit in unbaked pie shell.

Strawberry Glaze Pie

This pie is made with fresh whole or sliced uncooked strawberries in the pie and cooked crushed berries in the glaze.

INGREDIENTS

1 recipe Emily Stewart's Pie Crust, baked and cooled

4 cups fresh strawberries, rinsed with leaves and stems removed. (sliced or whole)

1 recipe strawberry glaze (see recipe below)

1 cup heavy cream, whipped and flavored with 1 teaspoon vanilla and 2 tablespoons powdered sugar

Strawberry Glaze

2 cups fresh strawberries, greens removed

1 cup water

3 tablespoons cornstarch

3/4 cup sugar

Red food coloring, optional

Tax Bite

Sparkler Tax

In West Virginia, July 4th is greeted with a special tax on sparklers and other novelties in addition to the regular state-wide 6% sales tax. Businesses planning to sell these items must pay a special fee of $15 for each and every location where they sell such items, and may not sell them to anyone under the age of 16. The business will be issued a sticker or card that must be prominently placed for visibility.

Source: West Virginia State Tax Department

DIRECTIONS

Bring strawberries and water to boil in medium sized pot. Cook for about two minutes, stirring with spoon to mash the berries. Remove from heat and sieve through strainer. Return mixture to same pot. Mix sugar and cornstarch together in separate bowl, and stir into berries. Bring to boil, stirring constantly, until mixture is thickened and will coat the back of a spoon. Can add a few drops of red food coloring, to enhance color. Remove from heat and cool to room temperature.

Pie Assembly

Wash and remove stems from about 4 cups of fresh, ripe strawberries. Place half of the berries, whole or sliced–your preference, either way is pretty–in bottom of cooled crust. Pour ½ of the glaze over this layer of berries. Make a second layer with remaining berries and pour remaining glaze over this layer. Chill. Serve with a dollop of whipped cream. This pie should be eaten the same day, since the glaze can make the crust soggy if left overnight.

Summer Fruit Crisp

Have you ever tried a wheat-free, dairy-free recipe only to discover it tastes like a cardboard, lacking the key attributes of flavor and texture? If so, Lauren Hoover has just the cookbook for you. No Wheat, No Dairy, No Problem is a revolutionary cookbook filled with 150 tested recipes, which, in addition to being wheat and dairy-free, use only unrefined sugars, so diabetics can enjoy them too. Her book is available at www.nowheatnodairynoproblem.com

INGREDIENTS

Filling

3 pounds of stone fruit (nectarines, peaches, apricots, plums), 1 inch slices

1/2 cup agave nectar

1 teaspoon real vanilla extract

Zest and juice of 1 lemon

1 teaspoon tapioca starch or 2 tablespoons oat or barley flour

Topping

1 cup oat or barley flour, sifted

1/2 cup date sugar or maple sugar or sucanat (I substituted organic turbinado raw cane sugar)

1 stick vegan Earth Balance, cold or frozen and diced

Zest of one lemon

1 teaspoon vanilla powder, optional

1/4 teaspoon freshly grated nutmeg

1/4 teaspoon ground cinnamon

1/2 cup chopped nuts (walnuts, pecans, almonds)

1/2 cup old fashioned rolled oats (not quick cooking)

Tax Bite

California Tax Grab

This may sound preposterous, but the State of California passed a measure in 2004, Prop 1A, which was designed to protect property tax revenues paid to counties and municipalities. Voters probably never knew about the stealthy clause that allows the State to "borrow" up to 8% of that revenue in times of economic stress. And, the State may borrow the money twice in any 10-year period for up to 3 years each time, as long as the loan was paid in full prior to the second helping. This can result in a 6-year period of loss for counties and municipalities, because the State can pay the money back one day, and literally borrow it for the second time the following day. In addition, the State may simply take 8% from special incremental revenue districts, such as redevelopment districts, without ever paying it back! In my home town, that 8% is equivalent to 4.2% of the general fund revenue budget and 39.4% of the redevelopment general budget. This is quite a loss for small cities, with few alternative revenue sources.

Source: City of Auburn, Auburn Journal, CaliforniaCityFinance.com

DIRECTIONS

Preheat oven to 350ºF. Slice fruit and put in a large bowl and add the rest of the filling ingredients to the fruit, stir well. Place fruit mixture into a 9x12 glass baking dish or a 2-quart round soufflé dish or something equivalent-it can be a different shape, but the same size. Set fruit aside.

For the topping, place all ingredients into a food processor and pulse until it is crumbly and the size of cherries. This can also be done with a pastry cutter in a bowl. Pour evenly over fruit and bake for approximately 30 minutes or until the topping is golden brown and fruit is bubbling. Cool for one hour.

*Can prepare crisp ahead of time and freeze to bake at a later time. If frozen, increase baking time to approximately 1 hour.

Peach Cobbler

INGREDIENTS

6 tablespoons unsalted butter, melted
1 cup granulated sugar
1 cup all-purpose flour
2 teaspoons baking powder
1/2 teaspoon salt
1 cup milk
2 teaspoons vanilla
6 or so, ripe peaches, skinned, pitted and cut into 6-8 wedges
1/4 cup light brown sugar
1 teaspoon cinnamon
Dash cardamom

DIRECTIONS

Preheat oven to 375°F.

Grease an 8-inch square baking dish with cooking spray. Pour melted butter into the bottom of the dish. In a medium bowl, blend granulated sugar, flour, baking powder and salt. Slowly stir milk into the dry mixture with a whisk, stirring all the while to avoid lumps. Mix in vanilla. Pour batter over butter in baking dish. In a separate bowl, gently toss peaches with brown sugar and spices. Lay peaches over top of batter, doubling the layer of peaches if necessary.

Bake for 25-30 minutes, or until topping is golden brown and beginning to pull away from sides of dish. Serve warm with whipped cream, vanilla frozen yogurt or ice cream.

Tax Bite

Private College Student Tax

Like most municipalities across the country, obese government budgets outweigh revenues during lean economic times. Actually, this phenomenon is becoming more common even during boom years. In response to his city's budget shortfall, Mayor David N. Cicilline of Providence, Rhode Island has proposed a $150 per semester tax known as the "Student Municipal Impact Fee" on the 20,000 students who attend one of the City's four private colleges and universities. This tax would not be imposed on public university students. The fee would generate $6 million annually and is being promoted as a "moral" obligation of students, never mind that most students are already short-funded, as are their parents.

Source: The Providence Journal May 3, 2009 "Providence seeks student tax at private colleges" by Philip Marcelo

Baked Apples with Pecan-Raisin-Spice Filling

(Serves 6)

About 25 years ago, when I was in college, my roommate and I travelled through San Luis Obispo in central California on my way to San Diego. We stopped at the Apple Farm restaurant and devoured one of their baked apples for dessert. I never did request their recipe, because I've since learned to make my own, but I've never forgotten that delicious baked apple wrapped in pastry! This recipe is divided into three parts: apples, filling and sauce. Serve with vanilla frozen yogurt or ice cream and drizzle extra sauce over.

Tax Bite

Fresh Fruit Finance

In California, fresh fruit is exempt from tax unless it's purchased from a vending machine, where it is taxed 33% of the price.

Source: California State Board of Equalization; Accountingweb.com

Apples

3 Gala, or Fuji apples
1 tablespoon butter
1 tablespoon brown sugar

Filling

1/2 cup granulated sugar
1/4 teaspoon salt
1 tablespoon butter
1 cup pecans, coarsely chopped
1 cup raisins
1/2 teaspoon cinnamon
1/4 teaspoon cardamom
Dash allspice
1/2 cup apple juice

Sauce

1 tablespoon butter
2 tablespoons brown sugar
1/2 teaspoon cardamom
1/2 cup apple juice
1 tablespoon Calvados or apple brandy

Baked Apples with Pecan-Raisin-Spice Filling (top) and Chocolate Cream Pie (bottom)

DIRECTIONS

Preparing apples

Preheat oven to 425°F. Cut apples in half from top to bottom. Using a melon ball cutter, remove the core. (A paring knife will work, too.)

Melt butter in a heavy ovenproof skillet large enough to hold 6 apple halves. Add brown sugar to butter and stir. Place apples, cut side down, on top of butter-sugar mixture and cook over stove top on medium-high heat for 3-5 minutes. Transfer pan to oven and continue to bake until apples are tender when pierced with a knife, approximately 15 minutes. Remove from oven and set aside.

Filling

Mix sugar and salt and place in un-greased heavy skillet. Cook over medium-high heat for 2-3 minutes, undisturbed. Continue to cook, stirring with a fork, until sugar just begins to turn golden, 3-4 minutes. Add butter and melt into sugar, stir well. Mixture will become kind of grainy. Add spices, nuts and raisins and continue to cook, and stir, until nuts and raisins begin to brown. Add 1/2 cup apple juice and cook until liquid is evaporated and nuts and raisins are well coated. Remove mixture from pan, reserving pan scrapings for the sauce.

Sauce

In same pan as above, melt butter, stir in brown sugar and cook until sugar is dissolved. Add cardamom and Calvados, or brandy, and apple juice. Cook over medium high heat, stirring all the while, until sauce is thick like syrup. Remove from heat and set aside, in pan.

Assembly

When ready to serve, stuff filling into apple cavities. You will have extra filling, which can be sprinkled over the final dish at serving, or saved for snitching later! Place the apples into the pan with the syrup, stuffed side up. Heat through just until warm. Serve on dessert plate or bowl, with vanilla ice cream, or yogurt. Pour remaining syrup over apple and ice cream and sprinkle extra filling over top and around sides of apple.

DECADENT DESSERTS

Coffee Mud Pie

My favorite ice cream dish is this mud pie my mom used to make for very special occasions. My kids love it, too, and it's nice because you can substitute any ice cream flavor you like, or divide the pie up into multiple flavors. Just remember to mark each section by some identifying mark on the top of the whipped cream topping.

INGREDIENTS

Crust

30 Oreo cookies, pulverized in food processor
1/2 cup (one stick) melted butter

Fudge Sauce

4 one-ounce squares unsweetened baking chocolate
1 cup granulated sugar
2 six-ounce can evaporated milk
1/4 teaspoon salt

Ice Cream

1 gallon coffee ice cream or frozen yogurt

Whipped Cream Topping

1 cup heavy whipping cream
1 tablespoon kahlua
1/2 cup toasted pecans, coarsely chopped

DIRECTIONS

Crust

Combine above and pat into a well-greased 9" pie dish. Freeze for about 30 minutes.

Tax Bite

Bingo Tax

It's not so unusual to enjoy a little dessert while playing bingo, but in the state of Arizona, as in many states, there is a tax imposed on licensed bingo operations. There are three classes of licenses and therefore three tax rates. For the Class "A" license, with gross receipts $15K or less, the fee is 2.5 % of the adjusted gross receipts. For Class "B" receipts may not exceed $300K and for Class "C" with receipts over $300K, the tax rates are 1.5% and 2%, respectively.

Source: Arizona Department of Revenue

Ice Cream

Spoon 2 cups of your favorite ice cream, softened slightly, into shell. (Coffee is the traditional flavor, but any flavor will do.) Freeze until ice cream is hardened.

Fudge Filling

Place all fudge sauce ingredients in heavy saucepan and cook until thick like fudge, stirring constantly. Remove from stove and cool to room temperature. Spread cooled fudge sauce over frozen ice cream. Freeze again until hard.

Whipped Cream Topping

Whip 1 cup heavy cream until stiff. Add 1 tablespoon Kahlua. Spread over frozen fudge sauce and top with 1/2 cup finely chopped toasted pecans or walnuts. Freeze until time to serve. For you coconut lovers, simply replace the Oreo cookies with Mother's Coconut Macaroons and use coconut ice cream.

Tax Bite

Tax Wedge

The tax wedge is the difference between before-tax and after-tax wages. The Tax Wedge measures how much the government receives as a result of taxing the labor force. The term comes from the fact that a market inefficiency is created by the imposition of a tax on a product or service and the tax causes the supply and demand equilibrium to shift, thereby creating a "wedge" of dead weight losses. In progressive tax nations, the wedge increases as employee income increases, which decreases incentive to work and invest labor and money. The net result is higher costs and lower production.

Source: Investopedia.com

Chocolate Cream Pie

My godmother, Eva Kinney, is a fabulous dessert maker. Her chocolate cream pie was a favorite of mine growing up. Sometimes old favorites get hidden in the recipe file and don't see the light of day for a long time, but it's so wonderful when they resurface.

INGREDIENTS

1 recipe Emily Stewart's Pie Crust, patted into an 9-inch pie dish

Chocolate custard filling

1 cup sugar
3 1/2 tablespoons cornstarch
1 tablespoon flour
1/2 teaspoon salt
3 cups milk
2 ounces bittersweet chocolate, chopped (into milk mixture)
2 ounces 72% dark chocolate, chopped
3 egg yolks
1 teaspoon vanilla
1 tablespoon butter

DIRECTIONS

For crust, pat mixture into pie dish and bake at 400°F for 15 minutes or until crust is slightly browned. Cool completely before filling.

For Filling

Mix sugar, cornstarch, flour and salt in a saucepan, or the top of a double boiler. Add 1/4 cup milk to dries and stir well to make a paste. Then add rest of milk and chocolate. Heat over medium-high heat, stirring all the while, until mixture comes to a boil. In the meanwhile, beat the yolks until mixed. Once mixture comes to a boil, add 1/4 cup to yolks, and stir well. Then add this back to main mixture and bring to a boil for one minute, again stirring often. Remove pudding from heat and add butter and vanilla, stir until integrated. Put plastic wrap right on filling to prevent skin from forming and cool completely. Fill cooled pie dish with cooled pudding. Serve with a dollop of whipped cream and shaved chocolate curls.

Tax Bite

America's Sugar Tax

American consumers pay more than double the world price for sugar. The federal sugar program guarantees domestic producers a take of 22.9¢ per pound for beet sugar and 18¢ for cane sugar, while the world spot price for raw cane sugar is currently about 10¢ per pound. A 2000 study by the General Accounting Office estimated that (at that time) Americans paid an extra $1.9 billion a year for sugar due to import quotas alone.

Source: http://www.reason.com/news/show/36207.html

Chocolate Pots de Crème

This is a dessert my boss, Georgia Alison, made for our sales team when I worked for HealthAmerica in the mid-1980s. The company is now defunct but this recipe lives on. I can't vouch for the healthiness of this dessert, but I can tell you, the silky thick chocolate is divine!

INGREDIENTS

6 ounces fine quality bittersweet chocolate, finely chopped (do not use unsweetened)
1 1/3 cups heavy cream
2/3 cup milk
6 large egg yolks
2 tablespoons sugar

DIRECTIONS

Prepare 8 ramekins with cooking spray. (Should hold 4-5 ounces each) Preheat oven to 300ºF.

Place chocolate in glass or plastic bowl. Bring cream, milk and pinch of salt just to a boil in a small heavy saucepan. Pour over chocolate in bowl and mix until chocolate is melted and mixture is smooth.

Whisk together eggs yolks, sugar and a pinch of salt in a different bowl. Then add warm chocolate mixture in a slow steady stream, whisking constantly. Pour custard through a sieve into a glass container and cool completely, stirring occasionally. This should take about 15 minutes.

Line the bottom of a baking pan with a folded kitchen towel and place ramekins on top. Divide custard between ramekins, then fill baking pan with water just halfway up ramekins. Cover baking dish tightly with foil. Bake until custards are set around edge, but still a little jiggly in the center, approximately 35 to 40 minutes.

(continued on next page)

Tax Bite

Idaho "Use" Tax

You may not be aware of this, but whenever you buy goods online, over the telephone or from a mail-order catalog, and you live in a state that imposes sales tax, you owe "use tax" if you were not charged sales tax. If you purchase tobacco products online, you owe the tobacco tax in addition to the use tax. It is the buyer's responsibility to declare these items and file the tax. Every state with a sales tax also has a use tax and the tax is usually paid with the individual tax return.

Source: Idaho State Tax Commission

Transfer ramekins to a wire rack to cool, uncovered. Once cooled to room temperature, cover and chill for at least three hours or overnight. Custards will become very firm as they chill.

Serve with a dollop of whipped cream and top with chocolate shavings.

Eternal Pot of Chocolate Fudge Sauce

I always have a pot of chocolate sauce on the stove for emergency desserts. This is a rich, creamy sauce and is even good for dipping cookies or fingers.

INGREDIENTS

2 ounces unsweetened chocolate

11/2 cups bittersweet chocolate chips

1 cup water (if needed slowly add more water to obtain desired consistency)

1/3 cup light Karo syrup or agave syrup

1 tablespoon pure vanilla extract

DIRECTIONS

Melt chocolates in small saucepan with water, stirring constantly with whisk until chocolate is smooth. Add corn syrup and vanilla. Whisk again until smooth. Bring just to boil, whisk again, and remove from heat. Can be made ahead and stored for weeks in the refrigerator … or on the stove! Add more chocolate or water to reach desired consistency.

Tax Bite

"The Gift of Giving" Tax

Receiving a gift can create a maddening tax liability. Gifts from game show winnings, gifts of real estate, and cars, trips and other valuable items can be levied with a hefty tax. In many cases, the winner must liquidate the gift in order to afford the tax bill. In one case, a man caught a valuable baseball at a ballgame and was hit with a $210,000 tax bill. It is better, if given the option, to receive cash in lieu of the gift, because a certain amount of cash can be set aside to cover the taxes.

Source: National Taxpayers Association

Joel's Chocolate Lava Cakes

INGREDIENTS

8 ounces bittersweet chocolate (not unsweetened)
1 cup (2 sticks) unsalted butter
4 large eggs at room temperature
4 large egg yolks, at room temperature
7 tablespoons sugar
1/4 cup all purpose flour, sifted

DIRECTIONS

Preheat oven to 375°F and grease insides of 8 nine-ounce ramekins.

Melt chocolate and butter in bowl in microwave, or in saucepan on low, stirring until smooth. Remove from heat. Set aside. Meanwhile, beat eggs, yolks, and sugar in a bowl with electric mixer for 3 minutes until thick. Add melted chocolate at low speed and mix until well blended. Fold in sifted flour. Pour batter into prepared ramekins and bake for 12-16 minutes or until top is set, but center is still molten. Remove lava cakes from oven and un-mold each one onto a dessert plate. Serve immediately with a scoop of vanilla ice cream.

Tax Bite

Tapping Travel

Because visitors to Bermuda generally arrive by plane, I thought it appropriate to reveal how many different taxes are applied to a basic airfare, which considerably increases the total price of the ticket. On a recent family trip to visit Baja, California, my husband was very excited to learn our airfare would be $318 round trip per person on U.S. Airways. But, after the computer completed the ticketing, he was shocked to see the price was $115.30 more per person due to a plethora of interesting taxes and fees. Here is a list of those taxes:

$16.10 U.S. International Arrival Tax

$16.10 U.S. International Departure Tax

$17.80 Mexico Tourism Tax

$ 7.00 U.S. Immigration fee

$ 5.00 U.S. Animal & Plant Inspection Service Fee

$ 7.50 September 11 Security Fee

$13.50 U.S. Passenger Facility Charge

$32.30 Mexico-Departure-Intl-81 Fee

(continued)

Chef Cliff Crawford's Sticky Date Pudding with Toffee Sauce

(Serves 15-20)

While visiting Bermuda a few years ago, we were treated to a fabulous dinner at the Fairmont Hotel's Waterlot Inn by the president of my husband's company. Not wanting to look too greedy when the time came to make a dessert selection, I chose one my husband and I could share, which in this case was a safe apple crisp and not the tempting Sticky Date Pudding with Toffee Sauce. (Dates are not his favorite.) The next day, I went back and ordered the date pudding and the recipe!

INGREDIENTS

Date Pudding

3 1/3 cups water

16 ounces dates, pitted and roughly chopped

2 tablespoons plus 1 teaspoon baking soda

1 cube butter

2 1/4 cups granulated sugar

6 eggs

2 1/4 cup all-purpose flour

2 tablespoons baking powder

1/2 teaspoon ground ginger

Toffee Sauce

1 cube butter

1 cup, packed, dark brown sugar

3/4 cup heavy cream

1/2 teaspoon pure vanilla extract

DIRECTIONS

Bring dates and water to boil, reduce heat and simmer for five minutes until softened. Removed from heat and add the baking soda. Mixture will

Tax Bite

(continued)

Total in taxes and fees–$115.5 or $36.2% of the price of the airfare!

In reviewing my ticket with U.S. Airways, I learned from the agent that the Mexico Tourism fees have gone up since our trip in June 2009, and had almost doubled by August of the same year!

Source: USAirways

start to foam. Allow to sit and ferment for about 30 minutes and cool to room temperature.

Meanwhile, cream the butter and sugar together in a large mixing bowl. Add eggs, and beat on medium speed of electric mixer until smooth, approximately 2 minutes. Sift flour, baking powder and ginger together and stir into butter mixture. Finally, fold the date mixture into the batter until well-combined. The batter will be quite runny.

Grease or spray a 9x13 inch glass baking dish and pour batter into baking dish. Place the glass baking dish with batter inside a larger metal baking dish or roasting pan and surround the glass dish with water about 2/3 up the side of date pudding dish.

Bake in a 350ºF for 20 minutes, then reduce heat to 300ºF and continue to bake for another 50-60 minutes or until pudding feels done to the touch. It will spring back a little when cooked. The color of the pudding will darken considerably during cooking.

Serve warm from the oven, (reheat to warm if made ahead) with a scoop of vanilla ice cream and drizzle warm toffee sauce (recipe below) over both date pudding and ice cream.

For Toffee Sauce

Melt butter and add brown sugar, stirring until dissolved. Bring this mixture to a boil. Add cream, reduce heat to medium-low and simmer for about five minutes, or until emulsified, stirring occasionally. Remove from heat and add vanilla. Cool sauce until just warm and serve over Sticky Date Pudding and a scoop of vanilla ice cream.

CHAPTER XIII

The Pork That Broke the Patriots' Backs

Rise of the Tea Party Patriots

When I learned about the Boston Tea Party in school, I didn't give it much thought, really. It was an important event of great consequence, but one that took place ages ago and would not happen again in my lifetime.

Likewise, when I gave tea parties for my little daughter, we only thought it a cute, quaint gathering to spend time with her friends and mine. It never crossed our minds that a decade later, she and I would be attending tea parties of a different nature—Tax Day Tea Parties. But, we did and yes, we were among the Tea Party Patriots of modern times.

We had a grand time at these events, where citizens, most of whom like us, had never protested before in their lives, civilly stood up to be counted and spoke their minds about the way our fiscally irresponsible legislators seem bent on treating us. We were proud to be a part of it. At the Sac Day Tea Party in front of California's capitol building, we and thousands of other disgruntled taxpayers shared our distrust and utter disdain for those very politicians who take and take and take our hard-earned income to redistribute it to other citizens—after skimming the fat for themselves.

I believe, as others do, that politics should not be a career because it has become a pathological breeding ground for corruption. Certainly not all, but many politicians are tainted, and even many of those who enter politics with good intentions, run the risk of becoming swindlers. It's to the point where I fear for anyone entering the odious career, lest they become infected with "porkulus." Because paid politicians have job saving tendencies like the rest of us, they stop at almost nothing to win the vote of their constituencies, including lying and cheating and writing legislation far too long to read. The longer the bill, the less it is read, and the more taxpayers unwittingly spend. It has to end.

George Washington kept one foot in the real world, as did all of the founding fathers of this great nation. They understood the problems and joys of real work and were less susceptible to bribery and trickery as a result. They understood the common man. Our legislators do not. They live in a dream world, where they thrive on reprimanding executives for flying in corporate jets, yet they attempt to usher in eight brand new Gulfstream V and Boeing 747 jets to shuttle them around the world (at a cost of between $66 and $70 million apiece). And that's not counting the $5,700 per hour they cost to operate. This, during an economic crisis not seen since Jimmy Carter's days as president, opened our eyes and after much outcry from the American public, the aircraft acquisitions were temporarily tabled!

The Tea Party movement erupted shortly after President Obama's inauguration. The rushed passage of the 2009 American Reinvestment and Recovery Act, signed into law on February 17, 2009, ignited the masses. Legislators were given just hours to review the 1,400+ page bill, reversing an Obama campaign pledge to post legislation on the Internet for at least 48 hours prior to Congress voting on it.

The bill was laden with pork and entitlement programs, which were anything but economically "stimulating." The 2009 $3.6 trillion Omnibus Appropriations Act followed closely on the heels of the "Stimulus" package and boasted some 8,500 earmarks, a congressional habit Nancy Pelosi promised to break once she became Speaker of the House. She failed miserably on that promise. Tea Party Protestors had had enough. This was the pork that broke the patriots' backs.

The time was ripe for the birth of the Tea Party Movement and a live report by Rick Santelli, Business News On-Air editor of CNBC and veteran of the finance industry, was the catalyst. Voicing the frustration that many Americans were feeling about runaway government spending, Santelli went on a live rant from the floor of the Chicago Stock Exchange just two days after the "stimulus" bill was enacted.

He proclaimed, "The government is promoting bad behavior. How about this, President and new administration? Why don't you put up a website to have people vote on the Internet as a referendum to see if we really want to subsidize the losers' mortgages; or would we like to at least buy cars and buy houses in foreclosure and give them to people that might have a chance to actually prosper down the road, and reward people that could carry the water instead of drink the water?"

After a few minutes of dialogue between Santelli and floor traders, he opened the flood gates of tea party patriots with this line. "We're thinking of having a Chicago Tea Party in July. All you capitalists that want to show up to Lake Michigan, I'm gonna start organizing."

His message resonated with Americans, but it didn't take until July for the first Tax Tea Party to materialize. It occurred just days later, on February 27, when tea party protests were held in 48 cities across the nation. This turnout occurred with merely days to prepare, but the next tea party protest, scheduled for April 15, was a different story. Cities popped up daily to host tea parties and all told, more than 1 million people turned out to air their frustration in 800 or so cities across America. The Tea Party Revolution had begun.

By summer, these very same folks, who merely wanted to be heard by lawmakers, attended "town hall" meetings to complain and to ask questions of their representatives about Obama's 1,100 page, $1 trillion health care initiative, only to be tagged as Un-American by Nancy Pelosi and Steny Hoyer, congressional representatives from California and Maryland, respectively.

If our congressmen remember anything at all, they must remember this: They work for the citizens of this country. We do not work for them! After all, it is we who pay their salaries. It would behoove them to remember this important fact.

In honor of the new Tea Party Patriots, let's do tea!

TEA PARTY PATRIOT LUNCHEON MENU

Caramelized onion-walnut tart
Artichoke Heart Sandwiches
Arugula Salad with three cheeses and spiced nuts
Mumsie's Fruit Scones
Pecan Shortbread
Assorted Teas

CHAPTER XIV

Hallelujah! It's Tax Freedom Day

Celebration Feast

Tax Freedom Day is the day in the year when Americans have earned enough money to pay their tax bill for the entire year. In other words, if at the beginning of each calendar year, you were to pay for all of your tax obligations up front, before keeping a single dime for yourself, Tax Freedom Day would be the day you could start keeping your paycheck for yourself. This is quite a reason to celebrate!

Of course taxpayers don't operate this way, by necessity opting to amortize the tax burden throughout the year by deducting a portion from each paycheck. But, still, it is an interesting study to see how many months the average American works just to pay Uncle Sam and Mini Me.

Because the tax burden covers federal, state, and local obligations, and also must account for the progressive nature of the U.S. tax schedule, an individual's actual Tax Freedom Day may fall on a day other than the national celebration. For example, in 2009, it took 120 days to achieve tax freedom in Connecticut, while it took just 82 days to find tax freedom in Alaska. Consider this: in Connecticut, a taxpayer works 2.63 hours each day, just to pay taxes. This is before any of the hundreds of ancillary taxes including: excise tax, sales tax, license fees, etc.

In 2009, National Tax Freedom Day fell on April 13, 103 days into the year and eight days earlier than 2008. This was, in fact, the earliest Tax Freedom date since 1967. Why? This phenomenon was driven by three overriding factors: the Bush Tax cuts of 2001 and 2003, the economic recession, and temporary tax cuts included in H.R. 1, the 2009 American Recovery and Reinvestment Act. (Note the key word temporary!) This refers not only to the "stimulus" package, but also the Bush Tax cuts, which Congress failed to make permanent when they had the chance to do so. Still, Americans pay more in taxes than they do on food, clothing and shelter, combined!

The earliest Tax Freedom Day on record fell on January 20, 1903, when Americans spent just 20 days working to pay off the tax bill, which amounted to 5.3 percent of income. That figure soared to 33.6 percent in 2000 and was 28.2 percent in 2009. Next year's 2010 celebration depends upon many factors including the results of ObamaCare, Cap and Trade and runaway pork barrel spending on everything else under the sun. Any of these programs would be sure to add considerable tax burdens on Americans of all income levels, but together, they would break the tax back of Americans. Subject to increase are: federal income tax, payroll taxes, state income tax, capital gains and dividends taxes, and of course the stealth tax of increased energy costs for everything from turning on the lights, to filling up the old Honda, and every single manufactured item requiring electricity to be produced.

It could be worse. In 2007, France, Norway and Sweden celebrated National Tax Freedom Day on July 16th, 29th and 29th, respectively. Hmmm … do we really want the Europeanization of America? And, in Canada, our neighbors to the north waited until June 6, 2009 for National Tax Freedom Day (the day varies by province in Canada.) This is equivalent to 43 percent of the work year, or 3.44 hours of each working day. See what National Health Care can buy you?

In honor of our friends and neighbors, I'd like to propose a toast to National Tax Freedom Day … before alcohol taxes go up!

Cheers!

TAX FREEDOM DAY DINNER MENU

Apéritif

Income Tax Cocktail (Recipe below)

Appetizers

Olive-blue cheese Toasts

Crostini of goat cheese, caramelized onions and fig butter

Nutty Stuffed Mushrooms

Salad

Catalina Corn Salad

Entrée

Lime-basted barbecued Turkey

Side

Roasted Corn Poblano and White Cheddar Tart

Vegetable

Roasted Sweet Peppers

Dessert

King of Coconut Cake

Strawberry Glaze Pie

Income Tax Cocktail

By Colleen Graham,
About.com Guide to Cocktails

INGREDIENTS

2 oz. gin
1/4 oz. sweet vermouth
1/4 oz. dry vermouth
1 oz. orange juice
Angostura bitters to taste
Orange twist for garnish

DIRECTIONS

Pour the ingredients into a shaker with ice cubes.
Shake well.
Strain into a chilled cocktail glass
Garnish with orange twist
Toast to the end of your taxes for the year!!!

Tax Bite

Your Tax Dollars @ Work

The National Institute of Alcohol Abuse and Alcoholism (NIAA), a part of the National Institutes of Health (NIH), will pay $2.6 million in U.S. tax dollars to train Chinese prostitutes to drink responsibly on the job. Phewf! We were getting concerned about this issue.

Source: CNSNews.com

CHAPTER XV

One More Reason to Celebrate!

Final Thoughts

Happy Cost of Government Day!

Cost of Government Day (COGD) is the day in the year, when the average American worker has earned ample gross income to cover his share of government spending and regulatory burdens for the combined federal, state and local levels. That date occurred on August 12 in 2009, a full 23 days later than the previous all-time high of July 20 in 1982. Reasons for the explosion in government spending included the $700 billion TARP (Troubled Asset Relief Program) the 2009 American Recovery and Reinvestment Act ("stimulus" package) the $100 billion Auto Bailout/Purchase Bonanza combined with the $3 billion "Cash for Clunkers" car trade-in program in addition to the $4 trillion Omnibus 6-month government spending bill. And, it will only get worse with ObamaCare now a reality. Not to spoil your celebration, but you can expect to see COGD pushed out toward the end of the year, say somewhere around Thanksgiving or Christmas!

Tax Bites

Public Pay Premium

The average compensation per hours worked for public sector workers in the U.S. is now 44.6% higher than average compensation for those in the private sector. On average, public employees receive $39.66 per hour, inclusive of wages, salaries and benefits, compared with $27.42 for private sector employees.

Source: WSJ Review & Outlook March 26, 2010, "The Government Pay Boom"

The calculation of Cost COGD varies for each state based upon the varying state and local government spending. Connecticut boasts the latest COGD, with the average worker working until September 7 to pay off all the costs of government at each level in 2009. New Jersey ranks second with COGD now falling on September 6, and New York is right behind on August 31. California and Maryland round out the top five!

Source: Center for Fiscal Accountability and Americans for Tax Reform.